HYMNS TO THE GODDESS

HYMNS TO THE GODDESS AND HYMN TO KALI

SIR JOHN WOODROFFE
(Arthur Avalon)

GANESH & COMPANY
Madras-600017

Reprint 2015

ISBN 978-81-8598-816-0

Price Rs. 350/-

Published by Ganesh & Co.,
An Imprint of Productivity & Quality Publishing Pvt. Ltd.
New No. 38, Thanikachalam Road, T. Nagar
Madras – 600 017
E-mail: service@kkbooks.com
Website: www.kkbooks.com

Printed at
Manipal Technologies Ltd.
2A, Industrial Aria, Manipal – 576 104
Udupi, Karnataka, India

SIR JOHN WOODROFFE

(At the Konarak Temple of Sun-god in Orissa)

Courtesy : Mr P. K. DUTTA

PREFACE

THE Goddess or Devī (as the Hindus call Her) is God (as the Western worshippers address Him) in Its Mother aspect. The latter not uncommonly deem such attribution of ſeminine quality to be " heathenish " ; but this condemnation (for the criticism has, of course, this intendment) is itself singularly foolish in that it is thereby implied that of two sets of terms (neither of which is in its strict sense applicable to the Deity as the Author of forms), one is, in fact, a more correct description than the other. In the Navaratneśvara it is said : " That Devī, who is existence, consciousness, and bliss, should be thought of as a female or as a male, or as pure Brahman. In reality, however, She is neither male nor neuter (that is to say, that She is not bound to any particular form). " No one contends that the Brahma-tattva in the supreme abode beyond appearances is masculine as opposed to feminine, or the latter as contrasted with the former. Like all else in this matter, words are but the babbling endeavour of our plane to express that which is above it. It is not easy, then, to explain the condemnation except upon the assumption that those who pronounce it think their mother's sex to be inferior to their own, and that thus Deity is unworthily described by any other terms than those of masculine excellence. But Hindus, who ever place the name of mother before that of father, and to whom *garbha dhāraṇapoṣābhyām pitur mātā garīyasī*, have no partiality for such mistaken notions. On the other hand, it is possible that they might not understand the Christian expression "Mother of God," nor approve it even after they had learnt the limited and special sense which theology gives to this epithet. The Tāntrika would least of all admit the insufficiency of the conception of God as Mother. For the Devī manifests in his own mother, in his prakṛti (as he calls his wife), and in all women. As the Kubjikā Tantra says: "Whosoever has seen the feet of woman let him worship them as those of his guru" (*Strīnām pādatalam dristvāguruvad-bhāvayet sadā*). Whilst male and female are both Her aspects, yet S'akti is, in a sense, said to be more revealed in the female than in the male form. And so the Muṇḍamāla Tantra says: "Wherever there is a śakti (female), there I am." On account of this greater manifestation, women are called S'akti. From this, however, it must not be supposed that S'akti is less present in such forms as S'iva and Kṛṣṇa and others. If, as the author of the Tantra Tattva says, a sādhaka who is a worshipper of the Kṛṣṇamūrti desires to see Him as as Kālī, Bhagavān, who fulfils the desires of devotees, will assume that form. All forms come into existence upon the manifestation of consciousness in the play of Her whose substance is consciousness.

Though the Sāktānandatarangiṇī says: Devī is worshipped on account of Her soft heart (*komalāntah-karaṇam*), yet the use of the term "Mother" has other grounds than those which are founded upon an appeal to the natural feelings which the sweetness of the word "Mother" evokes. The meaning of the term "Devī" is *prakāsātmikā*, or that which is by its nature Light and Manifestation. And the word is used in the feminine gender because the One, as S'akti and Prakṛti, bears and nourishes all things as their Mother. The Devī is therefore the Brahman revealed in Its Mother aspect (*S'rimātā*) as Creatrix and Nourisher of the worlds.

Worshippers of Devī or S'akti are called S'āktas. But those who have a true knowledge of S'akti-tattva without which, according to S'āstra, Nirvānamokṣa is unattainable, will in thought surpass the sectarianism which the terms " S'ākta ", " Vaiṣṇava " and " S'aiva " ordinarily connote. Whatever forms the Devī assumes in Her aspect with attributes are but Her forms. As the author last cited says, the sādhaka will know Her, whether the appearance be that of Kṛṣṇa, Durgā, or Mahādeva. The Vaiṣṇava may consider Her as Viṣṇu in the form of S'akti, or the S'ākta may look upon Her as S'akti in the form of Viṣṇu. To those who, immersed in the ocean of Her substance, which is citśakti, are forgetful of all differences which appertain to the world of form, Kṛṣṇaśakti, S'ivaśakti, or Kālīśakti, and all other manifestations of śakti, are one and the same. And so Rāmaprasāda, the Bengali poet and Tāntrik, sang : " Thou assumeth five principal forms according to the differences of worship. But, O Mother ! how can you escape the hands of him who has dissolved the five and made them into one ? "

The hymns to the Devī in this volume (introduced by a *stotra* to Her Spouse the Kālabhairava) are taken from the Tantra, Purāna, Mahābhārata, and S'ankarācārya, who was " the incarnation of devotion " (*bhaktāvatāra*) as well as a great philosopher ; a fact which is sometimes ignored by those who do not wish to be reminded that he, whose speculative genius they extol, was also the protagonist of the so-called " idolatrous Hinduism." As his great example amongst many others of differing race and creed tell us, it is not, from the view of religion, the mark of discernment (even though it be the mode) to neglect or disparage the ritual practice which all orthodoxies have prescribed for their adherents. *Stava* and *pūjā* are doubtless the *sādhana* appropriate to the first of the several stages of an ascent which gradually leads away from them; but they are in general as necessary as the higher ones, which more immediately precede the attainment of *brahmabhāva* and *siddhi*.

Apart, however, from this aspect of the matter, and to look at it from the point of view of that modern product, the mere "student of religions," who is not infrequently a believer in none, a knowledge of ritual (to use that term in its widest sense) will help to a greater and more real understanding of the *mahāvākya* of the Āryas than can be gained from those merely theoretical expositions of them which are now more popular. Those, again, whose interests are in what Verlaine called "mere literature" will at least appreciate the mingled tenderness and splendour of these Hymns, even in a translation which cannot reproduce the majesty of the sanskrit *ślokas* of the Tantra and Purāṇa, or the rhyme and sweet lilting rhythms of S'ankara.

Of the Hymns now published, those from the Mahābhārata and Candī have already been translated; the first, in the English edition of the Mahābhārata, by Protap Chandra Roy and by Professor Muir in his "Original Sanskrit Texts," and the second by Mr. Pargiter, whose rendering of the Mārkandeya Purāṇa (of which it is the most celebrated portion) has been printed by the Asiatic Society of Bengal.

Ādyākālīsvarūpastotra has also been previously published as part of a rendering by myself of the Mahānirvāṇa Tantra. The first two sets of Hymns have been translated afresh. In the translation of such works a Sanskrit dictionary (however excellent) is not either a sufficient or reliable guide. It is necessary to study the Hindu commentators and to seek the oral aid of those who possess the traditional interpretation of the *S'āstra*. Without this and an understanding of what Hindu worship is and means, absurd mistakes are likely to be made. I have thus, in addition to such oral aid, availed myself of the Commentaries of Nīlakaṇṭha on the Mahābhārata, of Gopāla Chakravarti and Nāgogi Bhatta on Candī, and of Nīlakantha on the Devībhāgavata. As regards the Tantra, the great Sādhana S'āstrā, nothing which is of both an understanding and accurate character can be achieved without a study of the original texts undertaken with the assistance of the Tāntrik gurus and pandits, who are the authorized custodians of its traditions.

The other *stotras* are now rendered in English for the first time; at least, I have come across no translation of them.

The text of the Tantrasāra which has been used is that edited by Shrījut Rasik Mohun Chatterjee. It is not free from faults, which have necessitated reference to other Manuscripts. A more correct text of the Tārāshtakam, from the Nīla Tantra, is given in the Brihatstotraratnākara, to which reference has also been made for the hymns of Vālmiki and Indra.

Both Ellen Woodroffe and myself have collaborated in the translation of the hymns by S'ankara. For the rest, as also for the Introduction and Commentary, I am alone responsible. Some of the notes deal with matter familiar enough to the Hindu reader but have been inserted for the use of his English friends. Other portions of the commentary will, I believe, be found to be of use to both.

March 1, 1913 JOHN WOODROFFE

CONTENTS

HYMNS TO THE GODDESS

HYMN TO KALI

HYMNS TO THE GODDESS

INTRODUCTION

SANĀTANA BRAHMAN is called *sakala* when with *Prakṛti*, as It is *niṣkala* when thought of as without *Prakṛti* (*prakṛteranya*), for *kalā* is *Prakṛti*.[1] To say, however, that S'akti exists in or with, the Brahman is an accommodation to human thought and speech, for the Brahman and S'akti are in fact one. S'akti is eternal (*anādirūpā*), and *Brahmarūpā*, and both *nirguṇā* and *saguṇā*.[2] She, the Goddess (*Devī*), is the *caitanyarūpiṇi devi* who manifests all *bhūta*; the *ānandarūpiṇi devi* by whom the Brahman, who She is, manifests Itself,[3] and who, to use the words of the S'āradātilaka, pervades the universe as does oil the sesamum seed. "*Sa aikṣata,*" of which *S'ruti* speaks, was itself a manifestation of S'akti, the *paramāpūrvanirvāṇaśakti*, or Brahman, as S'akti.

From the *paraśaktimaya* issued *nāda*, and from *nāda*, *bindu*[4]. The state of subtle body known as *kāmakalā* is the *mūla* of *mantra*, and is meant when the Devī is spoken

---

[1] S'āradā Tilakam (chap. i.). See *Introduction to Tantra S'āstra* by Sir John Woodroffe—*sub. voc.* "S'iva and S'akti," of which the above is in part (with added matter) an abbreviation.

[2] *Praṇamya prakṛtim nityām paramātmasvarūpiṇīm* (chap. i.). S'āktānandatarangini, both Tāntrik works of high authority.

[3] Kubjikā Tantra (First Paṭala).

[4] Sāradā (*loc. cit*).

of as *mūlamantrātmikā*.[1] The *Parambindu* is represented as a circle the centre of which is the *Brahmapada*, wherein are *Prakṛti-puruṣa*; the circumference of which is encircling *māyā*. It is in the crescent of *nirvāṇakalā* the seventeenth, which is again in that of *amākalā* the sixteenth, digit of the moon circle (*candramaṇḍala*), situate above the sun-circle (*sūryamaṇḍala*), the *Guru* and the *Hamsah* in the pericarp of the 1,000 petalled lotus (*sahasrārapadma*). The *bindu* is symbolically described as being like a grain of gram (*canaka*), which under its encircling sheath contains a divided seed—*Prakṛti-Purusa* or S'akti-S'iva. [2]

It is known as the S'abda Brahman. [3] A polarization then takes place in *paraśaktimaya*. The Devi becomes *unmukhi*. Her face is turned to S'iva. There is an unfolding which bursts the encircling shell.[4] The *devatāparaśaktimaya* exists in the threefold aspect of *bindu*, *bija*, and *nāda*, the last being in relation to the two former. An indistinct sound then arises[5] (*avyaktātmāravobhavat*). *Nāda*, as Rāghava Bhatta [6] says, exists in three states, for in it are the three *guṇas*. The S'abda Brahman manifests Itself in the threefold energies, *Jnāna*, *Ichhā*, and *Kriyā S'akti*. [7] For, as the Vāmakeśvara

[1] See Bhāskararāya's Commentary on the Lalitā Sahasranāma (verse 36), and the Pādukāpancaka in *The Serpent Power*.

[2] See Ṣatcakranirūpaṇa of Purnānanda Svāmi in *The Serpent Power*.

[3] S'āradā (*loc. cit*).

[4] *Ibid*.

[5] *Ibid*.

[6] See Commentary on verse 49 of the Ṣatcakranirupaṇa, and generally as to the subject-matter of this Introduction, my "*Introduction to Tantra S'āstra.*"

[7] See Goraksha Samhitā, Bhutaśuddhi Tantra, and Yogini Tantra, Part I, p. 10.

Tantra says, the Devī Tripurā is threefold, as Brahmā, Viṣṇu, and Īśa. Paraśiva exists as a septenary under the forms of S'ambhu, S'adāśiva, Īśāna, Rudra, Viṣṇu, and Brahmā. The last five are the *Mahāpreta*, four of whom form the support, and the fifth the seat, of the bed on which the Devī is united with Paramaśiva in the room of *cintāmaṇi* stone on the jewelled island clad with clumps of *kadamba*, and heavenly trees set in the ocean of ambrosia. [1]

S'akti is both *māyā* and *mūlaprakṛti*, whose substance is the three *guṇas*, representing nature as the revelation of spirit (*sattva*) ; nature as the passage of descent from spirit to matter, or of ascent from matter to spirit (*rajas*), and nature as the dense veil of spirit (*tamas*). The Devī is thus the treasure-house of *guṇas* (*guṇanidhiḥ*).[2] *Mūlaprakṛti* is the womb into which the Brahman casts the seed from which all things are born. [3] The womb thrills to the movement of the essentially active *rajoguṇa*, and the now unstable *guṇas* in varied combinations under the illumination of S'iva (*cit*)) evolve the universe which is ruled by Maheśvara and Maheśvarī. The dual principles of S'iva-S'akti, which are the product of the polarity manifested in *Paraśaktimaya*, pervade the whole universe, and are present in man in the *svayambhulinga* of the *mūlādhāra* and the Devī Kuṇḍalinī, who in serpent form encircles it. The *S'abdabrahman* assumes the form of the Devī Kuṇḍalinī, and as such is in the form of all breathing creatures (*prāṇi*), and in the form of letters appears in prose and verse. She is the luminous vital energy (*jīvaśakti*), which manifests as *prāṇa*. Through the

[1] See Ānandalaharī of S'ankarācārya, verse 8. The *dhyāna* is well known to the Tantrik *sādhaka*.

[2] Lalitā, verse 121.

[3] Bhagavadgītā (chap. xiv., verses 3,4).

various *prakṛta* and *vaikṛta* creations, issued the Devas, men, animals, and the whole universe, which is the work and manifested form of the Dẹvī. For, as the Kubjikā Tantra says, " Not Brahmā, Viṣṇu, and Rudra create, maintain, and destroy, but Brāhmī, Vaiṣṇavī, Rudrāṇī. Their husbands are but as dead bodies. "

The Goddess (*Devī*) is the great S'akti. She is *māyā*, for of Her the *māyā* which produces the *samsāra* is. As Lord of *māyā*, She is Mahāmāyā.[1] Devī is *avidyā* (nescience), because She binds; and *vidyā* (knowledge), because She liberates and destroys the *samsāra*.[2] She is Prakṛti,[3] and, as existing before creation, She is the *ādya* (primordial) śakti. She is the *vācaka-śakti*, the manifestation of *cit* in Prakṛti; and the *vācya śakti* or *cit* itself. The *ātmā* should be contemplated as Devī.[4]

S'akti or Devī is thus the Brahman revealed in its Mother aspect (*srīmātā*)[5] as creatrix and nourisher of the worlds. Kālī says of Herself in Yoginī Tantra:[6] "*Saccidānandarupāham Brahmaivāham sphuratprabham.*" So the Devī is described with attributes both of the qualified[7] Brahman, and (since that Brahman is but the manifestation of the Absolute), She is also addressed

1 *Mahāmāyā* without *māyā* is *nirguṇā*, and with *māyā*, *saguṇā*. S'āktānandatarangini (chap. i.).

2 S'āktānandatarangini (chap. i.).

3 Brahmavaivarta Purāṇa (chap. i.); Prakṛtikhanda. Br. Nāradiya Pr.

4 See chap. ii. of Devī Bhāgavata.

5 Devī is worshipped on account of her soft heart. S'āktānandatarangini (chap. iii.).

6 Part I., Chapter X.

7 Such as Mukunda, an aspect of Viṣṇu. Lalitāsahasranāma, verse 838.

with epithets which denote the unconditioned Brahman.[1] She is the great Mother (*ambikā*) sprung from the sacrificial hearth of the fire of the Grand Consciousness (*cit*) decked with the Sun and Moon; Lalitā—"She who plays"—whose play is world-play; whose eyes, playing like fish in the beauteous waters of Her Divine face, open and shut with the appearance and disappearance of countless worlds, now illuminated by Her light, now wrapped in her terrible darkness.[2] For Devī, who issues from the great Abyss, is terrible also in Her Kālī, Tārā, Chinnamastā, and other forms. Śāktas hold that a sweet and complete resignation of the self to such forms of the Divine Power denotes a higher stage of spiritual development.[3] Such dualistic worship also speedily bears the fruit of knowledge of the Universal Unity, the realization of which dispels all fear. For the Mother is only terrible to those who, living in the illusion of separateness (which is the cause of all fear), have not yet realized their unity with Her, and known that all Her forms are those of beauty.

The Devī as Parabrahman is beyond all form and *guṇa*. The forms of the Mother of the universe are threefold. There is first the Supreme (*para*) form, of

---

[1] *Ibid*, verse 153, and Commentator's note to Chapter II., where Devi is addressed as Supreme Light (*paramjyotih*), Supreme Abode (*paramdhāma*), Supreme of Supreme (*parātparā*).

[2] See the Lalitā.

[3] See the saying of Rāmaprasāda, the poet-devotee of Kālimā, quoted at p. 714 in Babu Dinesh Chunder Sen's "History of Bengali Literature."

"Though the Mother beat him, the child cries 'Mother! O Mother!' and clings still tighter to her garment. True, I cannot see Thee, yet am I not a lost child. I still cry 'Mother!'"

which, as the Viṣṇu Yāmala[1] says, "none know." There is next Her subtle (*sūkṣma*) form, which consists of *mantra*. But, as the mind cannot easily settle itself upon that which is formless,[2] She appears as the subject of contemplation in Her third or gross (*sthūla*) or physical form, with hands and feet and the like, as celebrated in the *Devīstotra* of the Purāṇas and Tantras. Devī, who as *Prakṛti* is the source of Brahmā, Viṣṇu, and Maheśvara,[3] has both male and female forms.[4] But it is in Her female forms that she is chiefly contemplated. For, though existing in all things, in a peculiar sense female beings are parts of Her.[5] The Great Mother, who exists in the form of all Tantras and all Yantras,[6] is, as the Lalitā says, the "unsullied treasure-house of beauty," the sapphire Devī[7] whose slender

---

1 *Mātastvatparamamrūpam tanna jānāti kashchana* (see chap. iii. of S'āktānandatarangini)

2 *Amurtauchitsthironasyāt tatomurtim vichintayet* (*ibid.*, chap. i., as was also explained to Himavat by Devī in the Kurma Purāṇa).

3 *Ibid.*, and as such is called Tripurā (see Bhāskararāyā's Commentary on Lalitā, verse 125).

4 *Ibid.*, chap. iii., which also says that there is no eunuch form of God.

5 So in Candi (Mārkaṇḍeya Purāṇa) it is said:

"*Vidyāh samastāstava devī bhedāh,*
Stryah samastāsakalā jagatsu."

The Tāntrika, more than all men, recognizes the divinity of woman, as was observed centuries past by the author of the Dabistan. The Linga Purāṇa also, after describing Arundhati, Anasūyā and Shachi to be each the manifestation of Devi, concludes: "All things indicated by words in the feminine gender are manifestations of Devī." Similary the Brahmavaivarta Purāṇa.

6 *Sarvatantrarūpā Sarvayantrātmikā* (See Lalitā, verse 53).

7 Padma Purāṇa says: "Viṣṇu ever worships the sapphire Devi."

waist,[1] bending beneath the burden of the ripe fruit of her breasts,[2] swells into jewelled hips heavy[3] with the promise of infinite maternities.[4] Her litanies depict Her physical form from head to foot, celebrating Her hair adorned with flowers and crowned with gems; Her brow bright as the eighth-day moon; Her ruby cheeks and coral lips; teeth like to "the buds of the sixteen-syllabled *mantra*," and eyebrows curved as are the arches at the gate of the palace of Kāmarāja; Her nose; Her teeth; Her chin; Her arms; and "Her twin breasts offered in return for that priceless gem which is the love of Kāmeśvara"; Her waist girdled with jewelled bells; Her smooth and faultless limbs rounded beneath the "jewelled disc of the knee like the

---

1 *Āpīvarastanatatimtanuvrittamadhyām* (Bhuvaneśvarīstotra), *tanumadhya* (Lalitā, verse 79). *krishodari* (Ādyakālisvarūpāstotra, Mahānirvāṇa Tantra, 7th Ullāsa).

2 *Stotra* and *dhyāna* commonly represent Her as having large, full, and erect breasts—*pīnastanādye* (in Karpurādistotra), *pīnonnatapayodharām*) (in Durgā-dhyāna of Devī Purāṇa), *bakshojakumbhāntarī* (in Annapurṇāstava) *āpīvarastanatatim* (in Bhuvaneśvaristotra)—which weight her limbs—*kuchabharanamitāngim* (in Sarasvatidhyāna), *annapradānaniratāngstanabhāranamrām* (in Annapūrṇastava). And the Lalitā , verse 15, says: "Her golden girdle supports Her waist, which bends under the burden of Her breasts, thrice folding the skin below Her bosom" (*trivalīvalayopetām*).

3 So it is said in the tenth *śloka* of the Karpūrākhyastava *samantādāpīnastanajaghanadhrikyauvanavatī*. S'ankarācarya, in his Tripurāsundaristotra, speaks of Her *nitamba* (buttocks) "as excelling the mountain in greatness" (*nitambajitabhūdharām*). The Javanese also call Her Loro Jongram. "The pure exalted virgin with beautiful hips."

4 The physical characteristics of the Devi in Her swelling breasts and hips are emblematic of Her great Motherhood, for She is *S'rimātā*.

sapphire-studded quiver of the God of Love" descending in lines of grace to Her bright louts feet, [1] which dispel the darkness of Her worshippers.[2] For moonlight is She, yet sunbeam, soothing all those who are burnt by the triple fires of misery (*tāpatraya*). Her face, Her body from throat to waist, and thence downwards, represent the *vāgbhava* and other *kūta*. The colour of the Devī varies according to the form under which She is contemplated. Thus, in conferring liberation, She is white; as controller of women, men, and kings, She is red; and as controller of wealth, saffron. As creatrix of enmity, She becomes tawny; and in the thrill of love, passion (*śṛngāra*), She is of the colour of the rose. In the action of slaying She becomes black. Thus, Devi, the Supreme Light, is to be meditated upon as differently coloured according to Her different activities. [3]

After the description of the form of the Devi in *brahmāṇḍa* follows that of Her subtle form, called Kuṇḍalinī in the body (*piṇḍāṇḍa*). As the Mahādevī [4] She exists in all forms as S'arasvatī, Lakṣmi, Gāyatrī,

---

[1] See the Lalitāsahasranāma, verse 4 *et seq.* "Her brow (*aṣṭamīcandravibhrājadalika sthala śobhitā*), Her eyebrow (*vadanasamara māngalyagrihatoranacillika*), Her twin breasts (*kāmeśvarapremaratnamani pratiphalastani*), Her waist (*ratnakinkinikarabhyarashanādāma bhūṣitā*), "Her thighs, known only to Kameśa" (*Kāmeśajnātasaubhāgya mardavorudvayānvitā*), Her lower limbs (*indragopa parikṣipta smaratunā bhajandhikā*); Her instep 'arched like the back of a tortoise,' the bright rays from her nails and the soles of Her feet in beauty shaming the lotus."

[2] From the beautiful litany to the Devi in the Lalitāsahasranāma.

[3] Bhāskararāya's Commentary on Lalitā, verse 170.

[4] She whose body is, as the Devī Purāṇa says, immeasurable.

Durgā, Tripurasundari, Annapurnā, and all the Devi who are *avatāra* of the Brahman.[1]

Devi, as Sati, Umā, Pārvati, and Gouri, is spouse of S'iva. It was as Sati, prior to Dakṣa's sacrifice (*dakṣayajna*) that the Devi manifested Herself to S'iva[2] in the ten celebrated forms known as the *daśamahāvidyā*—Kāli, Bagala, Chinnamastā, Bhuvaneshvari, Mātangini, Shorosi, Dhumāvati, Tripurasundari, Tārā, and Bhairavi. When at the *dakṣayajna* She yielded up Her life in shame and sorrow at the treatment accorded by Her father to Her husband, S'iva took away the body, and, ever bearing it with him, remained wholly distraught and spent with grief. To save the world from the forces of evil which arose and grew with the withdrawal of His divine control, Viṣṇu, with his discus (*cakra*), cut the dead body of Sati, which S'iva bore, into fifty-one fragments, which fell to earth at the places thereafter known as the fifty-one[3] *mahāpithasthānas*, where Devi, with her Bhairava, is worshipped under various names.

Thus the right and left breasts fell at Jalandhara and Ramgiri, where the Devi is worshipped as Tripuramālini; the *yoni* at the celebrated shrine at Kamrup in Assam, where the Devi is worshipped as Kāmākṣā or Kāmākhyā (see *ibid.*);[4] the throat, shoulders, nose, hands,

[1] S'āktānandatarangini (chap. iii.).

[2] In order to display Her power to Her husband who had not granted, at Her request, His permission that She might attend at Dakṣa's sacrifice (see "*Principles of Tantra*" and for an account of the *daśamahāvidyā*, their *yantra* and *mantra*, the Daśamahāvidyā upāsanārahasya of Prasanno Kumar Shastri).

[3] The number is variously given as 50, 51, and 52.

[4] Here at Her shrine the menstruation of the earth which, according to Hindu belief, takes place in the month of Assar, is

arms, eyes, fingers, tongue, buttocks, lips, belly, chin, navel, cheeks, thighs, teeth, feet, ears, thumbs, heels, toes (some at Kālighat), waist, hair, forehead, with skeleton (several of these parts being themselves divided), fell at other *pīṭha*, at each of which the Devi is worshipped under different names in company with a Bhairava or S'iva, also variously named. Thus, the Devī at Kālighat is Kālikā, and the S'iva Nakuleśvara, and the Devī at Kamrup is Kāmākshā, and Her Bhairava is Ramānanda.

These are but some only of Her endless forms. She is seen as one and as many: as it were, but one moon reflected in countless waters.[1] She exists, too, in all animals and inorganic things, since the universe, with all its beauties, is, as the Devī Purāṇa says, but a part of Her. All this diversity of form is but the infinite manifestations of the flowering beauty of the one Supreme Life—a doctrine which is nowhere else taught with greater wealth of illustration than in the S'ākta S'āstras and Tantras. The great Bharga in the bright sun, and all Devatā, and, indeed, all life and being are worshipful, and are worshipped, but only as Her manifestations.[2] And he who worships them otherwise is, in the words of the great Devībhāgavata,[3] "like unto a man who. with the light of a clear lamp

---

said to manifest itself. For three days during *ambuvāchī* no cooked food is eaten by the women, nor does any cooking take place in the house.

[1] Brahmabindu Up, p. 12.

[2] See chap. iii. of the S'āktānandatarangini, where it is said: "The Parabrahman, Devi, S'iva, and all other Deva and Devi are but one, and he who thinks them different from one another goes to Hell."

[3] Hymn to Jagadambikā in Chapter XIX.

in his hands, yet falls into some waterless and terrible well." It is customary nowadays to decry external worship, but those who do so presume too much. The ladder of ascent can only be scaled by those who have trod all, including its lowest, rungs. The S'akti-rahasya summarises the stages of progress in a short verse, thus: "A mortal who worships by ceremonies, by images, by mind, by identification, by knowing the self, attains *kaivalya*." Before *brahma-bhāva* can be attained the *sādhaka* must have passed from *pūjābhāva* through hymns and prayer to *dhyāna-bhāva*. The highest worship[1] for which the *sādhaka* is qualified (*adhikāri*) only after external worship, and that internal form known as *sādhāra*[2] is described as *nirādhāra*. Therein Pure Intelligence is the Supreme S'akti who is worshipped as the Very Self, the Witness freed of the glamour of the manifold universe. By one's own direct experience of Maheśvarī as the Self, She is, with reverence, made the object of that worship which leads to liberation.

J. W.

[1] Sūtasamhitā, 1, 5, 3, which divides such worship into Vedic and Tāntrik (see Bhāskararāya's Commentary on Lalitā, verse 43).

[2] In which Devī is worshipped in the form of *mantra* according to the instructions of the Guru.

HYMN TO KĀLABHAIRAVA

BY

S'ANKARĀCĀRYA

KĀLABHAIRAVA

(KĀLABHAIRAVĀṢṬAKA)

1

I WORSHIP Kālabhairava,[1] Lord of the city of Kāśi,[2]
Whose sacred lotus feet are worshipped by the
King of Devas,[3]
The compassionate One,
Whose sacrificial thread is made of serpents,
On whose forehead shines the moon.[4]
The naked one,[5]
Whom Nārada[6] and multitudes of other Yogis adore.
Kāśikāpurādhinātha kālabhairavam bhaje.[7]

2

I worship Kālabhairava, Lord of the city of Kāśi,
Blazing like a million suns,

---

[1] S'iva as such.

[2] Benares. The Kāśipanchakastotra of S'ankara says that the pure Ganges is the flow of knowledge and Kāśi is S'iva's mind (*Jnānapravāhāvimalādigangā sakāśikāham nijabodharūpah*).

[3] Devarāja or Indra.

[4] Hence S'iva is called Candraśekhara.

[5] *Digambaram,* as are the *Yogis* of whom He is Master. For He is clothed with space itself.

[6] The *Ṛṣi* of that name.

[7] The refrain is : "I worship Kālabhairava, Lord of the city of Kāsi."

Our great Saviour in our voyage across the ocean
of the world.[1]
The blue-throated,[2] three-eyed[3] grantor of all
desires,
The lotus-eyed, who is the death of death,[4]
The imperishable One,
Holding the rosary of human bone[5] and the trident.[6]
Kāśikāpurādhinātha Kālabhairavam bhaje.

3

I worship Kālabhairava, Lord of the city of Kāsī,
The primeval cause,[7]
Holding in His hands trident, axe, noose, and staff[8]
—Him of the black body,[9]
The first of all Deva[10], imperishable, incorruptible,
Lord formidable and powerful,

---

[1] A constant simile. The world is a storm-tossed ocean not free of danger, even in moments of calm, for therein many dangers, perils, and terrors lie.

[2] For S'iva swallowed the poison which issued at the churning of the ocean to save the earth from its dangerous presence.

[3] For with the ordinary eyes He bears in the forehead the eye of wisdom.

[4] S'iva is the conqueror of death ("*mrityunjaya*"), for he gives that knowledge which frees man of its terrors.

[5] Even often of the low-caste Candālas and others, for S'iva is the adored and protector of all.

[6] His peculiar weapon.

[7] For all causes potentially lie in His destructive energies, the manifestation of which is the prelude of re-creation.

[8] *S'ūla, tangka, pāśa, daṇḍa,* His implements.

[9] As Kālabhairava. Usually he is white and smeared with ashes "shining like a mountain of silver."

[10] Hence He is called Mahādeva.

Who loves to dance wonderfully.[1]
Kāśikāpurādhinātha kālabhairavam bhaje.

4

I worship Kālabhairava, Lord of the city of Kāśi,
Of great and beautiful body,
The giver of both enjoyment and liberation,[2]
Who loves and smiles upon all His devotees,
Whose body is the whole world,
Whose waist is adorned with little tinkling bells;[3]
Beautiful are they, and made of gold.
Kāśikāpurādhinātha kālabhairavam bhaje

5

I worship Kālabhairava, Lord of the city of Kāśi,
The protector of the bridge of *dharma*,[4]
Destroyer of the path of *adharma*,[5]
Liberator form the bonds of *karma*,[6]
The all-pervading giver of welfare to all,

---

1 *Vichitratāṇḍavapriyam.* S'iva is often pictured dancing as Natarāja. The place of the dance is the body of the individual and the world spoken of as *vanam* (the forest), on account of the multitude of its components. He as the inner *ātman* causes all things to dance into and out of life, and again into it. All life and activity comes through Him, " the unseen Lord of the stage."

2 *Bhuktimuktidāyakam*—that is, He gives both worldly and heavenly enjoyment, and that release from both which is the unending bliss of liberation.

3 Hung on a girdle.

4 Righteousness. For *dharma*, religion, law, and duty, are the bridge whereby the dangerous waters of the world are passed.

5 Unrighteousness.

6 The cause and fruit of action whereby man is bound to the phenomenal world until by knowledge, *karma* is exhausted and destroyed, and liberation (through S'iva, with whose essential being His worshipper becomes one) is attained.

Whose golden body is adorned with serpent coils.
Kāśikapurādhinātha kālabhairavam bhaje.

6

I worship Kālabhairava, Lord of the city of Kāśi
Whose feet are beautiful with the lustre of the gems thereon—
The stainless, eternal Iṣṭadevatā, [1]
One without a second, [2]
Destroyer of the pride, and liberator from the gaping jaw of the God of Death. [3]
Kāsikāpurādhinātha kālabhairavam bhaje.

7

I worship Kālabhairava, Lord of the city of Kāśi, [4]
Whose loud laughter broke the shell of many an egg of the lotus-born; [5]
Strong ruler, at whose glance the net of sin is broken; Giver of the eight powers, [6]
Whose shoulders serpents garland.
Kāśikāpurādhinātha kālabhairavam bhaje.

---

[1] The desired (or patron) Deity of the devotee.

[2] For He is the Supreme Unity.

[3] See *ante*, p. 16, note 4.

[4] Each world (for there are many) is called an egg of Brahmā the creator (*brahmāṇḍa*). S'iva the great Destroyer by His loud laughter shatters them.

[5] Brahmā.

[6] *Siddhi*—namely, *aṇimā*, *mahimā*, *garimā*, *laghimā*, *prāpti*, *prākāmya*, *iṣitva*, and *vaṣitva*. The power to become very small, vast, light, heavy, power of vision and movement, the powers of creation and control over the worlds and their Lords. These *siddhi* are powers of the all-pervading *ātmā*, and to greater or less degree may be acquired by S'ivayogins according as they realize their unity therewith.

8

I worship Kālabhairava, Lord of the city of Kāśi,
The Saviour of all, giver of great fame,
The all-pervading One,
Who purifies of both sin and virtue the people of Kāśi;[1]
The ancient Lord of the world,
Wise in the wisdom of all moralities.[2]
Kāśikāpurādhinātha kālabhairavam bhaje.

---

[1] *Kāśivāsiloka puṇyapāpaśodhakām*: for to the liberated there is neither sin nor virtue which are qualities of the phenomenal *jivātma* only. The liberated are above both.

[2] *Nītimargakovidam.*

HYMNS TO THE DEVĪ
FROM TANTRA

BHAIRAVĪ[1]

(BHAIRAVĪSTOTRA)

From the TANTRASĀRA[2]

1

Thus shall I pray to Thee, O Tripurā,[3]
To attain the fruit of my desires,
In this hymn by which men attain that Lakṣmi,[4]
Who is worshipped by the Devas.

2

Origin of the world thou art,
Yet hast Thou Thyself no origin,
Though with hundreds of hymns.
Even Brahmā, Viṣṇu, and Maheśvara[5] cannot
know Thee.[6]
Therefore we worship Thy breasts, Mother of all
S'āstra,[7]
Shining with fresh saffron.

---

[1] Fem. of Bhairava, a name of S'iva.

[2] P. 596, Ed. Rasik Mohun Chatterjee.

[3] See Tripurasundari—*post*.

[4] Devi of prosperity.

[5] S'iva.

[6] In the Viṣṇu Yāmala, Viṣṇu says of the Devi: "Thy supreme form none know" (*mātastvatparamarūpam tannajānāti kashchana*), (*see* chap. iii S'āktānandatarangini).

[7] *Vāngmaya*.

3

O Tripurā,[1] we adore Thee,
Whose body shines with the splendour of a thousand risen suns,
Holding with two of thy hands a book[2] and rosary of *rudrākṣa* beads,[3]
And with two others making the gestures
Which grant boons and dispel fear.[4]
With three lotus eyes is Thy lotus face adorned.
Beauteous is Thy Neck with its necklace of large pearls.[5]

4

O Mother, how can the ignorant, whose minds are restless with doubt and dispute,
Know Thy form ravishing with its vermilion,[6]
Stooping with the weight of Thy breasts,[7]
Accessible only by merit,
Acquired in previous birth?

---

[1] See *post*.

[2] *Vidyā*.

[3] Seed of a plant sacred to the worship of S'iva.

[4] That is, She makes the *mudrā vara* and *abhaya*. In the first the hand is held forth in front of the body with the palm upward and horizontal, the fingers together, and the thumb crossing the palm to the fourth finger. In the second the hand is held up with the fingers and thumb in the same positions with the palm towards the spectator.

[5] *Tārā*, the ordinary pearl, is called *muktā*.

[6] *Sindūra*, the Bhairavi's body is painted with vermilion and Her garments also are red.

[7] *Kuchabharaṇamrām* (see Introduction).

5

O Bhavānī,[1] the *munis*[2] describe thee in physical form;[3]
The *S'ruti* speaks of Thee in subtle form;
Others call Thee presiding Deity of speech;
Others, again, as the root of the worlds.
But we think of Thee
As the untraversable ocean of mercy, and nothing else.

6

Worshippers contemplate Thee in their heart
As three-eyed, adorned with the crescent moon,
White as the autumnal moon,
Whose substance is the fifty letters,[4]
Holding in Thy hands a book, a rosary, a jar of nectar, and making the *vyakhya mudra*.[5]

---

[1] The Devi is Bhavānī as the spouse and giver of Life to Bhava.

[2] Sages.

[3] There are three forms of the Devī—the gross or physical, with hands, feet, etc.; the subtle (*sūkṣma*), consisting of *mantra* and the supreme (*parā*), which is the real or own (*svarūpā*). The form of the Devī has both *prakāśa* and *vimarśa* aspects—that is real and secondary or manifested. Thus the Vāmakeśvara Tantra says: "The Devī Tripurā is Her real form. She who is of a red colour is the manifested one."

[4] Of the alphabet or *mātṛkā* (*panchāśadākṣaramayīm*). These letters stand for the *vṛtti* (functions and qualities of being). The Devī is thus *mātṛkāmayī*, or composed of *mātṛkā*.

[5] *Vyakhya.* according to the S'abda Kalpadruma = *vivaraṇam* (description), or *grantha* (book), and also commentary, but here denotes a *mudrā* of that name.

7

O Tripurā, Thou art S'ambhu[1] united with Pārvatī.[2]
Thou art now Viṣṇu embraced by Kamalā,[3]
And now Brahmā born of the lotus.[4]
Thou art again the presiding Devī of speech,
And yet again art the energy of all these.

8

I, having taken refuge with the four—
Bhāvas,[5] *Parā*, and others[6] born of the *vāgbhava* (*bīja*),[7]

---

[1] S'iva, one of the forms of the four *mahāpreta*, whose bija is "*Hsau.*"

[2] The androgyne form, called *ardhanārīśvara*, half being S'iva and the other half S'akti. According to Hindu belief, the wife is the pure and sacred (*puṇyā*) half of her husband's body, and besides shares the purity and merits of her husband according to the common saying *S'arīrārdham smṛtā jāyā puṇyā puṇyāphale samā.*

[3] Lakṣmī.

[4] That is, the power of destruction, maintenance, and creation.

[5] The four *bhāvas* are states or conditions of Kuṇḍalinī appearing as sound and its subtle elements, and are *Parā*, whose abode (*sthāna*) is the *mūlādhāra*; *Paśyantī* in the *svādhiṣṭhāna*; *Madhyamā* in the *anāhata*; and *Vaikharī* in the *viśuddha* issuing through the the throat (see next note). There appears, however, to be some difference as to the location of the second.

[6] *Parā* is the first condition of Kuṇḍalinī in the form of tāmasik sound in the *Mūlādhāra*; *Paśyanti* is the *bhāva* when Kuṇḍalinī, associated with *manas*, reaches the position variously stated as the *svādiṣṭhāna* or *manipūra*; *Madhyamā*, when it reaches the *anāhatacakra*, associated with *buddhi*; and *Vaikharī* is when Kuṇḍalinī issues through the throat in the form of the fifty letters. It is said that though there are thus four kinds of speech, the gross-minded do not understand the first three, and think speech to be *Vaikharī* alone.

[7] That is, *Āim* the *bīja* of Sarasvatī. The Devī is 'three syllabled' (*Tryakṣarī*)—that is, the *bīja* of the three divisions of the

Shall never in my heart forget Thee, the supreme
Devatā,
Whose substance is existence and intelligence,[1]
And who expresseth by Thy throat and other organ
The *bhāva* appearing in the form of letters.[2]

9

The blessed, having conquered the six enemies,[3]
And drawing in their breath,[4]
With steady mind fix their gaze on the tip of their
nostrils,
And contemplate in their head Thy moon-crested
form,[5]
Resplendent as the newly risen sun.

10

The Vedas proclaim that Thou createth the world,
Having assumed the other half of the body of the
enemy of Kāma.[6]
Verily is it true, O Daughter of the mountain and
the only World-mother,
That had this not been so,
The multitude of worlds would never have been.

Panchadaśi, *Vāgbhava*, *Kāmarāja* and *S'akti*. According to the Vāmakeśvara Tantra, Vāgiśvari is the *jnānā śakti*, which is in the *vāgbhava* division, and confers salvation, the *kāmarāja* and *śakti* divisions being the *kriyā* and *ichchhā sākti* (see the Lalitā, verse 126).

[1] *Sacchinmayī*, the Brahman being *sat* and *chit*.

[2] That is, they ultimately so appear, though previously existing as subtle elements of sound.

[3] The six sins: Lust (*kāma*), anger (*krodha*), greed (*lobha*), delusion (*moha*), pride (*mada*), envy (*mātsaryā*).

[4] *Akunchya vayam* by *pūraka* of *prāṇāyāmā*.

[5] As S'akti of S'iva.

[6] S'iva. The Androgyne form *ardhanārīśvara*.

11

In company with the wives of the Kinnaras,[1]
The Siddha women,[2] whose eyes are reddened by wine[3]
Having worshipped Thee with the flowers of celestial trees[4]
In Thy *pitha*[5] in the caverns of the golden mountain,[6]
Sing Thy praises.

12

I worship in my heart the Devi whose body is moist with nectar,[7]
Beauteous as the splendour of lightning,
Who, going from Her abode to that[8] of S'iva,[9]
Opens the lotuses on the beautiful way[10]

---

[1] A lower order of Devas (*devayoni*).

[2] Wives of the Siddhas, also celestial spirits (*devayoni*) inhabiting the atmospheric plane (*bhuvah*).

[3] *Asvāditāsavarasāruna netrapadma.*

[4] *Pādapa,* so called because the tree drinks by its roots. As to the celestial trees (see " Wave of Bliss " *post*).

[5] Seat or shrine.

[6] Sumeru.

[7] For She as Kuṇḍalinī goes from the *mūlādhāra* to the *śivasthāna* in the *sahasrāra* and returns moist with the nectar of Her union with Him.

[8] *Rajādhani.* Literally capital city of S'iva.

[9] That is from the *mūlādhāra cakra* to the *śivasthāna.*

[10] The *suṣumnā* is the central " nerve " (*nādī*), or, rather, channel of energy in the body in which the lotuses (*ṣaṭcakra*) are threaded with their heads normally downwards. As Kuṇḍalinī becomes stirred by the yoga process, She ascends from the

of the *suṣumnā*.[1]

13

O Tripurā, I take refuge at Thy lotus feet,
Worshipped by Brahmā, Viṣṇu, and Maheśvara;
The abode of bliss, the source of the Vedas,
The origin of all prosperity;
Thou whose body is Intelligence itself.[2]

14

I shall never forget Her who is the giver of happiness;
She it is, O Mother, who, in the form of the Moon,
Creates the world full of sounds and their meanings,
And again, by Her power in the form of the Sun,
She it is who maintains the world.
And She, again, it is who, in the form of Fire, destroys the whole universe at the end of the ages.[3]

---

mūlādhāra and enters the higher *cakra*. As She does so, the lotuses upturn and expand again, closing on her departure.

1 The text which has *sausuvartma kamalāni vikāshayantim*, is not, however, intelligible, and the metre is short. Possibly it is a misprint for *saumyang*.

2 That is, nothing but intelligence *caitanyamātra tanu*.

3 *Nādā*, as Rāghava Bhatta says, exists in the three states of *nibodhikā* or *bodhinī*, *nāda*, and in the form of *bindu*, according to the predominance of the *guṇa*. These three and the *śaktis*, *jnānā*, *kriyā* and *ichhā*, of which they are special manifestations, are said to be in the form of sun, moon, and fire respectively. The moon (*indu*) is *ichchhā* (will and desire), the eternal precursor of creation. *Kriyā* is like the sun, which makes all things visible. *Jnānā* is fire, as it burns up all actions (see Ṣatcakranirūpaṇā, verse 49, and Sāradā Tilaka, chap. i.).

15

Men worship Thee under various names—
As Nārāyaṇa [1]; as She who saves from the ocean of Hell;[2]
As Gauri;[3] as the allayer of grief;[4] as Sarasvati,[5]
And as the three-eyed giver of knowledge.[6]

16

O Mother of the world, such as worship Thee with twelve Verses of this hymn attain to Thee, and gain all powers of speech [7] and the supreme abode.

---

[1] As Viṣṇu.

[2] *Narakārnatārini*.

[3] Spouse of S'iva. The Devi Purāṇa says; "She who was burned by the fire of *yoga* was again born of Himālaya; as She has the colour of the conch, jasmine, and moon, she is called Gauri." Her colour is golden. S'iva said to Pārvati: "O Daughter of Himālaya, I am white as the moon and thou art dark. I am the sandal-tree, and thou art, as it were, a snake entwined round it." Pārvati, taking umbrage at this remark upon Her dark complexion, went away to the forest, and there, by the performance of austerities, gained for herself a golden complexion beautiful as the sunlit sky.

[4] *Khedāshāmine*.

[5] S'iva.

[6] Devi of speech and learning.

[7] *Vāksiddhi* or *siddhi* of words.

BHUVANES'VARI[1]

FROM THE TANTRASĀRA[2]

1

Now I pray for the attainment of all blessings to Bhuvaneśvarī,
The cause and Mother[3] of the world,
She whose form is that of the S'abdabrahman,[4]
And whose substance is bliss.

2

Thou art the primordial One,[5]
Mother of countless creatures,
Creatrix of the bodies[6] of the lotus-born,[7] Viṣṇu and S'iva.
Who creates, preserves, and destroys the three worlds.
O Mother! by hymning Thy praise I purify my speech.

---

[1] The Devi in her aspect as Lord and Ruler of the world.

[2] P. 567.

[3] *Ambikā.*

[4] *Sākṣātśabdabrahmasvarūpiṇī*: the "sound" or manifested Aparabrahman, as opposed to the absolute, the Parabrahman. The Devi and the S'abdabrahman are, in fact, one, though men speak of Her as His S'akti (power).

[5] Ādyā.

[6] *Vapuḥpratipādayitrī.* The Devas have bodies, subtle though they be, as the S'abdabrahman Himself has.

[7] Brahmā.

3

O Daughter of the Mountain-King,[1]
Thou art the cause of the world-destroying energy of S'iva,[2]
Who manifests in earth, water, fire, ether, the sacrificer, the sun and moon,[3]
And who destroyed the body of Manmatha.[4]

4

O Mother! men only worship the triple-streamed Gangā[5]
Because She shines in the matted hair of S'iva,[6]
Which has been purified
By the dust of Thy lotus feet.

5

As the moon[7] delights the white night lotus[8] and none other,

---

[1] Himavat, whose daughter, as Pārvati, the Devi was.

[2] For they derive their power from the Devi, the All-Mother, whose children they are, and who also manifests as their Spouse.

[3] These constitute the eight-fold forms (*aṣṭamūrti*) of S'iva, viz, Sarva, Bhava, Rudra, Ugraha, Bhīma, Paśupati, Īśāna, Mahādeva.

[4] The Deva of Love.

[5] *Trisrotah*, for there are three Ganges: the heavenly (Mandākinī), earthly (Alakanandā), and that of the nether world (Bhogavatī).

[6] As to the descent of Gangā into the *jaṭa* of S'iva (see Hymn to Ganga, *post*).

[7] Literally Lord of *Kalā*. *Kalā* is a digit of which there are sixteen in the moon. The *amākalā* is that from which the nectar is distilled.

[8] *Kumudinī*, which blooms and opens at night.

As the sun delights the day lotus [1] and none other,
As one particular thing only delights one other,
Thou, O Mother! delightest the whole universe by
Thy glances.

6

Although Thou art the primordial cause of the
world,
Yet art Thou ever youthful;
Although Thou art the Daughter of the Mountain-
King,[2]
Yet art Thou full of tenderness.
Although Thou art the Mother of the Vedas,[3]
Yet they cannot describe Thee.[4]
Although men must meditate upon Thee,
Yet cannot their mind comprehend Thee.[5]

7

O Mother of the worlds!
Those who have reached that birth amongst men
Which if so difficult to attain,
And in that birth their full faculties,
Yet nathless do not worship Thee,

---

[1] *Kamalini*.

[2] Mountain (*S'aila*), which is that which is made of masses of stone (*S'ilā*)—a rhetorical comparison between the hardness of stone and Her tenderness.

[3] *Trayā*. The whole Veda is so called because it consists of song, prose, and verse; or because the Rik, Yajus, and Sāma are alone referred to as Veda.

[4] *Cf.* verse 2 of Mahimnastava of Puṣpadanta.

[5] Literally, "Though thou art to be meditated upon, thou dost not stay in the path of mind" (*cf.* Mahimnastava, *loc. cit*, and S'ruti, which says, "*Yato vāco nivartitante aprāpya manasā saha.*")

Such, though having ascended to the top of the stairs,
Nevertheless fall down again.[1]

8

O Bhavānī!
Such as worship Thee with fragrant flowers and sandal paste,
Ground with cool water[2] and powdered camphor,
Gain the sovereignty of the whole world.

9

O Mother! like the sleeping King of serpents,[3]
Residing in the centre of the first lotus,[4]
Thou didst create the universe.
Thou dost ascend like a streak of lightning,[5]
And attainest the ethereal region.[6]

---

[1] That is, as the subsequent fall makes the ascent useless, so human incarnation is without avail for those who, without excuse in such incarnation, do not worship the Devī.

[2] Kālidāsa in the Ritusamhāra says that in the hot weather women should wear fine cloth, powder their hair with fragrant scent, and smear their breasts with sandal, ground with cool water.

[3] She as Kuṇḍalinī resembles a sleeping serpent with three and a half coils abiding in the *mūlādhāra*.

[4] The *Mūlādhāra cakra* (see last note).

[5] *Vidyullatā balaya vibhramamudvahanti*. This is the sense of the passage which may literally mean that the Devī carries the beauty (*vibrahma*) of wristlets, like a streak of lightning, or "the Devī is sporting like a streak of lightning."

[6] *Khamasnuvānā*. Kham is here S'iva in the *Sahasrāra*, whither the Devī repairs when Her passion is aroused by the lightning of the *Kāmāgni* around Her fanned by the leftward revolution of the red *Kandarpavayu*.

10

Thy body, having been moistened with the nectar flowing from That,[1]
Thou dost again reach Thy abode[2] by that way.[3]
O Mother and Spouse of Maheśvara!
They in whose heart Thou glitterest are never reborn.

11

O Gaurī! with all my heart
I contemplate Thy form,
Beauteous of face,
With its weight of hanging hair,
With full breasts[4] and rounded slender waist,[5]
Holding in three hands a rosary,[6] a pitcher,[7] and a book,
And with Thy fourth hand making the *jnānamudrā*.[8]

12

O Bhuvaneśvarī
Yogis who have restrained their senses
And have conquered the six enemies,[9]
In *yoga* with calm minds behold Thee
Holding noose and a goad,

---

[1] That is the *Sahasrārapadma*.

[2] *Mūlādhāra*.

[3] *Margenātena*—that is, the *nādi suṣumnā*.

[4] *Apīvarastanataṭīm*.

[5] *Tanuvrittamadhyām*.

[6] *Japamāla*, with which *japa* or recitation of *mantra* is done.

[7] *Kalaśa*.

[8] Literally, holding *cintā*, which is a name for the *jñāna mudrā*, or manual gesture so called.

[9] The six sins (see p. 27, n. 3).

And making the *vara* and *abhaya mudrās*. [1]

13

Thou art Lakṣmī,
Rivalling the lustre of molten gold,
Holding two lotuses in two of Thy hands,
And with the other two making the gestures which
grant boons and dispel fear. [2]
Four elephants holding jars (in their trunks),
Sprinkle Thy head with nectar. [3]

14

O Bhavānī ! Thou art Durgā,[4] seated on a lion,
Of the colour of *durvā* grass,[5]

---

[1] That is, the gestures (*Mudrā*) which grant boons and dispel fear. In the first the hand is held horizontally, the palm open, the fingers close to each other, and the thumb across the palm and touching the root of the third finger. The second is the same, but the hand is held upwards vertically, the palm being shown to the spectator.

[2] That is, the *vara* and *abhayamudrās*, *ante*.

[3] In this form the Devī is respresented as being surrounded by four elephants, which pour nectar over her from jars held in their trunks.

[4] One of the names of Bhuvaneśvarī (see p. 171 of Prosanna Kumar Shastri's "Daśamahāvidyā ").

[5] Of a dark green. It is not clear why this colour is here mentioned, as the colour of Durgā is a golden yellow. It is, however, the colour of other forms, which are those of the one and the same Devī. Thus the colour of Kālī is that of *anjana* (black, collyrium), Tārā is *nīlā* (dark blue), Mātanginī is *asitā* (black) or *shyāmāngī* (dark green). The hue of Shodashī (S'ri) is that of the rising sun (*bālārkākanti*), at it is that of Bhuvaneśvarī (*uddaddinakaradyuti*). The colour of Bhairavī is said to be that of a thousand rising suns; of Chinnamastā that of a million suns;

Holding in Thy eight hands various kinds of
dreadful weapons,
And destroying the enemies of the immortals.[1]

15

I remember again and again the dark[2] primeval
Devi[3] swayed with passion,[4]
Her beauteous face heated and moist with the sweat
(of amorous play),[5]
Bearing a necklace of *Ganjā* berries,[6] and clad with
leaves.

16

O Spouse of S'rīkaṇṭha,[7]
I place on my head Thy blue lotus feet,
Which are followed by[8] the Vedas,

Dhūmāvati is of an ashen colour (*vivarnā*); Bagalāmukhī is all yellow (*pītavarṇā*), and Kamalā is said to be like lightning (*saudāminisannibhā*)—see Prosanna Kumar Shastri's "Daśamahā-vidyā".

[1] The Daityas, enemies of the Devas, whose Protectress the Devī is.

[2] *Asitakānti*. It is difficult to arrive at English translations for some Sanskrit words of colour. Mātanginī here referred to is also spoken of as *shyāmāngī* or dark green; and dark green and dark-blue seem also to be used interchangeably.

[3] Mātanginī, one of the *Daśamahāvidyā*.

[4] *Anangatantrām*—influenced or swayed by Ananga ("the bodiless one"), a name of the Hindu God of Love, Kāma.

[5] *Avirnidāsha jalashikharashobhivaktrām*. The cause is shown in the preceding line—play and union with her Lord.

[6] Red and black berries used as goldsmiths' weights.

[7] S'iva, the "beautiful throated," also called Shitikaṇṭha ("peacock-throated"), from the colouring caused by His drinking the venom which arose at the churning of the ocean.

[8] *Anugamyamānau*—that is, the Vedas worship and adore Her.

As swans are lured by the tinkling sound of an
anklet.

17

O Bhavānī! I worship thy body from ankle to
knee, [1]
Upon which the bull-bannered one [2] gazes with
great love,
And who, as if not satiated by looking thereon with
two eyes,
Has yet made for himself a third. [3]

18

I call to mind thy two thighs, [4]
Which humble the pride of the trunk of an elephant,
And surpass the plantain-tree in thickness and
tenderness. [5]
O Mother! youth [6] fashioned those thighs
That they may support as two pillars the weight of
thy (great) hips, [7]

---

[1] *Janghā. cf.* Lalitāsahasranāma, verse 18, where the Devi's calves are compared to "the sapphire-studded quiver of the God of Love, with rounded ankles and instep arched like the back of a tortoise."

[2] S'iva, also called *Vriṣaddhvaja.*

[3] S'iva is always represented with three eyes, the third being the eye of wisdom, which in man opens on the realization of divinity.

[4] *Uru* (*cf.* Lalitāsahasranāma, verse 17. "The symmetry and smoothness of Her thighs are known only to Kāmeśa (S'iva). Her knees shine like jewelled discs."

[5] *Cf.* First Canto of Kālidāsa's Kumāra Sambhavam.

[6] *Madhyamenabayasā.*

[7] *Shroni.*

19

Looking at thy waist,[1] it would seem as if it had
been absorbed
And become the great bulk of thy breasts and
hips.[2]
By the youth[3] which clothes the body with hair,[4]
May it ever be resplendent in my heart!

20

O Devi! may I never forget thy navel,[5]
As it were a secure inviolate pool,[6]
Given to Thee by Thy blooming youth,
Filled with the liquid beauty[7] of the beloved of
Smara,[8]

---

[1] *Murtirmadhyastava.*

[2] *Shronyaustanauchayugapat prathayishyatochchairbālyāt parena bayasā parihristasārah*—that is, the waist is so slender and the breasts and hips so heavy that it would seem that the greater part of the body, which goes to the making of the waist, had been taken away and put into the breasts and hips, and formed their bulk.

[3] *Bālyātparenabayasā.* Literally the age which follows childhood, which is the cause of these changes in woman's body.

[4] *Romāvalivilāsitena,* which appears with puberty (*cf.* verse 15 of the Lalitā).

[5] *Nābhi,* which also means any navel-like cavity.

[6] *Pallalamapradhriśyam*—from all but S'iva: a similar idea to that of verse 17 of the Lalitā, where it is said that the beauty of the Devi's thighs are known only to Her Lord Kāmeśa (S'iva).

[7] *Lāvanyavāribharitāng.*

[8] That is, Rati, Spouse of Kāma or Smara, the God of Love, son of Kṛṣṇa and Rukmini. The son of Kāma is Aniruddha, and his companion is Vasanta, the spring. He is armed with a bow-and-arrows, the bow string being a line of bees, and the arrows flowers of different plants.

He who was fearful of the fire from the eyes of
Hara.[1]

21

Thy two lotus-like breasts, smeared with sandal,
Which bear ashes telling of S'iva's embrace,[2]
Call to mind the vermilion-painted temples moist
with ichor[3]
Of some (impassioned) elephant
Rising from his bath in waters,
Flicked with foam.[4]

22

O Mother! Thy two arms, beauteous with the water
Dripping from Thy body bathed from neck to throat,
Seem to have been formed by the crocodile-bannered One,[5]
As long nooses wherewith to hold the throat of his
enemy[6] (S'iva).

---

[1] When the Devas desired a commander for their forces in their war with Tāraka, they sought the aid of Kāma in drawing S'iva towards Pārvatī, whose issue alone could destroy the demon. Kāma undertook the mission, and shot his arrows of love at S'iva, when the latter was doing *tapas*. S'iva, however, who was offended at this disturbance of his devotions, burnt Kāma down with a flash from the fire of His third eye. Subsequently Kāma was reborn in the form of Pradyumna at the request of Rati.

[2] For S'iva's body is covered with ashes.

[3] *Samadasyakumbhau*, the ichor which exudes from the temples of elephants in rut.

[4] The ashes are thus compared to foam, and the sandal paste to the vermilion with which the temples and foreheads of fine elephants are painted.

[5] That is, Kāma, the God of Love.

[6] For S'iva burnt him (see *ante* n. 5). The Devī's arms embrace the neck of S'iva.

May I never forget them!

23

O Daughter of the Mountain-King,
Again and again have I looked upon Thy shapely neck,
Which has stolen the beauty of a well-formed shell,
And is adorning with pleasing necklace and many another ornament;
Yet am I never satiated.

24

O Mother! he has not been born in vain [1]
Who oft calls to his mind
Thy face, with its large round eyes and noble brow,
Its radiant cheeks and smile,
The high, straight nose,
And lips red as the *bimba* fruit. [2]

25

Whoever, O Devi! contemplates upon Thy wealth of hair,
Lit by the crescent moon, [3]
Resembling a swarm of bees hovering over fragrant flowers,
Is freed of the ancient fetters which bind him to the world. [4]

---

[5] *Sa eva jātah.* Literally, "He is indeed born." His birth is fruitful.

[1] The fruit of the tree called *tyālākucho* in Bengali, which, when ripe, is very red, and to which the lips of young women are often compared (*cf.* Meghadūta, verse 2, "*Pakvabimbādharoṣṭhī*").

[2] The Devī bears the crescent moon on her head as does S'iva.

[3] *Tasya svayam galati Devī purāṇapāshā*—that is, he is freed of rebirth, the fruit of *Karma.* Here commences the *phala* (fruit or result portion) of the *stotra.*

26

The mortal who in this world
Devoutly from his heart reads this hymn,
Sweet to the ears of the wise,
Attains for ever all wealth in the form of that Lakṣmi
Who attends the crowned kings who are prostrate at Her feet.

ĀDYAKĀLI

(ĀDYAKĀLĪSVARŪPASTOTRA)[1]

FROM THE MAHĀNIRVĀṆA TANTRA

1. *HRĪM*,[2] O destroyer of time ![3]
2. *S'RĪM*,[4] O terrific onc ![5]
3. *KRĪM*,[6] Thou who art beneficent,[7]

---

[1] From the Mahānirvāṇa Tantra, Seventh Ullāsa, verses 12 *et seq*. This hymn to the primordial Kālī contains a hundred of her names all beginning with " K. " Thus Kālī, Karālī, Kalyānī, Kalāvatī, Kamalā, Kalidarpaghni, Kaparddīśakripanvitā, etc. *Kādi* is that which has " Ka " in the beginning. In the Tantrarāja, Devī says to S'iva : " The syllable ' Ka ' is in Thy form, and that S'akti confers all *siddhis* " (see Lalitā Sahasranāma, where a number of the following names occur).

[2] The *Māyābija* (see Fifth Ullāsa, verse 10).

[3] Kālī (see Fourth Ullasa, verses 30 *et seq*.). She is thus called *Kālakarshinī*.

[4] *Bīja* of Lakṣmī, Devī of prosperity or beauty.

[5] Karālī.

[6] The Bījābhidāna says *Ka* = Kālī, *Ra* = Brahmā, *Ī* = Mahāmāyā. The half circle of *candrabindu* is the universal Mother, and the point is the destroyer of misery.

[7] Kalyāṇī, or She who bestows peace and happiness (see the Lalitā, verse 73). According to the Padmapurāṇa, Devī is worshipped as Kalyāṇī in the Malaya mountains.

4. Possessor of all the arts,[1]
5. Thou art Kamalā,[2]
6. Destroyer of the pride of the Kali Age.[3]
7. Who art kind to him of the matted hair,[4]
8. Devourer of Him who devours,[5]
9. Mother of Time[6]
10. Thou art brilliant as the fires of the final dissolution.[7]
11. Spouse of Him of the matted hair.[8]
12. O Thou of formidable countenance,[9]
13. Ocean of the nectar of compassion,[10]

---

[1] Kalāvati (see the Lalitā, verse 74). The *Kalā*, or arts, are sixty-four in number. The S'akti should always be *Kalāvatī*. Devī is also called *Kalāmālā*, or garland of the arts. Kalāvati may also mean possessed of all arts complete.

[2] A name of Lakṣmi-Devī is Kamalā, for She is all S'aktis. In verse 73 of the Lalitā, Devi is called Kāmakalārūpā, on which Bhāskararāya says that there are three *bindus* and the *hārdakala*. The first *bindu* is called Kāma, and the last Kalā ; but according to the rule *pratyāhāra*, Kamalā includes all four. Kālikā Purāṇa says, Devi, is alone indicated by Kāma.

[3] Kalidarpaghnī.

[4] Kapardīśakripanvitā. *Kapardīśa* is a title of S'iva derived from his matted hair.

[5] Kālikā, because She devours S'iva as Mahākāla (see Mahānirvāṇa Tantra, Fourth Ullāsa, verse 31).

[6] Kālamātā.

[7] Kālānalasamadyuti.

[8] Kapardinī. Spouse of S'iva, called *Kapardi* from his matted hair (see Lalitā, verse 151). The Viśva says that *Kaparda* means the matted hair of S'iva and the cowdung cakes. When S'iva incarnated, as Mailāra, his spouse was decked with a garland of cowdung-cakes.

[9] Karālāsyā.

[10] Karunāmritasāgarā (see Lalitā, verse 73).

14. Merciful,[1]
15. Vessel of mercy,[2]
16. Whose mercy is without limit,[3]
17. Who art attainable alone by Thy mercy,[4]
18. Who art fire,[5]
19. Tawny,[6]
20. Black of hue,[7]
21. Thou who increaseth the joy of the Lord of creation,[8]
22. Night of darkness,[9]
23. In the form of desire,[10]
24. Yet liberator from the bonds of desire,[11]
25. Thou who art dark as a bank of cloud,[12]

---

[1] Kripāmayi.

[2] Kripādhārā.

[3] Kripāpārā.

[4] Kripāgamā.

[5] Kṛṣānu. *Kṛṣānuretas* is an epithet of S'iva whose male seed is fire.

[6] Kapilā.

[7] Kṛṣṇā.

[8] Kṛṣṇānandavivardhini. Kṛṣṇa is here the supreme Lord.

[9] Kālaratri. The Lalitā, verse 101, speaks of the Devī as attended by hosts of S'aktis, Kālarātri, and others—that is the twelve S'aktis from Kālarātri to Tankāri, one in each petal of the *anahāta padma*. The Varāha Purāṇa says that Raudri, who was born form darkness and went to the Blue Mountain to perform penance (the S'akti causing destruction) is called Kālarātri.

[10] Kāmarupā (*ibid.*, verse 73), Kalika Purāna-says that Devi is called Kāma because She came to the secret place in the Blue peak of the great mountain (Kāilāsa) along with S'iva, for the sake of desire, and because She fulfils desires and destroys and restores the body of Kāma.

[11] Kāmapāśavimocini.

[12] Kādambini. In the heat of India the rain-cloud is welcome, and in some of Her forms She is dark.

26. And bearest the crescent moon,[1]
27. Destructress of sin in the Kali Age,[2]
28. Thou who art pleased by the worship of virgins,[3]
29. Thou who art the refuge of the worshippers of virgins,[4]
30. Who art pleased by the feasting of virgins,[5]
31. And who art in the form of the virgin,[6]
32. Thou who wanderest in the Kadamba forest,[7]
33. Who art pleased with the flowers of the Kadamba forest,[8]

---

[1] Kalādhārā.

[2] Kalikalmaṣanāśinī (see Lalitā, verse 113), Kūrma Purāṇa says that the repetition of the names of Devī destroys the multitude of sins in the Kali Age.

[3] Kumārīpūjanapritā. The *Kumārī pūjā*, or worship of virgins, is a *pūjā* common in Bengal. The worship is by men, whereas the *sadhavapūjā*, or worship of married women, is done by women. Or Kumārī may directly refer to the Devī Herself. She is known as the unmarried Kumārī. A *sūtra* of the S'iva Sūtras runs *Iccāśaktiḥ Umā kumārī*. The energy of desire is Umā, the unmarried. Bhāskararāya (Commentary, Lalitā, verses 25, 40) says: "As play She creates the universe, hence She is Kumārī, or She destroys (*mārayate*) the ground (*ku*) of the great illusion. Hence She is Kumārī; Kumārī is the enjoyer and not to be enjoyed, as She is one with the *Yogi*, the enjoyer.

[4] Kumārī pūjakālayā, or "who art the refuge of such worshippers."

[5] Kumārībhojanānanda. The *Kumārīs* are feasted at the *Kumārī pūjā*.

[6] Kumārīrūpadhārinī. So a very young marriageable girl is called Gaurī.

[7] Kadambavanasanchārā (see Hymn to Tripurasundarī, *post*).

[8] Kadambapuṣpasantoṣā (see Lalitā, verse 73).

34. Who hast Thy abode in the Kadamba forest,[1]
35. Who wearest a garland of Kadamba flowers,[2]
36. Thou who art youthful,[3]
37. Who hath a soft low voice,[4]
38. Whose voice is sweet as the crv of a *Cakravāka* bird,[5]
39. Who drinkest *Kādambarī* wine,[6]
40. And art pleased with the *Kādambarī* wine,[7]

---

[1] Kadambavanavāsinī (see the Lalitā, verse 23). The palace of *Cintāmani* is surrounded by a gallery of gems (*maṇimaṇḍapa*). Around this is the grove of Kadamba trees, which in the Purāṇās are said to be seven yojanas in height in the space between the walls of gold and silver. The Bhairavayāmala says the abode of Bindu is the ocean of nectar. The five *yonis*—that is, the five *śakti* angles in the *śricakra* — are the divine trees. There is the grove of *Nīpa* trees. Within that is the gallery of gems. Within that is the palace of *Cintāmaṇi*.

[2] Kadambapuṣpamālinī. The Lalitā, verse 8, speaks of Devī as decked above her ears with clusters of Kadamba flowers.

[3] Kishorī.

[4] Kālakaṇṭhā. Devī is also called Kālakaṇṭhi, or wife of Kālakaṇṭha, a name of S'iva whose throat was coloured by the poison he swallowed at the churning of the ocean. According to Devī purāṇa, Kālakaṇṭha was worshipped at Kālanjara.

[5] Kalanādaninādinī. Water-birds which sing to one another at night—the male to the female and the latter to the male—sitting on opposite banks of the river. Their passionate devotion is often alluded to by the poets.

[6] Kādambarīpānaratā.

[7] Kādambarīpriyā. *Kādambarī* is mead. Bhāskararāya (Commentary, Lalitā), dealing with the Tripura Upanishad, which prescribes that mead, fish, flesh, and cooked cereals should be offered to the Devatā, says that it enjoins those who are allowed to take wine, flesh, etc., that they should do so after first dedicating them to the Brahman, and minimize the habit by gradation (see the same idea expressed in Manu v., 56, Bhāg. Pr. XI., 5-11).

41. And whose cup is a skull,[1]
42. Who wearest a garland of bones,[2]
43. Who art pleased with the lotus,[3]
44. And who art seated on the lotus,[4]
45. Who abidest in the centre of the lotus,[5]
46. Whom the fragrance of the lotus pleases,[6]
47. Who movest with the swaying gait of a *hamsa*,[7]
48. Destroyer of fear,[8]
49. Who assumeth all forms at will,[9]
50. Whose abode is at Kāmarūpa,[10]
51. Who ever dallies at the Kāmapītha,[11]
52. O Beautiful One,[12]
53. O creeper which givest every desire,[13]

---

[1] Kapālapātraniratā.

[2] Kamkālamālyadhārini.

[3] Kamalāsanasantuṣṭā.

[4] Kamalāsanavāsini.

[5] Kamalālayamadhyasthā.

[6] Kamalāmodamodini.

[7] Kalahamsagati. *Hamsa* is variously translated goose, swan, flamingo. A swaying waddle like that of a duck is admired. As the swans live in the celestial lake called Mānasa, so She lives in the minds (*mānasa*) of Her devotees.

[8] Klaibyanāśini.

[9] Kāmarūpini (see also *post*).

[10] Kāmarūpakritavāsā (see next note).

[11] Kāmapīthavilāsini. Kāmarūpa, the great Tantrika centre in Assam, one of the *Mahāpīthas*, where the genital organ of the Devī fell on the severance of Her dead body by Viṣṇu after the *Dakṣa Yajna*. Kāmarupa is also one of the *Ādibhuta*, which are in the *Mūlādhāra* and other tattvik centres (see the Lalitā, verse 82).

[12] Kamaniyā.

[13] Kalpalatā. The *Kalpa* tree is one of the celestial trees in the heaven of India, which yielded whatever one desired. Woman is likened to a creeper (*latā*) embracing and depending on her

54. Whose beauty is Thy ornament,[1]
55. Adorable as the image of all tenderness,[2]
56. Thou with a tender body,[3]
57. And who art slender of waist,[4]
58. Who art pleased with the nectar of purified wine,[5]
59. Giver of success to them whom purified wine rejoices,[6]
60. The own Deity of those who worship Thee when joyed with wine,[7]
61. Who art gladdened by the worship of Thyself with purified wine,[8]
62. Who art immersed in the ocean of purified wine,[9]
63. Who art the protectress of those who accomplish *vrata* with wine,[10],

---

husband (see also the Lalitā, where the Devī is called *Bhaktimatkalpalatikā*, the *kalpa* creeper of the devotee).

[1] Kamanīyavibhūṣanā, or "who art the possessor of beautiful ornaments."

[2] Kamanīyagunārādhyā; or it may mean that the Devī is to be worshipped by the worshipper with all best and tender feeling.

[3] Komalāngī.

[4] Krishodarī. Literally, small of belly (see Bhuvaneśvarī *stotra*, *apivarastanatating tanuvrittamadhyām*, and the Lalitā, verse 79, *tanumadhyā*).

[5] Kāranāmritasantoshā. *Kārana* is one of the technical terms given to the purified wine consumed as an element of the Tāntrika pancatattva.

[6] Kāranānandasiddhidā.

[7] Kāranānandajapeshtā.

[8] Kāranārchchanaharshitā.

[9] Kāranārnavasangmagnā.

[10] Kāranavratapālinī. *Vratas* are ritual acts and devotional exercises which do not belong to the obligatory (*nitya*) *karma*.

64. Whom the fragrance of musk gladdens,[1]
65. And who art luminous with a *tilaka* mark of musk,[2]
66. Who art attached to those who worship Thee with musk,[3]
67. Who lovest those who worship Thee with musk,[4]
68. Who art a mother to those who burn musk as incense,[5]
69. Who art fond of the musk-deer,[6]
70. And who art pleased to eat its musk,[7]
71. Whom the scent of camphor gladdens,[8]
72. Who art adorned with garlands of camphor,[9]
73. And whose body is besmeared with camphor and sandal paste,[10]
74. Who art pleased with purified wine flavoured with camphor,[11]
75. Who drinkest purified wine flavoured with camphor,[12]

---

[1] Kastūrisaurabhāmodā. Musk is used in worship to scent *candan*, etc.

[2] Kastūritilakojjvalā. The *tilak* is the mark worn by sectarian Hindus on the forehead.

[3] Kastūripūjanaratā.

[4] Kastūripūjakapriyā.

[5] Kastūridāhajananī.

[6] Kastūrīmrigatoshinī.

[7] Kastūribhojanapritā.

[8] Karpūrāmodamoditā. Camphor is burnt in worship during *ārati*, and is used to scent the *pādya*, betel leaf, etc., offered to the Devi.

[9] Karpūramālābharanā. Balls of camphor are strung together in a garland.

[10] Karpūracandanākshitā.

[11] Karpūrakāranāhlādā.

[12] Karpūrāmritapāyinī.

76. Who art bathed in the ocean of camphor,[1]
77. Whose abode is in the ocean of camphor,[2]
78. Who art pleased when worshipped with the *bīja* "*Hūm*,"[3]
79. Who threatenest with the *bīja* "*Hūm*,"[4]
80. Embodiment of *Kulācāra*,[5]
81. Adored by Kaulikas,[6]
82. Benefactress of the Kaulikas,[7]
83. Observant of *Kulācāra*,[8]
84. Joyous one,[9]
85. Revealer of the path of the Kaulikas,[10]
86. Queen of Kāśi,[11]
87. Allayer of sufferings,[12]

---

[1] Karpūrasāgarasnatā.

[2] Karpūrasāgarālayā.

[3] Kūrchchabījajapapritā. *Hūm* is the *Kūrchhabīja*.

[4] Kūrchchajapaparāyayanā—that is, She who mutters "*Hūm*" when conquering the demons. The Devī then constantly uttered the *hūmkāra* with its threatening, roaring sound.

[5] Kulīna. *Kula*, according to the Tantra, means S'akti. *Akula* = S'iva. The union of *Kula* with *Akula* is called Kaula, the essence common to both S'iva and S'akti. Hence Devī is *Kaulinī* (see Lalitā, verse 37). Both *Kula* and *Akula* are in the *Sahasrāra*. *Kulācāra* is the way of the *Kaula* division of Tantrik worshippers.

[6] Kaulikārādhyā. The *Kaulikas* are followers of *Kulācāra* (see last note). So also in the Lalitā, verse 17, the Devī is addressed as "adored by *Dakṣinas* and *Adakṣinas*."

[7] Kaulikapriyakārinī.

[8] Kulacārā, *v. ante*.

[9] Kantukinī.

[10] Kulamārgapradarshinī.

[11] Kaśiśvarī. Kāśi is Benares, the sacred city of S'iva.

[12] Kartahartrī; and thus the Lalitā speaks of the Devī as the moon-light which soothes those burned by the triple fires of misery.

88. Giver of blessings to the Lord of Kāśi,[1]
89. Giver of pleasure to the Lord of Kāśi,[2]
90. Beloved of the Lord of Kāśi,[3]
91. Thou whose toe-ring bells make sweet melody as Thou moveth,[4]
92. Whose girdle bells sweetly tinkle,[5]
83. Who abidest in the mountain of gold,[6]
94. Who art like a moonbeam on the mountain of gold,[7]
95. Who art gladdened by the recitation of the *mantra* "*Klim*,"[8]
96. Who art the *Kāma Bija*,[9]

---

[1] Kāśiśavaradayini ("Lord" is S'iva).

[2] Kāśiśvarakritāmodā.

[3] Kāśiśvaramanoramā.

[4] Kalamanjiracaranā.

[5] Kvanatkāncivibhūṣanā.

[6] Kāncanādrikritāgarā (the mountain Kāncana or Sumeru). Durvāsa says in his Lalitāstavaratna (verses 2-4): "Let the gold mountain be victorious whose body is the universe resounding with the music of celestial women living in the golden bowers of creepers of the mountain peak. We salute the three peaks which are the seats of Brahmā, Viṣṇu, and S'iva, extending to the four quarters of the earth. In their midst is another peak 400 yojanas (a yojana is eight or nine miles) in height, making the place beauteous with the golden rays of its flowers, and I worship it." The Lalitā Sahasranāma (verse 22) also addresses Devī as dwelling on the middle peak of Mount Sumeru.

[7] Kāncanācalakaumudi.

[8] Kāmabijajapānanda. The *Kāma bija* is "*klim*." When the "*Ka*" and "*La*" are eliminated, the remaining "*im*" is called *kāmakalā*, which is in the *turiya* state. In the Lalitā, verse 225, Devī is called creatrix of the *mantra klim* ("*klimkari*"). *Klimkāra* is *S'ivakāma*, and She is His wife.

[9] Kāmabijasvarūpinī—that is, She is "*klim*" itself.

97. Destructress of all evil inclinations,[1]
98. And of the afflictions of the *Kaulikas*—[2]
99. Lady of the Kaulas,[3]
100. O Thou who by the three *bījās*, "KRĪM" "HRĪM" "S'RĪM" art the Destructress of the fear of death[4]—
(To Thee I make obeisance.)

[1] Kumatighnī. Devī is also (Lalitā, verse 78) *Sadācāra pravarttakā*, because She makes men move to right action.

[2] Kulinārtināśinī.

[3] Kulakāminī.

[4] *Krīm, Hrīm, S'rīm mantravarṇena kālakaṇṭakaghātinī.*

LAKṢMĪ[1]

(LAKSMĪSTOTRAM)

From the TANTRASĀRA[2]

O Devī Kamalā,[3] beloved of Viṣṇu,
Adored by the three worlds,
As Thou art constant to Viṣṇu, be Thou constant to me.
Whoever worshipping Lakṣmi, reads these twelve names of Her—
Īśvarī, Kamala,[4] Lakṣmi, Calā,[5]
Bhūti,[6] Haripriyā,[7] Padmā,[8] Padmālayā,[9] Sampat,[10]

---

[1] Lakśmi, commonly called S'rī, Devī of prosperity and beauty: the S'akti, or Spouse of Viṣṇu, who rose resplendent from the sea at the churning of the ocean by the Devas and Asuras, and then reclining on the breast of Hari, gazed upon the enraptured Devas. As her Lord assumes various forms, so does She.

[2] P. 577.

[3] Because She appeared from the lotus.

[4] Feminine of Īśvara, or Lord, or Ruler.

[5] Or Cancalā, the fickle one, for nothing is so fickle as wealth and prosperity—" here to-day and gone to-morrow."

[6] Prosperity.

[7] Beloved of Hari (Viṣṇu).

[8] Lotus.

[9] Who dwells in the lotus.

[10] Wealth.

Uchaih,[1] S'ri[2] Padmadhārini,[3]
With such an one, his wife and children,
Laksmi ever abides.

[1] The exalted One, for prosperity exalts.
[2] Beauty and prosperity.
[3] Holding the lotus in her hands.

TĀRĀ[1]

(TĀRĀṢṬAKAM)[2]

From the NĪLA TANTRA

1

O Mother, Devi Nilasarasvatī[3] Tārā,

---

[1] The Matsyasūkta, Tārārṇava, and Nīla Tantras deal with particulars or Tārā or Tāriṇī, one of the Mahāvidyā, whose *bija* is *Hrim Strim, Hūm* (*Kurccha*), *Phat* (see verse 4). She is called Nīlasarasvatī, because She playfully gives the power of speech. She is called Tārā on account of her being deliverer or saviour (*tārakatvāt*). She gives both pleasure (*sukha*) and liberation (*mokṣa*). She is called also *Ugratārā*, because She saves from formidable and horrible calamities. Ṛṣi Vaśiṣṭha is said to have cursed this *vidyā*, and then raised the curse so that *siddhi* might be gained from Her by *japa* of the *bija Hrīm, Strīm, Hūm, Phat*, after which She again became glorious. Her Mantra is also given as *S'rīm, Hrim, Strim, Hūm, Phat* (giver of wealth and beauty); another is *Hrīm, Hrīm, Strīm, Hūm, Phat* (giver of all desires); another is *Aim, Hrīm, Strīm, Hūm, Phat* (giver of speech), and *Hrīm, Strīm, Hūm, Phat* (giver of liberation). Her Yantra is an eight-petalled lotus surrounded by a circle, with inverted triangle in the centre with *Hūm*. On the petals are *Hrim, Strim, S'rim, Hūm*. There is also a *Yantra* (*Tārāṣatkoṇa*) of two superimposed triangles, making a star.

[2] From the Nīla Tantra (see also Tantrasāra, p. 610, R. M. Chatterjee's edition, and the Brihatstotraratnākara, p. 283, where a more correct text is given).

[3] The blue Sarasvatī, Devi of speech (see note 1,*ante*). Nīla Tantra says She is in the form of all language (*sarvabhāṣā ayī*). The Nīlasarasvatī Yantra is figured at p. 93 of the Dashamahāvidyā.

Refuge with Thee I crave.
Giver of prosperity and wealth art Thou
To those who worship Thee. Standing on S'iva,
Thy right foot upon His breast and left upon His thigh.
Ever art Thou, with smiling lotus-like face.
Thy three eyes are, as it were, full-blown lotuses.
In Thy hands Thou holdest a knife,[1] a skull, a lotus, and a sword.

2

Thou art the presiding Devī of speech.
Thou art the creeper which grants all desires.[2]
Thou art the giver of all *siddhi*,[3]
And the power to write both verse and prose.
Three are Thine eyes, as it were blue lotuses.
Ocean of kindness and compassion art Thou.
I pray Thee of Thy mercy shower upon me the nectar of prosperity.

3

O Sharbhā,[4] I pray Thee remove my fears.
Proud Lady, brilliant are Thy garments,
Bright with coiling serpents.
Thou art clad in tiger skin.
Thy waist is adorned with tiny tinkling bells.
Thou holdest the heads of two demons
Dripping with blood, just severed by the sword.
Thy waist is girdled with heads of demons,

---

[1] *Karttri* (for *dhyāna* see p. 94 Daśamahāvidyā).

[2] As did the celestial *Kalpa* tree in Indra's heaven.

[3] Material success, psychical powers, spiritual attainment.

[4] Spouse of S'iva (Sharbha).

As it were with a garland.
Thus art Thou beautiful, O formidable One.[1]

4

O Devī Tārā, attained with difficulty,
I take refuge with Thee.
Thou art beautiful with form both amorous and
          charmful.[2]
Thou art *Bindu* and the half-moon,[3]
Whose substance is *Hrīm* and *Phat*.[4]
Thou art *mantra*[5] and the shelter of all.
Thy forms are threefold—
Gross, Subtle, and Supreme.
Thou art beyond the reach of Veda.[6]

---

[1] Her *dhyāna* is given as follows : The Devī is in the midst of four blazing funeral pyres ; Her feet as described in verse 1 ; formidable, with garland of severed heads ; short of stature ; big-bellied ; tiger skin round the waist ; youthful ; four-armed ; protruding tongue ; giving *vara* ; holding the articles mentioned in verse 1 (the skull and lotus in left hands); a *ṛṣi* Akshobhya in the form of a serpent on her head ; her body lustrous as that of the moonbeams ; formidable teeth ; smiling face ; three eyes blazing like the morning sun.

[2] *Māyānanga vikārarūpalalane.*

[3] *Ardhacandrātmike* —that is, the crescent sign below the bindu in *candra bindu*. She is both bindu and Nāda (see Introduction). It is also said that there are eight *varṇa* above the *bindu* of Hrīm, commencing with *ardhacandra*, and ending with *unmani*, of which the third is *Nāda*. Here, as the Mahāsvachchanda Tantra states, the Devī should be contemplated.

[4] Two tantrik *bīja mantras* : as to *Hūm* (see p 56, note 1, *ante*). *Phat* is the *astra* or weapon *mantra* (see note 1, p. 50, *ante*).

[5] *Mantrātmike* (see p. 2, *ante*).

[6] *Vedanāngnahigocharā*, as to her three forms (*vide ante*).

5

By the service of Thy lotus feet,
Men of good deed attain *sāyujya*[1] liberation.
O Parameśvari, Thou art the Spouse of Him[2]
Who is Brahmā, Visnu, and the three-eyed One.
O Mother ! he who neglects to serve Thy lotus feet,
But serves instead the Devas, Indra, and others,
Who are themselves plunged in the ocean of *samsāra*,[3]
Is indeed and most truly ignorant.

6

O Mother ! those Devas who receive on their crowns
The pollen which comes from Thy lotus-like feet,[4]

[1] Literally, "becoming one with the Deity." Identification of the self and the Deity with attributes ; one of the four forms of qualified liberation—*Sālokya, Sārūpya, Sāmīpya, Sāyujya.* Those who know the Brahman and such worship to be imperfect reject them, and attain the unconditioned bliss (*kaivalya*) which transcends all other states. But these others must be passed before the end is reached, which the S'aktirahasya summarizes by a short verse : "A mortal who worships by ceremonies, by images, by mind, by identification, by knowing the self attains *kaivalya*."

[2] That is Parameśvara, in whom the threefold energies which manifest in the *trimūrti* are contained *tasyastri parameśvari trinayanabrahmādi samnyātmanah.*

[3] The Deva, in this like man, is a *samsārin* or inhabitant of of the *samsāra,* which comprises earth, the *antarikṣa,* and heaven (*svarga*), the abode of the Deva. The latter has wife and children, is engaged in conflict with demons, and so forth. When the merit which gains the Deva heaven is exhausted, he descends to earth again.

[4] That is, the Deva bow their heads at the feet of the Devī, receiving on their heads the dust of Her feet.

Are able to keep their promise of conquest,
And to gain victory over their enemies in battle—
Such, without a doubt, are sheltered in Thy lap.
But their enemies who send forth the defiant challenge,
"I am a Deva, and none is equal to me in the whole world,"
Perish and meet such death as befits them.

7

Bhūta, Preta, Piśācha, Rākṣasa,
Daitya, foremost of Dānava, Yakṣa, Lords of Naga,[1]
Wrathful Dākinī, great birds,[3] tigers, and other dreadful creatures
Forthwith take flight at but the remembrance of Thy name,
And are powerless to do aught of evil.

8

Who serves Thy lotus feet, to him *siddhi*[4] is given.
He surpasses the Lord of speech,[5]
And obtains the beauty of Kāma.[6]
He can charm and paralyze[7] multitudes of elephants upon the field of battle,

---

[1] Various spirits and inferior divinities of more or less evil and malignant character.

[2] A form of S'akti attendant on the Devī in Her terrible forms.

[3] *Khacara* (vultures, eagles, etc.).

[4] *Vide ante*, p. 57. note 3,

[5] Brihaspati.

[6] Deva of Love.

[7] He has the powers of *mohanam* and *stambhanam*, the latter being one of the *Tāntrika Ṣatkarma*.

And has power to stay the flow of water.[1]
The Siddha[2] and prosperity are under his control.

PHALAŚLOKA.[3]

Whoever, being pure and self-controlled,
Reads this eight-versed hymn to Tārā,
At morn, at noon, at evening,
To him is given
The power to write beautifully in prose or verse,[4]
Knowledge in all *S'āstra*,
Imperishable fortune,
The enjoyment of whatsoever he may desire,
Fame, beauty, and wealth,
The love of all men,
And at the end liberation.

---

1 A particular form of *Stambhanam* called *jalastambha*.

2 Devayoni of that name inhabiting the *antarikṣa*.

3 Fruit or result of the stotra.

4 *Labhate devyām kavitvām*.

MAHIṢĀMARDINĪ[1]

(MAHIṢĀMARDINĪSTOTRA)

FROM THE TANTRASĀRA[2]

1

O CANDĪ![3] wander in my heart,
By whom the act of formidable Asura[4] was shattered,
Destroy the calamities which deeply pierce me,
Arising from the mass of malice and fears (which assail me),
So that, free from danger,
And protected by the lotus cluster of Thy feet,
My swan-like[5] mind may swim and rejoice in the ocean of bliss.

---

[1] A title of Durgā, S'akti of S'iva as the powerful victrix of demons. She is Mahiṣamardinī, as the slayer of Mahiṣa. The Daitya S'umbha attacked Her in the form of a buffalo (*Mahiṣa*; see Candi).

[2] P. 574.

[3] A form of the Devī assumed for the destruction of the Daitya Canda, and who assisted in the destruction of the demon Raktabīja (see Mārkandeya Purāṇa).

[4] Mahiṣa.

[5] *Manohamsa*, the *hamsa*, is variously described as a swan, goose, and flamingo.

2

What fear of his enemies has he who worships Thee?
The Devas who worship Thy feet stamping on beast and noose,[1]
Having abandoned the form of Narasimha,[2]
Whose towering mane reached the summit of Mount Sumeru,
And whose fingers are outstretched to tear (the breast of) Hiraṇyakaśipu,[3]
Now worship the lion,[4] the enemy of the elephant.[5]

3

O Caṇdī! when the syllables, the letters of which speak of Thee,
Reach the ear, then Brahmā and other Devas
Sing the truth, touching Puruṣa and Prakṛti.[6]

---

[1] The Devī is standing on Her lion (*v. post*) with the noose (*pāśa*) beneath Her feet.

[2] The Man-lion (*Avatāra*) of Viṣṇu, in which He destroyed the Daitya Hiraṇyakaśipu, father of His devotee Prahlāda.

[3] See last note. The *avatāra* is generally represented with the King of the Daityas across his knees, tearing asunder with his hands and claws the latter's belly.

[4] Which accompanies the Devī as Durgā. After the destruction of Hiraṇyakaśipu, Viṣṇu's wrath was not appeased. The world trembled, fearing what he might do. The Devas asked the help of S'iva, who assumed the Sharabha form—that of a lion with wings and eight feet—who tossed up Viṣṇu into the air and held him there until he had become powerless. The lion then went to the feet of Durgā, whom he accompanies.

[5] *Gaja*, the elephant form subsequently assumed by the Asura, Mahiṣa.

[6] S'iva and S'akti, the "Male" and "Female" elements, from whose union springs the universe (see *Introduction to Tantra S'āstra* and *Principles of Tantra*.)

O Devī ! be to-day gracious to me,
Devoted as I am to the kissing of Thy beautiful lotus feet,
The one and only glittering abode of the essence of the nectar of all Devatās.

4

If, because of my following your way of Kula,[1]
I suffer reproach better is it that I shall thus be without fame.
Let me not have that which comes of the worship of Keśava [2] and Kauśika ; [3]
Rather, O Mother ! let my heart rest in meditation on Thy lotus feet,
Worshipped by Brahmā, Hari, the enemy of Smara[4] and the enemy of the Daityas.[5]

5

O Mother ! if I be engaged in the rightful [6] contemplation of Thy lotus feet,

---

[1] That is, *Kulācāra,* one, and the highest, of the divisions of Tāntrik worshippers often misunderstood, and therefore subject of reproach ; and which is contrasted in the next line but one with the more popular and conventional worshipper of Keśava and Kauśika.

[2] Viṣṇu.

[3] An epithet both of S'iva and Indra, probably here the former.

[4] Smara, the God of Love ; S'iva, who slew him, is his "enemy."

[5] *Daityāri* : usually an epithet of S'ri Kṛṣṇa, but as Hari has already been mentioned, possibly the reference may be to Indra.

[6] *i. e.,* orderly, according to the direction and sequence of the dhyāna or stotra.

[7] Literally, "If I be deprived of."

What matters it if I know not[7] other sacred places?[1]
May Thy lotus feet be ever present to my mind—
Thy feet which are the wealth of our wounds![2]
O propitious Mother! do Thou forgive me.

6

Verily and without doubt, even the Lord of Bhūtas[3] would have perished,[4]
Maddened as He was with the joy of the embrace of (Thee who art) His own self,[5]
Had He not enjoyed the lotus fragrance of Thy feet,
Full of honey from which drop liquid sandal,
And the nectar, there haply fallen from the moon.[6]

---

[1] *Siddhāspada*, where the perfect (*siddha*) are, or where *Siddhi* (power and perfection) may be gained.

[2] That is, they are the healers of our pain.

[3] S'iva Bhūteśvara or Bhūtanātha. *Bhūta*, which in a general sense means "beings," specifically refers to the spirits and ghosts by whom S'iva is surrounded and of whom He is Master.

[4] It is by the Devī's aid that S'iva is Parameśvara, for without S'akti He is nothing, and without Her life-giving energy and support cannot exist. As the Kubjikā Tantra says: "Without their S'aktis the husbands are but *preta*" (inert corpses). So also the Jnānārnava: "O beloved, pure Sadāśiva without S'akti is without motion like a corpse, for without S'akti He can do nothing."

[5] *Svātmānam parirabhya.* Literally, having embraced Himself. The Devī is, however, in a dualistic sense, His sacred half, and in reality one with Him and His own self (see Mahānirvāṇa Tantra, chap. i.).

[6] *Daivādvichyuta candra candanarasaprāgalbhya garbashravat*— "Haply" in the poetical sense, as the nectar should be in the moon, but it happens to be dropping from the sacred feet of the Devī. Moreover, the Parambindu, which is S'ivaśakti, is in the crescent of Nirvāṇakalā, which is by Amākalā the sixteenth digit

7

O Mother ! let the stream of heavy showers of holy devotion torwards Thee
Be ever shed upon me,
Struggling and drowning, alas! as I am in the endless ocean of illusion,[1]
Without taste of the springing water of the Bliss of Brahman,[2]
Which dispels the weight of mental afflictions from numbers of Devas.

8

May (Thy) glory,[3] dark as collyrium cloud,
Be ever in my heart.
From its glittering lustre were born the three Devatās,
Who create, maintain, and destroy the world,
Whose substance is pure intelligence and bliss,[4]
Dispelling the darkness which overspreads the heart
By the (glory of the unnumbered) millions of their rays !

9

May[5] Devī Mahiṣāmardinī, who hath power to destroy

---

of the moon-circle (*Candramaṇḍala*), whence flows the nectar which, as Ichchhā, is the eternal precursor of creation (see Commentary, verse 49, of the Ṣatcakranirūpaṇa in *The Serpent Power*).

[1] *Viddhā*, not as the original has it, *Siddha*.

[2] *Brahmānandasarābhiṣeka* in the original should be *Brahmānandarāsābhiṣeka*.

[3] *Mahas*, not *maham*, as in the text.

[4] *Nirmalacidānandatrayamdaivatam*.

[5] Verses 9 to 12 are a free rendering of a text which in parts is so corrupt as to be untranslateable with accuracy.

The proud enemies of the Devas,
And is the slayer of many another demon,
Ever conquer!
She it was who, having severed the head of the Asura Mahiṣa,
Seized upon him who assumed the form of a buffalo by his magic art
Upon the field of battle,
Now bellowing, now running, now lowering his head downward,
Falling upon the battlefield, and then vanishing from it for a while.

10

She kills the Asuras upon the battlefield.
Terrible it was, with the dancing of the weapons and streamers[1] of the enemy.
With a cloud of thrown discus and other missiles.
There the copper-coloured weapon[2] dashed and flashed from the enemy's arrows—
Enemies so stout, strong, and tall, proud of wealth and power,
The field of battle thus seemed to have been swept by a tempest,
Most hideous it was, thickly spread with limbs and dead bodies of Asuras,
In whose blood and flesh birds slaked their thirst and appeased their hunger.

11

Let the Sādhaka meditate upon Devī Mahiṣā-mardinī.

---

[1] Chowrie.

[2] That is, fire.

Rushing now here, now there on the field of battle
for the slaughter of the enemies,
Attended by eight companion Mātrikas,[1]
Ear-ringed with eight-petalled lotuses,
Within each petal of which are writ the eight
syllables
Mahiṣāmardinyai namah.[2]
Formidable was that field with the tossing of the
huge curved horns of Mahiṣa,
Deeply black, maddened, wandering to and fro,
horribly roaring
Whose instant death was desired of the Devas.

12

Let the Sādhaka meditate
Upon the auspicious black *Bhagavati*[3] Mahiṣā-
mardini,
Holding in Her hands discus, lance, axe, shield,
arrow, bow, and trident,
Making the gesture[4] which dispels fear ;
Her long, matted hair is like a bank of cloud,
Covering Her face most formidable,
Loudly screaming, now with peals of terrible
laughter,
And then with Her threats greatly frightening the
Daitya heroes.

13

O Devi ! such as in this manner
Meditate upon Thy faultless form,

---

1 The Devīs so called.

2 Salutation to the Devī slayer of Mahiṣa.

3 For She has all powers.

4 Tho *abhaya mudrā* (see p. 36, note 1).

Worshipped by Indra and other Devas,
To them it is given to attack the cities of their enemies,
And, conquering their enemies, to gain a kingdom;
They, too, acquire nectar of the knowledge of poesy,
And power to arrest, banish and slay.[1]

14

O Mother! salutation to Thee!
May Thou conquer!
Whosoever, meditating upon Thy lotus feet,
Utters this Thy hymn,
In the palms of the hands of all such
Are forthwith wealth, fulfilment of desire, and liberation.

---

[1] *Stambhanam, uchchātanam,* and *māraṇam,* three of the Tāntrik *Ṣaṭkarma.*

ANNAPŪRṆA[1]

(ANNAPŪRṆĀSTOTRA)

FROM THE TANTRASĀRA[2]

1

SALUTATION to thee, O Devi!
Dispenser of blessings, beloved of S'ankara,[3]
Dear to devotees,
Annapūrṇe.

2

Thou hast assumed form by *māyā*[4]
Beloved of S'ankara.
Salutation to Mahesvarī,[5]
O Annapūrṇé! obeisance to Thee.[6]

---

1 A name of the Devī as She who bestows food, whose sincere devotee will never want rice. In one hand She holds a rice-bowl, and in another a spoon for stirring the boiled rice.

2 P. 570.

3 S'ivé.

4 All forms of the Devi, as also the forms of all *Devatā*, whether in the strict sense *avatāra* or not, are māyik, but to the worshipper none the less real.

5 Feminine of Mahesvara, a title of S'iva as great Lord and Ruler of the worlds.

6 *Annapūrṇé namostute*—the refrain.

3

O Mahāmāyā ![1] beloved Spouse[2] of Hara,[3]
Giver of the fruit of desire,
Queen of *Suras*.[4]
O Annapūrṇé ! obeisance to Thee.

4

O Mahādevī with the lustre of a thousand rising suns,
Three eyed,
Crested with the crescent moon.[5]

5

O Devī ! clad in fine garment,
Ever giving rice,[6] Sinless One,
Who delights in the dance of S'iva.
Crested with the crescent moon.[5]
O Annapūrṇé ! obeisance to Thee.

6

O Devī ! fulfiller of the desires of devotees,[7]
Destructress of worldly pain,
Bending under the weight of Thy breasts.[8]

---

1 The Devī as She who yields and is yet Herself unaffected by *māyā*.

2 *Dharmapatī*—that is, a wife married with religious rites. There are other forms of marriage.

3 S'iva.

4 *Devas*.

5 As is S'iva.

6 *Annadānaratā*, or food generally.

7 *Sādhakas*, those who practise *sādhanam* (see *Introduction To Tantra S'āstra*)

8 *Kucabhārānate* (see Introduction).

O Annapūrṇé! obeisance to Thee.

7

Thou residest in the centre of the six-petalled lotus,[1]
And art in the form of the six-fold *śakti*,[2]
Thou art Brahmāni and all others,[3]
O Annapūrṇé! obeisance to Thee.

8

O Devi! adorned with crescent moon,
All empires[4] are Thy gifts,
Giver of delight to Sarva[5],
O Annapūrṇé! obeisance to Thee.

9

Thy lotus feet are worshipped by Indra and other *Devās*;
Thou assumest the form of Rudra and other *Devas*,
Giver of wealth.
O Annapūrṇé! obeisance to Thee.

---

1 That is, the *svādhishṭhāna padma.*

2 *Sharangayuvatīmaye*, which equals *sharangaśaktisvarūpe*. The sixfold *śaktis* are: *Hṛdayānga śakti, śirongga śakti, śikhānga śakti, netrānga śakti, avachānga śakti*, and *astrānga śakti* which refer to the *Tāntrika nyāsa*, done on the heart, head, crownlock, eyes, the body, and the concluding gesture with the palms of the hands, accompanied by the *astra bija* or "*phat.*"

3 That is, Indrāṅi, Kaumāri, and other *Mātrikas.*

4 *Sāmrājya.*

5 *Sarvānandakare.* Sarva is one of the eight forms (*aṣṭamūrti*) of S'iva; or it may literally mean "giver of delight to all."

10

Whoever[1] at time of worship
Devoutly reads this hymn,
In his house Lakṣmī[2] ever abides;
True is this and without doubt.

11

Whoever having recited[3] the *mantra* daily,
Reads this hymn at dawn of day,
Obtains wealth of rice
And prosperity.

12

Not to all and any should this hymn be revealed,
For be it made known to one who is unworthy,
Then ills fall upon him,
Therefore should it be carefully concealed.

---

[1] This is the *phala* (fruit or result) portion of the *stotra*. All devotional works contain a *phala* chapter or verse, which states the result or reward (*phala*) to be obtained by their perusal, recitation, or hearing. If any worshipper invokes Devī by any particular name, such as Annadā, he obtains the corresponding fruit. So the Sūta Samhitā (iv, 33, 29, 30) says: "All names are attributed by His own *māyā* to Brahman, yet some apply specially by the wish of S'iva Himself. O sages! by the repetition of such names one becomes the supreme Lord Himself and before His lotus face Sadāśiva dances with His Spouse" (see Bhāskararāya Commentary, Introduction to second Chapter of the Lalitā-sahasranāma).

[2] Devi of prosperity and wealth.

[3] Literally, "made *japa* of"

SARASVATĪ[1]

(SARASVATĪSTOTRA)

From the TANTRASĀRA[2]

1

HRĪM, HRĪM[3] is Thy most pleasing *bija*,[4]
O Thou whose moon-like[5] beauty is heightened

[1] Devī of speech, eloquence, knowledge, and learning, and S'akti of Brahmā; but formerly, according to the Purāṇic account, the Spouse of Viṣṇu, represented as a fair woman with either four or two arms, and often as seated on a lotus holding a *vinā*. The Bhāradvaja Smr. says: "Sarasvatī is She who ever resides in the tongue of all beings and who causes speech." According to the Vasiṣṭha Rāmā, cited in the Lalitā, verse 137, She is called Sarasvatī as the possessor (*vati*) of the *saras* (flow of nectar from the *brahmarandhra*). The Brahma Purāṇa says the Devī created Sarasvatī from Her tongue, and from Her shoulders the science of love.

[2] P. 579.

[3] The *bīja*, or "seed" mantra of the Devī whose other *bīja* is the *vāgbhava bīja* or "*aim.*"

[4] See last note.

[5] The colour of Sarasvatī is white. Thus She is elsewhere represented as "white, holding the *vinā*" (*Svetavīnādharā*), "adorned with white flowers" (*svetābharaṇabhūṣitā*), "holding a white rosary" (*svetākṣasūtrahastāca*), "besmeared with white sandal paste" (*svetacandanacarcitā*), "clad in white raiment" (*svetāmbaradharā*), and the like. Here Her whiteness is compared to the moon.

By the lotuses (which surround Thee).[1]
O auspicious and favourable Devī!
Forest fire[2] of the forest of evil thoughts,
Whose lotus feet are worshipped by the universe.
O lotus seated upon a lotus,
Joy dost thou cause to those who salute Thee,
Destroyer of Ignorance,
Spouse of Hari,[3]
Substance of the world.[4]

2

AIM, *AIM*[5] is Thy favourite *mantra*,
Thou who art both form and formlessness,[6]
Who art the wealth of the lotus face of the lotus-born,[7]
Embodiment of all *guṇas*,[8] yet devoid of attributes,[9]
Changeless, and neither gross nor subtle.[10]

---

1 She is seated on and represented as surrounded by lotuses.

2 *Dāvāgni*. She destroys such thoughts.

3 Viṣṇu

4 *Samsārasāre*. The *samsāra* is the illusory world of birth and rebirth, which is said to be *asara* (unreal, unsubstantial, fleeting). The reality behind this phenomenal illusion is the Devī, who plays, and whose play is world-play.

5 The *vāgbhavabīja*.

6 *Rūpārūpaprakāśe*.

7 Brahmā, whose Spouse She is.

8 The "qualities," or conditions, which are the substance of *Prakṛti* or *sattva*, *rajas*, and *tamas*.

9 She is *nirguṇā*, for She and the *Parabrahman* are in Their essence one.

10 The forms of the Devī are threefold: *parā* (supreme), *sūkṣmā* (subtle), which consists of *mantra* and *sthūla* (gross or physical), with hands and feet. But She is neither of these in the sense that the only true form (*svarūpa*) is above and beyond them both.

None know Thy nature, nor is Thy inner reality known.[1]
Thou art the whole universe ;
And Thou it is who existeth within it.
Thou art saluted by the foremost of Devas.
Without part Thou existeth in Thy fulness everywhere.[2]
Ever[3] pure art Thou.

3

Greatly art Thou pleased with the recitation[4] of the *mantra HRĪM.*[5]
Thy crown is white as snow.[6]
Thy hands play with the *vīnā.*[7]
O Mother ! Mother ! salutation to Thee.
Burn, burn my sloth and grant me great intelligence.[8]
Thou art Knowledge itself.
The *Vedānta* ever sings of Thee.

---

[1] *Nāpivijnātatattve* ; another reading being *nāpivijnānatattve.* The reference is to Her supreme (*para*) form, of which the Viṣṇu Yāmala says "none know" (*Mātastvatparamam rūpam tannajānāti kashcana* (see chap. iii. of the S'āktānandatarangini).

[2] She as the Brahman is *akhaṇḍa* "everywhere" and yet in the limited sense "nowhere," in the sense that She is at some particular place and not elsewhere, or partly here and partly there.

[3] In past, present, and future.

[4] *Japa,* which includes that which would not be understood as recitation in the English sense—viz., *manasa* or mental, and the inaudible *japa.*

[5] The bīja of the Devi.

[6] Her colour is white

[7] A stringed musical instrument.

[8] *Dehibuddhimprashastām* ; the great prayer to Her.

S'ruti[1] speaks of Thee.
O giver of liberation ! O way to liberation !
Whose power is beyond all understanding.
O giver of happiness,[2] adorned with a white necklace,[3]
Grant to me Thy favours.

4

Thou art intelligence, intelligence, intelligence,[4]
Thy names are memory, resolution, mind, and hymn of praise.[5]
Eternal and fleeting,[6]
Great cause, saluted by *Munis*,[7]
New and old ;[8] sacred current of virtue,[9]
Saluted by Hari and Hara.[10]
Ever pure, beauteous of colour,
The subtlest element[11] of things—

---

[1] Revelation ; generally applied to the Vedas in which Sarasvatī is spoken of (see Muir, O.S.T., verse 339). She is also called Mother of Vedas.

[2] *S'āradā.*

[3] See note 5, p. 74, *ante*.

[4] *Dhī.*

[5] *Dhāranā, dhriti* (or constancy), *mati*. She is the "hymn of praise," for it is composed of words, and She is the Devī thereof, and word and speech itself.

[6] She eternally exists as the reality behind all appearance, and is the cause of the fleeting appearance itself.

[7] Sages.

[8] See note 6 *ante*. She ever appears in new forms, and yet Herself in Her aspect as *Atmā*, persists as the one and same.

[9] *Punya.*

[10] Viṣṇu and S'iva.

[11] *Mātra*—the atomic part of things.

Yea, even the very half thereof.[1]
Thou art the giver of intelligence, intelligence, intelligence.
Who art the giver of joy to Mādhava.[2]

5

In the form of *HRĪM*, *KṢĪM*, *DHĪM*, *HRĪM*,[3]
Thou holdest a book,
Thou art joyful, of smiling face, and of good fortune.
Innocence, current of charm,[4]
With all powers of arrest[5].
Burn, burn my sin,
And dispel the darkness of my evil thoughts.
O praiseworthy of all!
Thou art *Gīh*, *Gauh*, *Vāk*, and *Bhāratī*.[6]
It is Thou who grantest success to the tongue of the greatest of poets,

---

[1] *Mātrārdhatattve*. She is so very subtle: or alternatively the Mātrārdha below the *Sāhasrāra*.

[2] The husband of Mā or Lakṣmī—that is, Viṣṇu, whose Spouse She was. She as Prakṛti gives joy to the *paramātmā*, who is the enjoyer (*bhoktā*).

[3] The mantra, as currently recited is *Om Om Kshīm, Kshīm, svarupe*. "*Kshīm,*" for She is the destructress of sin.

[4] *Mohemugdhapravāhe*. *Mugdhā* is generally used in connection with *nāyikā*—that is, a simple, artless innocent maiden, as yet unacquainted with love. The general and correct reading is *mugdhemohapravāhe*.

[5] *Stambhanam*; one of the six "magical" powers known as the *ṣatkarma*, whereby a person may be paralyzed in action or speech. So a disputant might seek the power of *stambhanam* to close the mouth of, or confuse his adversary.

[6] Various words which all mean "word" or "speech."

As also in the attainment of all (forms of) knowledge.[1]

6

I pray to Thee, I pray to Thee, I bow to Thee,
Come to my tongue and never leave me.
May my intelligence[2] never go astray,
May my sins be taken away,
May I be free from sorrow.
In time of peril may I never be bewildered.
May my mind work freely without impediment[3]
In *Śāstra* disputation and verse.

7

He who chastely[4] lives, observing silence[5] and religious devotions,[6]
Abstaining from flesh and fish[7] on the thirteenth day of the month,[8]
And bowed with devotion, early each morning
Praises Thee with the most excellent verse.
Will, skilful in speech, surpass even Vācaspati.[9]
The uncleanliness of his sins will be swept away.
Such an one gains the fruit of his desires,

---

[1] Literally, the giver of *siddhi* (success) in all knowledge of which She is the presiding Devi.

[2] Both *buddhi* and *manas*.

[3] *Prasaratu* ("flow freely").

[4] He who is *brahmachārin*. Here commences the *phala* portion of the *stotra*.

[5] *Maunin*.

[6] *Vratin*. The *vrata* are voluntary religious practices and devotions as distinguished from the obligatory daily ritual.

[7] *Nirāmishah*.

[8] The *trayodaśi*; the *Sarasvati vrata* day.

[9] Or Brihaspati, the Lord of Speech.

The Devī protects him as though he were Her
own child.
Poetry flows from his mouth,
Prosperity attends his house,
And every obstacle to success will disappear.

8

Whoever reads without interruption the whole of
this hymn
Twenty-one times on the thirteenth day of the
month,[1]
Both on the dark and the light side of the month,[2]
And meditates on Sarasvatī garmented in white,
Adorned with white ornaments,
Such an one attains in this world the fruit of his
desires.
This auspicious hymn has been made by Brahmā
himself;
Whoever daily reads it with care acquires
immortality.[3]

---

1 *Trayodaśī*

2 The month is divided into two halves (*pakṣa*), according as the moon is waxing or waning.

3 *Amṛtatvam*—that is, liberation (*mukti*).

DURGĀ[1]

(DURGĀS'ATANĀMA STOTRA)[2]

From the VIS'VASĀRA TANTRA

1

Saith Īśvara : [3]

I shall tell thee the hundred names of Durgā.

By the grace of this hymn the chaste[4] Durgā is satisfied.

Listen, then, thereto.

2-13

OM.

Chaste one.[5]

---

[1] Manifestation of the S'akti of S'iva in warrior form as the Destructress of demonic beings, enemies to *Devas* and men. According to one account, She is so called as having slain the Asura Durgā, son of Ruru (Skanda Purāṇa). Another account of the origin of Durgā is given in Candi (Mārkandeyapurāṇa), where the combined *tejas*, like a mountain of all the Devas, manifested as the Devi Durgā for the destruction of the *Asura* Mahiṣa.

[2] P. 573, Tantrasāra from the Viśvasāra Tantra.

[3] The Lord S'iva.

[4] *Satī*.

[5] *Satī*, or faithful. The name of the daughter of Dakṣa. Brahma Pr. says: " The faithful Spouse Satī became Umā, who ever dwells with S'iva."

Virtuous one.[1]
Beloved of Bhava.[2]
Spouse of Bhava.[3]
The Manifested Brahman.[4]
Liberatrix from the world of births and deaths.
Destructress of distress.[6]
Victorious one.[7]
Primordial one.[8]
Three-eyed,[9]
Holder of the spear.[10]

---

[1] *Sādhvi*, or chaste. She is of unequalled virtue as being attached to none but Her Lord (see Lalitā, verse 43, where Bhāskararāya cites the Ācārya (Saundaryalahari), which says: "How many poets share the wife of Brahmā? Cannot everyone by means of wealth become the Lord of S'rī (Viṣṇu)? But, O virtuous one, first among faithful women, your breasts are untouched save by Mahādeva, not even by the paste of Kuravaka." (a kind of paste made of the leaves of the red amaranth used to redden the cheeks, breasts, palms, and soles of Hindu women). Devī Bhāg. Pr. also says: "Thou art praised as Sādhvi on account of Thy unequalled fidelity to Thy Lord."

[2] *Bhavapritā*. Bhava is S'iva

[3] *Bhavāni*.

[4] *Aryā*, which literally means noble, but which here means, as the commentator Nīlakaṇṭha says in reference to the hymn to Durgā in the Mahābhārata (see *post*) *prāpyabrahmasvarūpa*, the own form of the accessible Brahman as distinguished from the *Nirguṇa* Brahman beyond thought and speech. The very nature of the Devi is manifestation, and She is near to us in the world.

[5] *Bhavamochini*—that is, from the *samsāra* or phenomenal world.

[6] Durgā—that is, *Sa ya durgatim harati*.

[7] *Jayā*

[8] *Ādyā*.

[9] *Trinetrā*.

[10] *S'ūladhārinī*. The *śūla* is a weapon of the Devi.

Spouse of Him who holds the *pināka* Bow.[1]
Wonderful one.[2]
Whose bell sounds fearfully.[3]
Of great austerities.[4]
Manas.[5]
Buddhi.[6]
Ahamkāra.[7]
In the form of *citta.*[8]
Funeral pyre.[9]
Knowledge.[10]
Whose substance is all *mantras.*[11]
Reality.[12]

---

1 *Pinākadhārini*—that is, Spouse of S'iva, who wields the *Pināka* bow broken by Rāma ; hence he is called *Pinākin.*

2 *Citrā.*

3 *Candaghantā*, the first of the nine Durgās in the *Durgā Kavaca.*

4 *Mahātapāh.* For the Devi as Umā Aparṇā did great austerities to gain S'iva as Her husband.

5 See p. 87, note 5 *post.*

6 *Ibid.*

7 *Ibid.*

8 *Cittarupā.* *Citta* is mental substance.

9 *Citā*, which in Tantra has a twofold meaning (*smaśānam dvividham Devī citā yonimāheśvari*) for, whereas on the first the body is burnt, so in the second is the fire which consumes passion (Niruttara Tantra, chap. i.).

10 *Citih = jnānā.*

11 *Sarvamantramayī.*

12 *Satyā*, that which persists through the threefold time—past, present, and future—of which the opposite is *asatyā*. That which is real and not fictitious (*yathārthasvarūpa*). The epithet *Satyā*, which occurs thrice in this *stotra*, has also, besides "real," three other meanings: (1) Eternal, (2) the best (*uttamā*), and (3) *sthitiśila*, whose nature it is to exist.

Whose nature is the true bliss.[1]
Endless one.[2]
In whom are the three dispositions.[3]
Accessible by devotion.[4]
Auspicious.[5]
Pervading all things.[6]
Spouse of S'ambu.[7]
Mother of *Devas*.[8]
Contemplation.[9]
Fond of gems.[10]
All knowledge.[11]
Daughter of Dakṣa.[12]

---

1 *Satyānandasvarūpinī*.

2 *Anantā*.

3 *Bhāvini*. In the ordinary sense *bhāvini*, as sentimental, emotional, is a term which, according to the Amarakośa, is commonly applied to women, as are the terms *pramadā* (pleasing), *kāntā* and *lalanā* (beautiful), and *nitambinī* (possessing beautiful *nitamba* or buttocks). But here the word refers to the *bhāvas*, *paśu*, *vira*, and *divya*, which are each manifestations of Her.

4 *Bhāvagamyā*.

5 *Bhāvyā*.

6 *Sadāgatih*.

7 *S'āmbhavī*, Spouse of S'iva (S'ambhu).

8 *Devamātā*.

9 *Cintā*.

10 *Ratnapriyā*.

11 *Sarvavidyā*; and so also the Lalitā, verse 137, speaks of Her as being all the *S'āstras* (*śāstramayī*). The Brahma Pr. says that from Her breath came the Vedas; from the tip of Her throat the sixty-four sciences; from the rest of Her limbs all other Tantras; and from Her shoulders the science of love.

12 *Dakṣakanyā*. Dakṣa was one of the Prajāpatis and father-in-law of S'iva, who was married to his daughter Satī, a manifestation of the Devī.

Destroyer of Dakṣa's sacrifice.[1]
Who eat not even a leaf during Thy austerities.[2]
Of various colour.[3]
Red.[4]
Having a red colour.[5]
Clad in silken garment.[6]
Pleased with sweet-sounding anklets.[7]
Of unbounded power.[8]
Terrifying.[9]
Beautiful.[10]
House lady.[11]
Forest Durgā.[12]
Daughter of Matanga.[13]

---

1 *Dakṣayajnavināśinī*. Because on Her account S'iva, Her husband, destroyed the *dakṣayajna*.

2 *Aparṇā* (see Hymn entitled "May the Devi Grant Me Pardon", *post*).

3 *Anekavarṇā*.

4 *Pātalā*: a reddish-pink, the colour of the Bhairavimurti.

5 *Pātalavatī*.

6 *Pattāmbara paridhānā*.

7 *Kalamanjīraranjinī*.

8 *Amiyavikramā*.

9 *Krūrā*. Literally, "cruel"—that is, to the demonic beings which She destroyed, though even not truly so, for as Candī says, She destroyed them not only for the happiness of the world, but for their own happiness, so that being slain by Her hand they might go to heaven.

10 *Sundarī*.

11 *Purasundarī*.

12 *Vanadurgā*: the Devi of the forests. The foresters, before entering the forests, offer *pūjā* to Vanadurgā as protectress against their dangers and terrors.

13 *Mātangī*; that is, of the *Ṛṣi* Matanga.

Worshipped by the sage Matanga.[1]
Spouse of Brahmā.[2]
Great Ruler.[3]
Aindrī.[4]
Kaumāri.[5]
Vaiṣṇavī.[6]
Cāmundā.[7]
Varāhī.[8]
Lakṣmī.[9]
In the form of the Puruṣa.[10]
Pure one.[11]

---

1 *Matangamunipūjitā.*

2 *Brāhmī.*

3 *Maheśvarī* (feminine of Maheśvara), an appellation of S'iva.

4 Spouse of Indra, one of the eight Mātṛkās.

5 Spouse of Kārtikeya or Skanda, the leader of the celestial hosts. The Devī is also Mother both of Kumāra and Gananātha (Gaṇeśa), and is so called in the Lalitā, verse 94 (*Kumāraganana-thāmbā*), where it is said that the Devatā of egoism (*ahamkāra*) is Kumāra. The Varāha Pr. says: "Viṣṇu is the Puruṣa, or S'iva is so called, Avyaktā is Umā or Laksmī, the lotus-eyed. From the interaction of these two arises *ahamkāra*. This *ahamkāra* is the *guha* (*skanda*), the leader of the army."

6 The *vaiṣṇavī śakti.*

7 See Hymn entitled " May the Devi Grant Me Pardon ", *post.*

8 S'akti of Varāha, the boar incarnation, one of the eight *Mātṛkas.*

9 Devī of wealth, prosperity, and beauty.

10 *Puruṣākritih.* Puruṣa is man, male, or person; the primeval man; the spirit of the universe, manifesting as Brahmā, Viṣṇu, S'iva, etc.; the passive spectator of the acts of Prakṛti. But in their ground both are one. Therefore Devī is in such sense Puruṣa also. So Krṣṇa, to screen his action from Rādhikā, manifested as Kālī.

11 *Vimalā.*

Essence of all.[1]
Knowledge.[2]
Action.[3]
The Supreme One.[4]
Giver of *buddhi*.[5]
Who art all.[6]
Whose love is unbounded.[7]
Mounted on a bull.[8]
Destructress of S'umbha and Niśumbha.[9]
Slayer of the Asura Mahiṣa.[10]
Slayer of Madhu and Kaitaba.[11]
Destructress of Caṇḍa and Muṇḍa.[12]
And of all Asuras.[13]

---

1 *Utkārṣinī*,.

2 *Jnānā*, for the Devī is *jnānā*, *kriyā*, and *ichchhā śakti*.

3 *Kriyā*.

4 *Satyā* (see *ante*, p. 83, note 12).

5 *Buddhidā*. *Buddhi* (intellect), the function of which is determination (*niścayakārinī*), is part of the fourfold *antaḥkaraṇa*: constituted by *Buddhi* and *Manas* (aspects of mind), *Ahamkāra* (egoity) and *cintā* (contemplation).

6 *Bahula-bhumā*.

7 *Bahulapremā*.

8 *Sarvavāhanavāhanā*. Literally whose vehicle (*vāhana*) is the *vāhana* of Sarva (S'iva), or a bull.

9 *Niśumbhaśumbhahananī*. These were two *Daityas*, or enemies of the Devas, slain by the Devī (see Caṇḍī). The Daityas were sons of Diti and the Devas children of Aditi, hence they are called *Āditeya*.

10 *Mahiṣāsuramardinī* (*vide ibid.*).

11 *Madhukaitabahantrī*. Two *Daityas* (*ibid*).

12 *Caṇḍamuṇḍavināśinī* : two generals of S'umbha and Niśumbha (*ibid.*)

13 *Sarvāsuravinarśa*.

And of all Dānavas.[1]
Whose substance is all *S'āstra.*[2]
Existence.[3]
Holder of all weapons.[4]
In whose hands are various weapons.[5]
Holder of many weapons.[6]
Virgin.[7]
Maiden.[8]
Kaiṣori.[9]
Youthful.[10]
Ascetic one.[11]
Apraudhā.[12]

---

1 *Sarvadānavaghātinī.* The Dānavas were enemies of the Devas, children of Danu, a daughter of Dakṣa and Kāśyapa.

2 *Sarvaśāstramayī.*

3 *Satyā.*

4 *Sarvāstradhārinī. Astra* is a weapon which is thrown—a projectile ; and *śastra,* in the next verse, is a weapon which is held.

5 *Anekaśastrahastā* (see last note).

6 *Anekāstrasyadhārinī.*

7 *Kumārī.*

8 *Kanyā.*

9 A girl up to fifteen years of age is so called (*Kaiṣoram āpancadaśāt*). It is said that up to sixteen years one is known as *bālā.* At thirty one is *Taruṇī,* at fifty-five *praudhā,* and above that *vriddhā.* As the verse runs:

Aṣōdaśād bhaved bālā,
Trinśatā taruṇī matā,
Panca pancāśatā praudhā,
Bhaved vriddhā tatah param.

10 *Yuvatī.*

11 *Yati*: one who controls the passions is an ascetic. The Devī practised great austerities to gain S'iva as Her husband.

12 That is, below fifty-five years old, an adult woman who is no longer bashful or timid in the presence of her lord.

Praudhā.[1]
Old mother.[2]
Giver of strength.[3]

14

For him who daily reads[4] these 108[5] names of Durgā
There is nothing impossible in the three worlds.
He obtains wealth, crops, sons, wife, horses, and elephants;
He accomplishes the *caturvarga*,[6]
And gains lasting liberation.

15

Having worshipped the Devī Kumārī,[7]
And meditated upon Sureśvarī,[8]
The devotee should worship,[9]
And then read with devotion the 108 names of Durgā.
O Devī! such an one gains the fruition[10] which *Devas* have;

---

[1] Over fifty-five years old.

[2] *Vriddhamātā*.

[3] *Balapradā*. The litany in the Tantrasāra here ends at the 87th name, short of the prescribed number of names.

[4] Here commences the *phala* portion.

[5] *Sic*; *vide ante*. Wherever 100 or 1,000 is mentioned (the former in the title of the present hymn) 108 or 1,008 is to be understood, for zero is an inauspicious number.

[6] *Dharma, artha, kāma*, and *mokṣa*—piety, wealth, desire, and liberation—(see *Introduction to Tantra S'āstra*).

[7] See "Hymn to Annapurṇā" *post*.

[8] Mistress of Suras (Devas).

[9] *i.e.*, make *pūja*.

[10] *Siddhi* (see *Introduction to Tantra S'āstra*).

Kings become his servants,
And he obtains a kingdom and all prosperity.

16

He who, versed in the *śāstric* injunctions
In accordance therewith, writes this *mantra*
With saffron mixed with cows' pigment,[1] red lac,[2]
camphor, and the three sweets,[3]
And then wears it, becomes himself Purāri.[4]

17

Whoever writes and then reads this hymn
On a Tuesday in *Amāvāsya*,[5]
At night, when the moon is in *S'atabhiṣā*,[6]
Attains all wealth and prosperity.

---

[1] *Gorocanā.*

[2] *Alakta.*

[3] *Madhutraya*—that is, ghee, honey, and sugar.

[4] S'iva.

[5] The fifteenth day of the dark half of the lunar month; a very dark day on which *S'avāsana* and similar rites are also accomplished.

[6] There are twenty-seven lunar mansions, of which *S'atabhiṣā* is the twentyfourth, containing a hundred stars.

TRIPUṬĀ[1]

(TRIPUṬĀSTOTRAM)

FROM THE TANTRASĀRA[2]

1

I CONTEMPLATE the good Guru who is Light itself,[3]
Sitting with his *S'akti*[4]
In the lotus of the head,[5]
Two-armed, gracious, very gracious,
Whose moon-like face is full of grace,
Making with his hands the gestures which grant boons and dispel fear.[6]

2

Such as recite[7] thy primordial golden *bija*

---

[1] Tripuṭā and Tripurā are separate Devis, but the former is *antargatā* of Tripurā—that is, forms part, is included in, and a particular manifestation of Tripurā. In the same way the Devis Ekajaṭa, Nilasarasvati, Ugratārā, Mahogrā, are each *antargatā* of Tārā.

[2] Tantrasāra, p. 571.

[3] *Prakaśasvarūpa. Prakāśa* is light and manifestation.

[4] Spouse.

[5] That is, the *Sahasrārapadma*.

[6] That is, he is making the two *mudrās* called *vara* and *abhaya* respectively.

[7] Literally, " make *japa* ".

SRĪM,[1]
Attain all prosperity and fortune.

3

O Mother!
He who contemplates Thy second *bīja*,
Adorned by numbers of Devas,
"*HRĪM,*"[2]
Gains all prosperity.

4

The chiefs of men who meditate upon Thy *bīja*,
Lustrous as the sun,

---

[1] As is frequently the case in Tāntrik works, the *mantra* is not given in the text, but must be spelt out. Thus the Sanskrit is *vakamvahnisamstham trimurtyā prajuṣtam śaśānkenayuktam*—that is, "*vakam* with *vahni* attended by *trimurti*, combined with *śaśāngka.*" *Vakam* = "S′" (*tālavya*). *Vahni* is the "fire." = "r," *trimūrti* = the long vowel ī, and *śaśāngka*, the moon in "whose lap is the hare," or "man in the moon" = "m" (*anusvāra*). S′+r+ī+m = *śrīm* the *Lakshmībīja* (see the Ādyakālīstotra of Mahānirvāṇa Tantra).

[2] Literally, *Nabhovahni* (not *vāyu*, as the text has it, for the *vāyu bīja* is *yam*); *miśram* (not *mitram* as Prasanna Kumāra Shāstrī's edition has it); *tatovāmanetram sudhā dhāmavimbam niyojyaikāvaktram*—that is, *nabhas* combined with *vahni*, and then *vāmanetra* and the receptacle of nectar (the moon) applicable in the case of Ekavaktra. *Nabhas*= "*ha*" or "*bha*" (here the former), *vahni* = "*ra*," *vāmanetra* = long *ī*, and the moon is *anusvāra* ("m"), H+r+ī+m = *Hrīm*, known as the *māyā bīja*. Then the *śloka* more clearly points to the *bīja* meant by saying it is that applicable to Ekavaktra. The latter is the Bhairava of Bagalāmukhī, whose *bīja* is also *Hrīm*.

" *KLĪM*,"[1]
Charm the three worlds,
And by recitation thereof become like unto Īśvara.

5

O beloved of the enemy of Smara![2]
Those who contemplate Thy body[3] thrice[4] and recite these three *bījas*[5]
Render their enemies speechless,
Lakṣmī shines in their house,
And they become the God of Love[6] to women.

6

The presiding Devatā of Speech
Blesses their mouth with poetry and prose.
Harmful animals cause them no harm,
Even the Suras[7] salute them.

---

[1] Literally, *Virinchim kṣitistham tatovāmanetram vidhum nādayuktam*—that is, *virinchi*, *kṣiti* and *vāmanetra*, together with moon combined with *nāda*. *Virinchi* = "*ka*", *kṣiti* = "*La*," *vāmanetra* = long ī, the moon = "m" (*anusvāra*). K + l + ī + m = *Klīm*. The three elements of the mantra are given—viz., *S'rīm, Hrīm, Klīm*—but the actual *bīja* of Tripuṭā is *S'rīm, Hrīm, Klīm, Hrīm, S'rīm, Klīm, Klīm, S'rīm, Hrīm*.

[2] The Deva of love (Kāma), of whom S'iva is described as the enemy, for he burnt him with the fire of his eye (see p. 40, note 1).

[3] *Anga*.

[4] Literally, make *japa*. "Thrice," as follows *S'rīm, Hrīm, Klīm, Hrīm, S'rīm, Klīm, Klīm, S'rīm, Hrīm*."

[5] See last note.

[6] The beautiful youth Kāma. *Cf.* Verse 5 of Karpūrādistotra.

[7] The Devas.

Their feet are the head ornaments of kings,[1]
The *siddhis*[2] are in their hands,
Malignant stars relinquish them.

7

Let the *Sādhaka* meditate upon an eight-petalled lotus[3]
Set upon a throne studded with various gems,
Placed upon an altar
Standing on the floor of a jewelled house
Amidst a forest of *Pārijāta* trees.[4]

8

Let him then meditate upon two angles[5] in the lotus,
And the Devi Herself in the lotus as follows:
Her lustre is that of molten gold,
With earrings[6] on her ears,
Three-eyed, of beauteous throat,
Her face like the moon,
And bending from the weight of Her breasts.[7]

9

She holds in many arms, decked with diamonds and other gems,

---

[1] That is, he sets his feet on the heads of kings.

[2] The great powers, *aṇimā*, *laghimā*, etc. (see p. 18, note 6).

[3] The heart lotus (not *anāhata*) in which the *Iṣṭadevata* is worshipped.

[4] One of the celestial trees (see HYMN "Wave of Bliss", *post*).

[5] *Yoni*. There are five *yonis* or *śakti* angles in the *S'rīcakra*.

[6] *Kuṇḍala*.

[7] *Subakṣojanamrām*.

Two lotuses, a noose,[1] bow, golden goad,[2] and
flowery arrows.[3]
Her body is adorned with great jewels,
Slender is She of waist[4] and beautifully girdled.

10

Her lotus feet glitter with beautiful anklets,[6]
Crowned, adorned, and gracious,
Holding two white fly-whisks,[7] a mirror, jewel-
case,[8] and a box filled with camphor.[9]

11

Creatrix of the three worlds,
Destructress of the pain of the world,
Destructress and ruler of the world,
Ever full of Bliss,

---

1 *Pāśakam.*

2 *Angkuśa.*

3 *Puṣpavānām* (see Comm. Lalitā, verse 2) According to the Yoginīhṛdaya, the noose is *Ichchā*; the goad, *jnāna*; and the bow and arrows the *kṛyā śaktis* respectively.

4 *Sumadhyām.*

5 She wears a *candrahāra*, so called because it has a moonlike ornament in its centre.

6 *Tulākota.*

7 *Cāmara* or chowrie, the bushy tail of the Cāmara (the yak; *bos grunniens*); used as a fly-whisk or fan, an insignia of royalty, and also used as a streamer on the heads of horses.

8 *Karanda—alangkāra pātra.*

9 *Samudgam*, translated in the Bengali as a *pān*-box with camphor, which is put into *pān* (betel).

Half of the letter *Hā*;[1] of the nature of the threefold *Bindu*,[2]
The threefold *S'akti*,[3]
It is Her I worship.

12

The *Sādhaka* who, having thus for a long time contemplated Her
On a *yantra*[4] set before him,
And welcomed[5] her with great deuotion,
Worshipping Her with *Svayambhu* flower[6]
Attains, even though he be of the lowest[7] *siddhi*[8] in the *caturvarga*.[9]

---

[1] *Hakārārddhavarṇām*—that is, She is *Kāmakalā-svarūpā* (see Ādyākālīstotram, p. 43, and the *Kāmakalāvilāsa*, cited in the Lalitā sahasranāma, verse 73.) Another name for *Kāmakalāsvarūpā* is *Kāmapurasvarūpā*. The half *Ha* resembles a *bindu*, of which there are three—viz., the *bindu* at the base of the triangle from which the *A-ka-tha trikoṇa* emanated and the *visargah* above. See Kālicarana's commentary on the Pādukāpancakam, in *The Serpent Power*.

[2] *Tribindusvarūpā*—there are three such in *Kāmakalā*.

[3] *Jnāna, ichchhā*, and *kṛyā śaktis* of the Devi.

[4] Diagram used in Tantrik worship (see *Introduction to Tantra S'āstra*.)

[5] With the *āvāhana mantra*—viz., *iha āgacha iha āgacha, iha tishtha, iha tishtha atra adishthānam kuru mama pujām, grihāna*. ("Come here, come here! Stay here, stay here! accept my worship").

[6] See Mātṛkābheda Tantra. The word *puṣpa* (flower) has here a technical sense. *Puṣpaśabdena atra riturucyate. Mātṛkābhedatantra pramānānusārena anurāyāh kanyāyāh prathama eva rituratrā ucyate. Tantrāntaretu vivāhitāyāh eva bālāyāh rituratra vivakṣitah.*

[7] *Pāmara*, one who is low or vile, a very contumelious term.

[8] Success, perfection, fruition.

[9] That is, *Dharma* (religion, piety), *artha* (wealth), *Kāma* (desire and its fulfilment), and *Mokṣa* (liberation). (See *Introduction to Tantra S'āstra*).

13

Whoever after having done worship[1]
Of S'rī,[2] S'rīpati,[3] Pārvatī,[4] Īśvara,[5] Rati,[6] and
Kāmadeva,[7]
Together with the *Ṣadānga* Devatā[8] of the Devī,
Recites[9] the *mantra* on Thy *yantra*,[10]
Becomes a King among men.

14

Having worshipped the two *nidhis*,[11] S'ankha and
Padma,
On the two sides of the lotus,

---

[1] *Pūjā*.

[2] *Lakṣmī*.

[3] *Viṣṇu*.

[4] Devī as daughter of Himavat.

[5] S'iva.

[6] Spouse of Kāma, the God of Love.

[7] The God of Love.

[8] That is, the six *āvarana* or attendant Devatās on the Devī.

[9] Makes *japa* of.

[10] See *Introduction to Tantra S'āstra*.

[11] There are eight gems or treasures (*nidhi*) of Kubera—viz., *padma, mahāpadma, makara, kachchapa, mukunda, nīla, nanda, śankha*. The Mārkaṇḍeya Purāṇa gives the meaning of *nidhi* in the followng *śloka* ("Lakṣmī is the presiding *Devatā* of the *vidyā*, called *Padminī*. The *nidhis* are Her supporters. Listen while I speak of them"):

Padminīnāma yā vidyā,
Lakṣmī stadadhi devatā,
Tadādhārāsca nidhaya,
Stan me nivadatah śrinu.

And the Mahiṣis,[1] regents of the quarters,[2] and
their weapons,
Attains, even though he be of the most vile,[3] the
eight *siddhis*[4] of S'iva.

15

Thou art the earth, *Vidhātri*,[5] creatrix of the world;[6]
Thou art water, and in the form of Viṣṇu preser-
veth the world;
Thou art fire, and in the form of Rudra destroyeth
the world;
Thou existeth in the form of *Aiśvarya*;[7]
Thou art the air of the world.

16

Thou art the primeval[6] and auspicious one,[8]
Spouse of S'ambhu,[9] refuge (of Thy worshippers).

---

1 That is, the S'aktis Brāhmi, etc.

2 The *lokapālas* or guardians of the points of the compass (N., N. W., W., S. W., N.E, E., S.E., and S. Indra, Yama, Varuna, Kubera, Vivasvat, Soma, Agni and Vāyu).

3 *Pāmara*.

4 *Aṇimā*, *Laghima*, etc.

5 *Vidhātrī* = Creatrix; but both the terms *Vidhātri* and Creatrix of the world are used in the text.

6 The six *aiśvarya* are *S'ri* (beauty and auspiciousness), *Vīrya* (power), *jñāna* (Wisdom), *Vairāgya* (dispassion), *Kīrti* (glory) and *Māhātmya* (greatness). Bhagavan is He who is possessed of these six *aiśvarya*. All these are in the Devī who is hence called Bhagavati (see Devī Bhāg. Pr., Saktirahasya; Bhāskararāya, *op. cit.*, verse 65), and as here, *Aiśvarya rūpā*.

7 *Ādyā*.

8 *S'ivè*, voc. of *S'ivè*, feminine of *S'iva*.

9 S'iva.

Who ever moves in the *Brahmarandhra*[1] of the world
The supporter of all, yet Thyself without support.
The only pure One in the form of ether.[2]
O Bhavānī ! be gracious to me.

17

Thou hast humbled the pride even of the *Ṛṣis*
By plunging them into the ocean of the world.
Thou art intelligence and bliss and light itself.[3]
How, then, can I know thee ?
O Bhavānī ! be gracious to me.

18

O Bhavānī ! even an ignorant man[4]
Who, meditating on Thy form, recites[5] Thy *mantra* a *lakh* of times
Acquires all poetic power,
And those things in the three worlds which are most difficult of attainment.
O Bhavānī ! be gracious to me.

19

Thou art that which supports[6] and that which is supported.[7]
Thou pervadeth the world,

---

1 The opening in the top of the head, whence in the case of *yogis* the soul on death issues.

2 *Ākāśakalpā*.

3 *Prakāśasvarūpā*.

4 *Mandaceta*.

5 Makes *japa*.

6 *Ādhāraśakti*.

7 *Tvāmādheyarūpā*.

And art in the form of the world which is pervaded
by Thee.[1]
Thou art both negation[2] and existence.[3]
O Bhavānī ! be gracious to me.

20

Thou art the atom[4] and ever-pervading.[5]
Thou art the whole universe.
No praise of Theẹ is sufficient.
Yet Thy qualities prompt me to sing Thy praise.
O Bhavānī ! be gracious to me.

21

To him who reads and recites [6] at morn, noon, and
evening
This most secret hymn,
There is nothing impossible in the three worlds,
Such an one attains Thy nature.[7]
O Bhavānī ! be gracious to me.

---

1 *Jagatvyāpyarūpā.*

2 *Abhāva,* the last of the seven categories of Kaṇāda's system (Vaiśeṣika Sūtra). Thus darkness is the *abhāva* of light.

3 *Bhāva.*

4 *Aṇu.*

5 *Vibhu.*

6 Makes *japa.*

7 *Svarūpam labhante*—that is, he attains that form of liberation which is known as *svārūpya mukti* (receiving the same form as that of the Devatā worshipped).

HYMNS TO THE DEVĪ

FROM PURĀṆA

MOTHER OF THE WHOLE UNIVERSE

(SARVAVIS'VAJANANĪ)

From the DEVĪBHĀGAVATA[1]

1

I call to mind the Mother of the whole universe,
Who has created this world, both real and unreal,[2]
And who, by Her own power with its three *guṇas*,[3]
Protects it, and having destroyed it, She then plays,[4]

---

[1] First Skandha, (chap. ii.).

[2] *Sadāsatsvarūpam*, on which Nīlakaṇṭha says: *Vyavahāra drishtyā sat, paramārthadarshanena asat*; that is the world is real (*sat*) from the point of view of practical life and reason; to all those, in short, who have not experimentally realized the *Advaita Tattva*; but to those who have, and from the transcendental standpoint, it is, in fact, unreal (*asat*).

[3] *Sattva*, *rajas*, and *tamas*, the substance of S'akti, as *Prakṛti* (see Introduction).

[4] *Ramate*—that is, "in her own self" (*svasminnevakrirate*) (*N*) She shines. Hence She is also called Lalitā. "She who plays;" Padma pr. says, "having passed beyond the worlds, She plays; hence She is called Lalitā." Beyond S'akti and S'iva there exist various manifestations of Parāśakti and Sadāśiva, each in its own sphere. But Mahāśakti, who is Paramaśiva, crossing all worlds in the supreme sphere of *Mahākailāsa*. She it is who is known as Lalitā and Kāmeśvari.

2

Commonly is it said that Brahmā creates the
universe,
Yet the learned in Veda and Purāṇā
Speak of His birth from the navel lotus of Murāri,[1]
Although it is said He creates, yet He is Himself
dependent therein.[2]

3

Even Murāri in the blossom of whose navel lotus,
Brahmā was born—
Deeply sleeps upon his serpent bed[3] at the time of
dissolution.
Therefore Ananta with his thousand hoods is His
support.
How can He who is Himself supported
Be called a leader[4] in the creation of the world?

4

Even the water of Ocean[5] which is a liquid sub-
stance
Cannot exist without a container; therefore[6]
I take refuge with Her, the Mother of all beings,

---

[1] Viṣṇu as Enemy of the Daitya Mura.

[2] Because He is born, He creates dependent on Bhagavati. In the next verse the argument is: "Let Brahmā be not the creator; why not, then, Viṣṇu?" To which the answer is given of His dependence on Ananta.

[3] Viṣṇu reposes on the 1,000-headed Serpent Ananta.

[4] *Netra*.

[5] Which is again the support of Ananta.

[6] And that container requires a support. Therefore the *ādhāraśakti* is the Mother of all. For this reason, in commencing any *pūja*, the Ādhāraśakti is worshipped on account of Her being the supporter of all, and that S'akti is none but the Mother of all.

Who exists in all things in the form of Power.[1]

5

Brahmā in the lotus,
Seeing that the eyes of Visṇu were closed in
deep slumber,[2]
Prayed to that Devi with whom I take shelter.[3]

---

1 *S'aktirūpā.*

2 *Yoganidra,* the sleep of *pralaya.*

3 That He might be roused from his sleep and take part in the cosmic process. Sūta continues; "Having meditated upon Her who is *Māyā* and *Saguṇā*, and giver of liberation and *Nirguṇā*, I will tell you, O *munis,* the whole Purāṇa, which is the best and the most sacred S'rimadbhāgavata of 18,000 Sanskrit S'lokas."

AMBIKĀ[1]

(ELEVENTH MĀHĀTMYA OF CAṆḌĪ)[2]

1

Devī, Thou who removeth the pain of Thy sup-
  pliants, [3]
Be gracious, Be gracious, O Mother of the world!
Be gracious, O Queen of the universe!
Protect the universe.
Thou art, O Devī! the Iśvarī of all moving and
  unmoving things. [4]

2

Thou art the only support of the world,
Because Thou wert in the form of earth.
By Thee who existed in the form of water
Is the whole universe pervaded.
Thou art She whose powers are unsurpassed.

3

Thou art the Vaiṣṇavī Śakti [5] of eternal power;

---

[1] Mother.

[2] When the great Lord of the Asuras was slain by the Devī,
Indra and other Devas (Agni at their head), with shining faces,
offered praise to Kātyāyanī, because of the fulfilment of their
desire.

[3] Literally, "Those who come to take shelter with Her."

[4] That is, the organic and inorganic world.

[5] The energy of Viṣṇu, the sustaining power of the Universe.

Thou art the seed of the universe,
And the supreme *Māyā*.
All this universe has been bewitched by Thee.
Thou, when pleased, art the cause of salvation to men.

4

All sciences are parts of Thee,
As also all women without exception[1] throughout the world.[2]
By Thee alone, O Mother! is the universe filled.
How can we praise Thee?
Art thou not beyond all Praise of highest speech?

5

When,[3] O Devi![4] being in the form of the universe,
And bestowing heaven[5] and liberation,[6]
Thou art worshipped,
What words, howsoever sublime, suffice for Thy praise?

---

[1] *Sakalā*. Nagoji Bhatta is not happy in his Commentary when he says that *sakalā* here means "endowed with the sixty-four arts" (*kalā*), such as dancing, music, painting, literature, acting, etc., and who are devoted to their husbands, modest, etc. The Devī is not, according to this noble line, in these only but in all women, however ignorant of the "arts" or low born they may be.

[2] *Vidyāh samastāstavadevi bhedāh.*
Striyah samastāh sakalā jagatsu.

The Devībhāṣyam of Panchānana Tarkaratna translates the verse as, "All sciences, all things (*bhedāh*), and all women are of Thee."

[3] The verse here changes from *upendra vajrā* to *anustup* metre.

[4] That is, She who is, as Nagoji says, of a shining nature (*dyotanaśīlā*).

[5] *Svarga*.

[6] *Mukti*.

6

O Thou who existeth in the form of *buddhi*[1]
In the heart of all beings,
Who art Giver of heaven and liberation—
O Devi Nārāyaṇi ![2] salutation to Thee.

7

In the form of moments, minutes, and other fractions of time,
Thou art the cause of (worldly) change.
At the time of the dissolution of the universe
Thou art all-powerful.[3]
Nārāyaṇi all reverence to Thee.

8

O Auspicious One ! auspicious with all auspiciousness,
Accomplisher of all successful things,
Giver of refuge, Three-eyed one ;[4]
O Gauri ![5] O Nārāyaṇi ! all reverence to Thee.

9

O Eternal One ! who art the energy[6]
Of creation, maintenance, and destruction ;

---

[1] That is, *nischayātmakam jnānam*.

[2] For she is the support of all beings ; *fem.* of Nārāyana, a name of Viṣṇu.

[3] For She is in the form of time.

[4] As is Her Spouse S'iva with his third eye of wisdom.

[5] Either as Nagoji says "white Devi," or the Devi of that name, who issued from the body of Mahādevi.

[6] The commentator says "that She is the possessor of it" (*śakti*) ; but there is in reality no difference between *śakti* and the possessor of *śakti,* though human understanding and speech may make such difference.

Who art the abode of the qualities,[1]
And are yet beyond them—[2]
O Nārāyani ! all reverence to Thee.

10

O Thou who ever savest those in poverty and pain,
Who take shelter with Thee !
O Remover of the pains of all !
Nārāyaṇi, all reverence to Thee.

11

Rider in an aerial car yoked with swans,[3]
Who assumed the form of Brāhmanī,[4]
Who sprinklest water in which *kuśa* grass[5] is steeped[6]—
Nārāyaṇi, all reverence to Thee.

12

Who holdeth trident, moon, and serpent,[7]
Riding on a great bull[8]
In the form of Maheśvari[9]—
Nārāyaṇi, all reverence to Thee.

---

[1] The *guṇas*—the three *sattva, rajas,* and *tamas,* and their derivatives, the *Tattwas.*

[2] Nagoji says that *gunāśraye gunamaye=gunāśraye agunamaye.* Though the *gunas* inhere in Her, She is not as is the *jīva,* affected by them.

[3] See next note.

[4] S'akti, or energy of Brahmā whose vehicle (*vāhana*) is a swan (*hamsa*), or flamingo, as it is variously rendered.

[5] Grass used in *pitṛ kryā and agni kṛyā.*

[6] As Brahmā does with the holy water (*śāntijalam*) from his pot called *kamaṇḍalu.*

[7] Associated with S'iva.

[8] The *vāhana* of S'iva.

[9] S'akti, or energy of Maheśvara or S'iva.

13

Who art attended by fowl and peacock.[1]
O faultless One!
Who holdeth a great *śakti*-weapon,[2]
And existeth in the form of Kaumāri,[3]—
Nārāyaṇi, all reverence to Thee.

14

Who holdeth Thy great implements,
Which are the conch, discus, mace, and bow;
Who art in the form of Vaiṣṇavi,[4]
Be gracious,
Nārāyaṇi, all reverence to Thee.

15

Who holdeth the formidable discus,
And hast uplifted the earth with Thy tusks[5]—
O auspicious One! in the form of a boar[6]—
Nārāyaṇi, all reverence to Thee.

16

O Thou who in the fierce man-lion form[7]
Didst put forth effort to slay the Daityas,

---

[1] Both the cock and peacock are said in the Mahābhārata to be the *vāhana* of Kārtikeya. Gopal Chakravarti renders it, however, as "the best of peacocks."

[2] A kind of missile, dart spear, lance, or pike.

[3] The S'akti of Kumāra, or Kārtikeya, son of S'iva and Pārvati and Commander of the celestial hosts.

[4] The S'akti of Viṣṇu, who holds the conch, discus (cakra), etc.

[5] See next note.

[6] Viṣṇu, in His boar-incarnation, uplifted on His tusks the world which had been submerged in the waters.

[7] As S'akti of Viṣṇu in the *narasimha* incarnation, in which He slew the Daitya Hiranyakaśipu.

And who hast delivered the three worlds—
Nārāyaṇi, all reverence to Thee.

17

Who weareth a diadem and beareth a great
thunder-bolt,
Who dazzles with Thy thousand eyes,[1]
Destructress of the life of Vritra,[2]
Who art Aindri,[3]
Nārāyani, all reverence to Thee.

18

Who art in the form of S'ivadūti,[4]
Destructress of the great host of the Daityas,
Of terrible form and loud and terrible voice—
Nārāyaṇi, all reverence to Thee.

19

Whose visage is formidable with its teeth,
Adorned with a garland of severed heads—
O Cāmuṇḍā ![5] destructress of Muṇḍa[6]—
Nārāyaṇi, all reverence to Thee.

---

1 The Devi is here invoked as Aindri, the śakti of Indra, who is crowned, and whose weapon, like that of Jupiter, is the thunder-bolt and who has a thousand eyes.

2 An Asura slain by Indra.

3 See note 1, *ante*.

4 The Devi is known as S'ivadūti, because S'iva was engaged by Her as messenger to S'umbha and Niśumbha.

yatoniyukto dautyena tayā devyā śivah svayam
śivadūtīti lokesmingstatah sā khyutim āgatā.

Caṇḍi, eighth Māhātmya.

5 Devi is so called because She slew the Asuras Caṇḍa and Muṇḍa (see verse 25, chap. vii. Candi).

6 *Muṇḍamathane*; not as one translation of the Caṇḍi has it, " who grindest shaven heads. "

20

Lakṣmi, modesty, great knowledge,[1]
Faith (in *śāstras*), nourishment, *svadhā*;[2]
Truth, permanent and unchangeable;
Great night of dissolution, great nescience[3]—
Nārāyaṇī, all reverence to Thee.

21

Understanding,[4] Sarasvatī, the Best of all.
All Powers,[5] Spouse of Babhru,[6] Dark One,[7]
Primeval S'akti.[8] Be gracious, O Lady!
Nārāyāṇī, all reverence to Thee.

22

Who art in the form of all things,

---

1 That is, as Nagoji says, the knowledge pertaining to the *Ātman* (*adhyātmavidyā*) contained in the Upaniṣads; not "wide knowledge," as last mentioned translator renders it.

2 *Mantra* of *Pitṛs*.

3 For Devi is both *vidyā* (knowledge) and *avidyā* (nescience), or *Prakṛti*.

4 *Medhā*, which Nagoji says = *dhāranāvati buddhi*, or firm, steady, concentrated *buddhi*.

5 *Bhūti*, which ordinarily means wealth = here, according to Gopal Chakravarti *aiśvaryarūpinī*—that is, the eighth *siddhi*; or, according to Nagoji, it is *sattvapradhāna* ("greatly excelling in *sattva guna*").

6 A name of S'iva, Viṣṇu, or Fire. According to Nagoji the *rajoguna śakti* is here indicated.

7 *Tāmasī*—that is, *tamogunayuktā*.

8 *Niyate*, which ordinarily means fate (*adriṣṭa*); but here denotes, according to Nagoji, the *Mūlaśakti*, the root or primeval S'akti. It does not mean, an stated in the last-mentioned translation, "O self-controlled Queen!". In the case of the Devi there is no self to be controlled. She controls others, not Herself.

Controller of all; who hast all power;
From the cause of all fear protect us, O Devī!
O Devī Durgā! reverence to Thee.

23

Beautiful is Thy face adorned with three eyes.
Guard us from all (formidable) beings.
O Kātyāyani![1]
Reverence to Thee.

24

May Thy trident most formidable with flame,
Slayer of countless Asuras,
Protect us from fear,
O Bhadrakālī![2]
Reverence to Thee.

25

May Thy bell which destroys the power of Daityas,
Filling the world with its sound,
Guard us from sin,
As a mother[3] protects her children!

26

May Thy sword glittering in Thy hands,
Besmeared with the blood and fat of Asuras as with mire,
Be for our welfare!
O Caṇdikā; to Thee we bow.

---

[1] According to Gopal, the Devī is so called because She was born in the hermitage of the *Muni* Kātyāyana, but the Vedantists say that *Kātya* is he who is devoted to the Brahman (*brahmaniṣṭa*), and She who is attained by them is Kātyāyanī.

[2] Auspicious Kālī.

[3] *Anah.*

27

Thou, when gratified, dost destroy all forms of
disease;
But if displeased, Thou dost destroy all longed-for
desires.
Such as take shelter with Thee need fear no danger,
Since they become verily a refuge to themselves.[1]

28

O Mother, who hast shown Thyself in many forms,
Who else than Thee is able to achieve
That destruction of the great Asuras,
Enemies of righteousness,[2]
Which Thou hast wrought to-day.

29

In the sciences,[3] in all scriptures,[4] and in the great
sayings'[5]
Which are the lamp of knowledge,[6]
Who else is there but Thee
Who makes this universe again and again[7] revolve

---

[1] As Gopal says, even Rajahs, not to mention others, become the slaves of such an one.

[2] *Dharma.*

[3] There are fourteen kinds of *vidya*—viz., four Veda, six Anga, Mimāmsa, Nyāya, Dharmaśāstra, Purāṇā. Gopal says *vidyā* and *upavidyā*, such as Indrajāla, Gārudakadyāh, Dhanurvidyā, etc.

[4] *S'āstra*—that is, *tarka* (logic), *niti*. etc.

[5] Literally; the "first sayings"—that is Veda or the Karmakāṇḍa.

[6] *Viveka=jnāna* (Gopal).

[7] *Ativa.*

In the pit[1] of delusion[2] steeped in darkness.

30

Where there are Rākṣasas[3] and greatly poisonous serpents;
Where there are (armed) enemies;
Where there are highway robbers;
Where there is the forest and ocean[4] fire,
There abiding,[5] Thou dost guard the universe.

31

Queen of the universe art Thou and its guardian;
In the form of the universe Thou art its maintainer.
By the Lords[6] of the universe art Thou worshipped.
They, its supporters, have great devotion to Thee.[7]

32

O Devi! be gracious;
Ever protect us from the fear of enemies
As Thou hast just now saved us by the slaughter of the Asuras.

---

[1] The reference is to the *samsāra*. It is a "pit," for men fall into it; and it is "dark," for it obstructs knowledge.

[2] *Mamatvam*, which Gopal defines as *asvakiye svakiyatvābhimānah*—the sense of ownness in respect of a thing not one's own —*e.g.*, to take the body to be the self; to think I am white, I am tall, etc

[3] Demonic beings.

[4] That is, the submarine fire.

[5] Because She pervades all things.

[6] Indra, Brahmā, etc.

[7] Gopāla Chakravarti renders it: "Those who are devoted to Thee are themselves worshipped—even by Indra, Brahmā, etc., the Lords of the Universe—therefore Thou art the supporter of the universe."

Make cease at once the sins of the whole world
And the great dangers which come of all portents.[1]

33

O Devi! who takest away the afflictions of the universe.
Be gracious to us who make obeisance to Thee.
O Thou who art worthy of all praise,
Grant boons to the dwellers in the three[2] worlds.[3]

---

1 Unusual phenomena, such as earthquakes, comets, hurricanes, etc.

2 *Bhuh, bhuvah, svah* (see *Introduction to Tantra S'āstra*).

3 Then Devi said: " Now I bestow a boon, O Devas " (Caṇḍi).

CAṆḌIKĀ

From the FOURTH OR SHAKRĀDI [1] MAHĀTMYA OF CAṆḌĪ (MĀRKAṆḌEYA PURĀṆA)

1

May that Devi by whose power this world was
spread,
The perfect form of the powers of countless Devas,[2]
The Mother [3] worshipped by Devas and Maharṣis,[4]
Do good to us.

2

May that Caṇḍikā whose peerless majesty and
power
Neither Bhagavān Ananta,[5] Brahmā, nor Hara[6]
can declare,
Turn Herself towards us for the destruction of the
fear of evil,
And the protection of the whole world.

---

[1] When the enemies of the Devas were vanquished by the Goddess, Shakra and the other Devas, bowing down before Her, their hair "erect with exultation," thus sang Her praises.

[2] Her form was that of their combined powers.

[3] *Ambika.*

[4] Great *Ṛṣis* or Seers.

[5] Viṣṇu.

[6] S'iva, for they, too, adore Her.

3

We bow to Her who is good fortune itself in the dwellings of the virtuous,
Ill-fortune in those of the sinful,
Reason[1] in the hearts of the intelligent, faith in those of the good,
Modesty in that of the high born.
Protect, O Devī ! this universe.

4

How can we describe Thy thought-transcending form,
Or, Thy greatly abounding strength which destroyed the Asuras,[2]
Or, O Devī ! those great deeds of Thine
Done in battle midst hosts of Devas, Asuras, and others ?

5

Thou art the cause of all the worlds,
Though Thy substance is the three *guṇas*,[3]
Yet is no fault known in thee.[4]
Incomprehensible art Thou even to Hari, Hara,[5] and other Devas,[6]

---

[1] *Buddhi.*

[2] Enemies of the Devas.

[3] *Sattva, Tamas, Rajas.* Nature as spirit, as the veil of spirit, and of descent and ascent from spirit to matter and matter to spirit (see *Introduction to Tantra Sāstra*).

[4] Ordinarily, the world which consists of the *gunas* is imperfect, but She who is it and yet transcends it, is perfect.

[5] Viṣṇu and S'iva.

[6] As the Viṣṇu Yāmala cited in the S'āktānandatarangini, says (*Mūlastvatparamam rūpam tanna jānāti kashchana*, chap. iii.) " Her supreme form is that which none know."

Thou art the refuge of all.
The whole world is but a part of Thee,[1]
Unmanifested,[2] primeval, supreme Prakṛti.[3]

6

O Devī ! Thou art *Svāhā*,[4]
By the utterance whereof all Devas in all sacrifices are satisfied.
Thou art also declared by men to be *Svadhā*,[4]
Which satisfies the *pitṛs*[5].

7

Thou, O Devi ! whose great *vrata*[6] surpasses all thought,
Art the supreme knowledge full of power
Which is the cause of liberation
Ever sought to be gained by those *Munis*[7] desirous thereof,
Who have strictly controlled their senses and are free of all faults.[8]

---

[1] Not as it has been rendered, "Thou art the entire world which is composed of parts"—the world is but a part of Her. Hindu belief is not pantheistic in the ordinary European sense of the word.

[2] *Avyākrita*, of which Nagoji Bhatta says: *Ṣadvidha vikāra-rahitatvāt*, on account of its being void of the six forms of change.

[3] Of whom the S'āktānandatarangini says: "*Pranamya prakritim nityām paramātma svarūpinīm*" (chap. i.).

[4] The *Mantra* of that name.

[5] The lunar ancestors of the human race and the earthly ancestors of the seventh degree, to whom offering is made in *pitṛkriyā*.

[6] Vow or voluntary rite(see *Introduction to Tantra S'āstra*).

[7] Sages.

[8] This passage has been rendered: "Thou studiest with Thy organs, which are the essence of strength well restrained." But the Devī does not study, nor has She organs restrained or otherwise.

8

Thou art in the form of sound.
The repository of spotless [1] Ṛg [2] and Yajus [2] hymns,
And of the Sāman [2] hymns wherein are the verses of the charmful *Udgitha*, [3]
Devī, Thou art the threefold Veda [4] and Bhagavatī;[5]
For the maintenance of the world Thou art the science of *Vartta* ; [6]
Thou art the supreme destroyer of its pains. [7]

9

O Devī ! Thou art the power of understanding [8]
By Which the essence of all *S'āstras* is known ;
Thou art Durgā, [9] the vessel wherein we cross the dangerous ocean of the world.
Devoid of attachment art Thou. [10]
S'rī [11] also, who hast made Thy abode in the heart of the enemy [12] of Kaiṭabha, [13]

---

[1] Because they were breathed out by Iśvara.

[2] Of the Vedas so named.

[3] Part of the Sāmaveda, the office of the Udgātri.

[4] See p. 33, note 3.

[5] For She has all powers.

[6] *i.e.*, agriculture, cattle-rearing, and trading.

[7] As the Lalitā Sahasranāma says, "She soothes like moonlight all those who are burnt by the triple fires of misery" (*tāpatraya*) of phenomenal existence.

[8] *Medhā*, which Gopal Chakravarti says = *Dhāraṇāvatī buddhi*.

[9] Nagoji says: "*Duhkhaprāpyatvena durgāsi iti uchyate*" (to be attained to with great difficulty).

[10] *Asangā-nirlepā* (G. C.) *cidānandamayitvāt* (on account of Her being *cit* and *ānanda*).

[11] Lakṣmi.

[12] Viṣṇu,

[13] The *Daitya* brother of Madhu.

Thou art indeed Gaurī,[1] who hast fixed Thy dwelling in the moon-crested Deva.[2]

10

Smiling spotless like unto the full moon,
Resplendent as the finest gold
And lovely was thy face.
Yet wonderful it was that swayed by wrath
The Asura Mahiṣa suddenly smote Thy face when he saw it.

11

Greatly marvellous indeed it was that when he had seen Thy face,
Wrathful, terribly frowning, beauteous as the rising moon,
Mahiṣa did not forthwith yield up his life,
For who can live after beholding the wrathful king of Death? [3]

12

O Devi, our supreme Lady
Be gracious for the sake of the world.
For when wrathful Thou dost suddenly destroy the generations of the enemies.[4]
It is but now made known to us
That the mighty army of the Asura Mahiṣa has met its end.

13

Those to whom Thou, O bestower of prosperity! art gracious,

---

[1] Daughter of guru, the Lord of the Mountains.

[2] S'iva, who bears on His head the crescent moon.

[3] Yama.

[4] That is, the *Daityas*.

Are esteemed in all lands,
Their wealth and fame increases,
And their *dharma*, *artha*, *kāma*, *mokṣa*[1] know no lessening.
Praiseworthy are they maintaining sons, servants, and wives.

14

By thy grace, O Devī! the virtuous man, ever honoured,
Does ever daily all religious acts,
And thereafter gains heaven by Thy grace;[2]
Therefore art Thou of a surety the giver of fruit in the three worlds.

15

O Durgā; the remembrance of Thee destroyest the fear of all creatures,
When called to recollection by those in health Thou dost bestow a truly good mind.
O remover of poverty, pain, and fear,
Who but Thee art ever compassionate for the good of all.

16

By the slaying of these foes the world gains happiness.
O Devī! Thou hast slain them with the desire
That they should not always sin so as to merit hell,[3]
But that by death in battle they may go to Heaven.

---

[1] The four aims of being.

[2] Nagojī Bhatta says *tatah* here means that after that (*svarga*), and in order of time they gain *mokṣa* (liberation).

[3] Not "Let these practise sin so as to descend to Hell for long." as it has been rendered. The Devī's desire is to save even Her foes. The translation of the alternative reading given by the translation referred to is nearer the sense of the text.

17

Seeing them, why dost Thou not (by Thy look) turn them to ashes?
Thou throwest Thy weapon among the enemies, the Asuras,
In order that, being purified by it,
Even these enemies may go to heaven.
Such is Thy merciful intention even towards them.

18

If by the glittering, formidable flashes of Thy sword,
And by the lustre of Thy spear-point,
The eyes of the Asuras were not destroyed,
It was because they gazed on Thy countenance,
Like unto the radiant moon.

19

O Devi! Thy nature it is to subdue the evil works of the wicked.
Thy form, destructive of the strength of those who destroy the Devas,
Surpasses all thought, and is comparable with none.
By this Thou hast manifested Thy kindness even to enemies.

20

Devi! with whom may this Thy valour be compared,
Or Thy most charming form striking fear among foes?
In Thee only, bestower of boons, even upon three worlds,

Are seen both kindness of heart and relentlessness
in battle.

21

By the destruction of their foes the three worlds
have been saved by Thee,
Thou hast led even these to heaven.
Having slain them in the front of battle.
And hast dispelled the fear besetting us from the
maddened enemies of the Devas.
Salutation to Thee, O Devi!

22

With Thy spear protect us, O Devi ![1]
O Mother ! protect us with Thy sword.
By the sound of Thy bell guard us,
And by the twanging of Thy bow-string
Protect us in the East and in the West,
Guard us, O Caṇḍikā ! in the South,
And in the North by the brandishing of Thy
spear.

23

Whatever gentle forms of Thine,
And whatever of Thy terrible forms
Wander in the three worlds,
By these forms protect us and the earth.

24

O Mother ! by Thy sword, spear, and club,

---

[1] Here follows the *prārthanā* (prayer).

And other weapons, in Thy soft and supple hands,[1]
Guard us on every side.[2]

---

[1] Literally, leaflike (*pallava*), soft, and supple.

[2] The *Ṛṣi* in Caṇḍī continued : Thus was the upholder of the world hymned by the Devas who did worship Her with celestial flowers, perfumes, unguents, and incense upon which the Devī, highly honoured with this hymn, said to the Devas : " Choose what ye desire of me ". On which the latter prayed that whenever they called upon Her She might come to their assistance, and that whatever mortal should praise Her with this hymn should prosper. Bhadrakāli said, " Be it so, " and vanished from their sight.

MAHĀDEVĪ[1]

(From the FIFTH MAHĀTMYA OF CAṆḌĪ)[2]

1

Reverence to the Devi,[3] to the Devi of the Great,[4]
To Her who is auspicious,[5] for ever reverence.
Reverence to Prakṛti[6] who maintains.[7]
Setting our minds wholly upon Her, we make
obeisance to Her.

[1] Here not the "Great Goddess," but as Commentator Nagoji Bhatta (cited *post* as N.B.) says, "The Goddess" (Devi) "of the great"—viz., Brahmā, Viṣṇu, and S'iva, for it is by Her power that they enjoy their abode, and it is She whom even they worship—the Mother of all.

[2] The Asuras S'umbha and Nisumbha bereft the Devas of their dominion whereupon the latter prayed to the Goddess for help as follows.

[3] Nagoji says that *Devī* = *prakāśātmika,* that which is by its nature light and manifestation.

[4] *Mahādevī* (see note 1, *ante*).

[5] Because She is the cause of all auspicious things.

[6] *S'ṛṣṭiśakti,* or *śakti* (power) of creation (N. B).

[7] *Bhadrāyai.* Literally, good = *rakṣanaśakti,* the *Vaiṣṇavaśakti,* which maintains (N. B.).

2

Reverence to Her who is eternal,[1] Raudrā,[2]
To Gaurī,[3] and Dhātrī,[4] reverence and again reverence,
To Her who is moonlight and in the form of the moon,[5]
To Her who is supreme bliss,[6] reverence for ever.

3

Bending low, we make obeisance to the auspicious One
Who is prosperity in the form of wealth,
To Siddhi,[7] Nairiti,[8] and to the good fortune of Kings.[9]
To Sarvānī[10] reverence, and again reverence.

---

[1] *Nityāyai* ; or She is the S'akti Nitya (N. B.).

[2] That is, She is *samhāraśakti* or *śakti* of dissolution, the *tāmasika śakti* (according the Commentator Gopal Chakravarti), as contrasted with Dhātri, the *rājasika śakti*, and *indorūpā* (moon form), the *sāttvika śakti* (*vide post*).

[3] Daughter of Guru, the Lord of the Mountains.

[4] Creator and upholder.

[5] The moon here stands for all luminous things : or it may mean *indorūpā* in the technical sense of *yoga śāstra*.

[6] *Sukhā* = *paramānandarūpā*.

[7] That is, *aṇimādirūpa* (G. C.), the eight *siddhis—aṇimā*, *laghimā*, etc.

[8] Gopal Chakravarti says this means *Rākṣasaśakti* (demonic power) ; also *alakṣmī* (misfortune). At the time of worship of of Lakṣmi (Devi of Prosperity) on the fifth day after *vijayadaśamī*, the Devī Alakṣmī is worshipped in the house in the form of a misshapen figure, and then thrown away.

[9] *Bhubritām*, which, according to G. C, means mountains, for wealth in the form of gems, etc., are found therein.

[10] Maheśvarī or S'ivaśakti.

4

To Durgā,[1] to Her who enables men to cross the
ocean[2] of the world,
Who is the life and strength[3] and cause of all.
Knower of the distinction between Puruṣa and
Prakṛti,[4]
And who is both black[5] and grey,[6] reverence for
ever.

5

We prostrate ourselves before Thee, who art at
once most gentle[7] and formidable,[8]
Reverence to Her, and again reverence;

---

1 Which means, according to Nagoji: "She who is known with difficulty (*duhkhajneyā*).

2 As N. B. says: *Durgātsamsārātpārāngkaroti*, etc. G. C. says it means She whose abode is not known in either time or space.

3 For She is not only *antaryāmini*, but remains even at the time of dissolution. She is feminine because She supports all things as their mother.

4 *Khyātihprakritipuruṣayor bhedajnānām* (N. B.). *Viveka khyātih* is a term in Sānkhya denoting the cause of liberation, the recognition of the self (Puruṣa) by the self; not as one published rendering runs, "to fame;"

5 As *tāmasika śakti*.

6 *Dhūmra*; that which is with smoke; the sacrificial rite; here the knowledge of the rites.

7 *Atisaubhāgyā*. As such She is (N. B.) *vidyārūpini*, as putting an end to the *samsāra*. For this reason She, as G. C. says, greatly delights all.

8 *Atiraudrāyā*, because, as N. B. says, She, as *avidyā*, is the cause of the *samsāra* with all its terrors.

Reverence to Her who is the material cause of the world,[1].
To the Devi, [2] who is in the form of action, reverence, and again reverence.

6

To the Devī who in all things is called Viṣṇumāyā,[3]
Reverence to Her, reverence to Her,
Reverence to Her, reverence, reverence. [4]

7

To the Devi who is known as intelligence [5] in all beings,
Reverence to Her, reverence to Her,
Reverence to Her, reverence, reverence.

8

To the Devī who dwells in the form of *buddhi* [6] in all beings,
Reverence to Her, reverence to Her,
Reverence to Her, reverence, reverence.

---

[1] *Jagatpratishtāyai* = (as N. B. says) *jagadupādānakāraṇam*; or, as, G. C. has it, She is *sarvāntaryāminī*, who dwells in the inmost being of all things.

[2] Which = (G. C.) *dyotanaśila*, whose nature it is to lighten, or (N.) *devaśakti*.

[3] Or *mulāvidyā* (Nagoji).

[4] *Namastasyai, namastasyai, namastasyai namo namah.* The refrain throughout the succeeding verses.

[5] *Cetana* = (Nagoji says) *chitśakti*, or mind. She Herself is *nirvikalpacitśakti*, but manifests as *savikalpacitśakti* in all worldly beings.

[6] The mind, as the aspect so named of the *antahkaraṇa*.

9

To the Devi who in the form of sleep abides [1] in all
beings,
Reverence to Her, reverence to Her,
Reverence to Her, reverence, reverence.

10

To the Devi who exists in all beings in the form of
hunger,
Reverence to Her, reverence to Her,
Reverence to Her, reverence, reverence.

11

To the Devi who exists in all beings in the form of
cāyā,[2]
Reverence to Her, reverence to Her,
Reverence to Her, reverence, reverence.

12

To the Devi who exists as energy [3] in all beings,
Reverence to Her, reverence to Her,
Reverence to Her, reverence, reverence,

---

1 *Nidrārūpena*. According to Nagoji, *nidrā* = *suṣupti*, the state of dreamless sleep where all sense functions are at an end. According to G. C., *svapna* or dreaming sleep also.

2 Nagoji says this word = *samsāratāpābhāvah*, or lack of worldly pain. The *samsāra* is like a burning flame. In its shadow there is coolness and peace. According to Gopal Chakravarti, however, it = *ātapābhāvah*. *Ātapāh* = *prakāśarūpatvātvidyā*, or knowledge on account of its giving light, and therefore as the lack of it She is *avidyā*.

3 *S'akti* : power, action.

13

To the Devī who exists in the form of thirst [1] in all
beings,
Reverence to Her, reverence to Her,
Reverence to Her, reverence, reverence.

14

To the Devī who in the form of forgiveness [2] exists
in all beings,
Reverence to Her, reverence to Her,
Reverence to Her, reverence, reverence.

15

To the Devī who exists in the form of race and
species in all beings,[3]
Reverence to Her, reverence to Her,
Reverence to Her, reverence, reverence.

16

To the Devī in the form of modesty in all beings,
Reverence to Her, reverence to Her,
Reverence to Her, reverence, reverence.

17

To the Devī existing in the form of peace [4] in all
beings,

---

[1] Which, as Nagoji says, is the desire for that which is not one's own (*anātmīyā*); thirst for enjoyment, possession, individual life, etc.

[2] Which is the desire not to return evil to those who have done us wrong, notwithstanding our power to do so (N. B.).

[3] *Jātirūpeṇa*: that which classifies and differentiates one body of beings from another.

[4] Which Nagoji says means the control of the senses and renunciation of all worldly things.

Reverence to Her, reverence to Her,
Reverence to Her, reverence, reverence.

18

To the Devī who exists in all beings in the form of faith,[1]
Reverence to Her, reverence to Her,
Reverence to Her, reverence, reverence.

19

To the Devī existing in the form of beauty in all beings,
Reverence to Her, reverence to Her,
Reverence to Her, reverence, reverence.

20

To the Devī who exists in all beings in the form of prosperity,[2]
Reverence to Her, reverence to Her,
Reverence to Her, reverence, reverence.

21

To the Devī who in all beings exists in the form of their respective callings,[3]
Reverence to Her, reverence to Her,
Reverence to Her, reverence, reverence.

---

[1] That is, Nagoji says, *āstikatvam* (belief in God's existence); or, according to Gopal Chakravarti, also a firm and strong faith in *Veda*.

[2] Wealth, etc.

[3] That is, *jīvikā*, the callings of husbandmen, merchant, cattle-rearing, etc.

22

To the Devī who in the form of memory exists in all beings,
Reverence to Her, reverence to Her,
Reverence to Her, reverence, reverence.

23

To the Devī who in all beings exists in the form of mercy,[1]
Reverence to Her, reverence to Her,
Reverence to Her, reverence, reverence.

24

To the Devī who in the form of contentment[2] exists in all beings,
Reverence to Her, reverence to Her,
Reverence to Her, reverence, reverence.

25

To the Devī who exists in all beings as (their) Mother,[3]
Reverence to Her, reverence to Her,
Reverence to Her, reverence, reverence.

26

To the Devī who in the form of error[4] exists in all beings,

---

[1] Which Nagoji says is the desire of removing the pain of others.

[2] Which Nagoji defines as satisfaction with that which one possesses as distinguished from longing for what one has not got.

[3] She is *jananī*, and, as Nagoji says, *pālayitrī* (protectress).

[4] *Bhrānti.* A thoroughly Indian conception, though some modern Hindus have lost the sense of it. Gopal Chakravarti gives as an example the classical instance of the *jīva* taking mother-of-pearl to be silver, etc.

Reverence to Her, reverence to Her,
Reverence to Her, reverence, reverence.

27

Reverence to the Devī
Who is the Presiding Deity over the senses of all beings,
Who is ever in all beings,
And who pervades all things.

28

To the Devī who in the form of consciousness,[1]
Having pervaded all the world, exists therein,
Reverence to Her, reverence to Her,
Reverence to Her, reverence, reverence.

29

Praised aforetime by the Devas,
By reason of their obtaining that which they desired;
Worshipped by Surendra[2] on days of victory.
May the Īśvari,[3] who is the cause of all good.
Do good and auspicious things for us,
And may She ward off all calamities.

30

And may She who is now saluted by us as our Queen,
As also by the Suras,[4] tormented by arrogant Asuras,[5]
Whom we call to mind
As we bow our bodies in devotion to Her,
Destroy at this very moment all our calamities.

---

[1] *Cit* = *citśakti* (N. B.), and according to Gopal Chakravarti, who says the *jiva* is here meant, *caitanya*.

[2] Indra.

[3] Queen and Ruler of the worlds.

[4] The Good Devas.

[5] Their evil enemies.

JAGADAMBIKĀ[1]

From the DEVĪBHĀGAVATA PURĀṆA[2]

1

It is by Thy power only
That Brahmā creates, Viṣṇu maintains,
And at the end of things S'iva destroys the universe.
Powerless are they for this but by Thy help.
Therefore it is that Thou alone art the Creatrix,
Maintainer, and Destructress of the world.[3]

2

Thou art fame, mind, remembrance,
And our refuge, the mountain-born,[4]
Companion, kindness, faith, and patience,
Earth, Kamalā,[5] health,[6] the arts, and victory,

---

[1] Mother of the world.

[2] Chap. xix., Skandha v., p. 27, of the Bombay Edition (Venkateshvara Press), edited by Khemarāja ; 1823, Shaka (1902), with Commentary by Nilakantha, hereafter referred to by the letter N.

[3] The Devi, who is the *mahākāraṇasvarūpā*, is also the *kārya-svarūpa*. As cause She is in the effect and is the *śaktirūpa* by which all things are done (N).

[4] Here is meant the S'akti of Rudra (N).

[5] Lakṣmi, Devi of Prosperity and Beauty.

[6] *Puṣṭi* : nourishment.

Contentment, ever victorious,[1] Umā,[2] Ramā,[3]
True knowledge, and the highest *buddhi*.[4]

3

Science, forgiveness, beauty, retentiveness art Thou,[5]
Who art Known in the three worlds as all in all.
Who is there that unaided by Thee can do ought?
Thou art the abode wherein all men dwell.[6]

4

Thou art the upholder.
Were Thou not so, how could the tortoise and serpent uphold the Earth?[7]
Thou art the Earth itself.
Were this not so, how could this weighty world rest on Ether?[8]

5

Those who through Thy *māyā* pray to Devas,
Such as[9] the four-headed One[10], Viṣṇu, Rudra,[11] Fire,

---

[1] *Vijayā.* The Devi Pr. says: "After conquering this very powerful King of the Daityas, named Padma, She is known in the three worlds as Vijayā and unconquerable (*aparājitā*)."

[2] See Hymn to Annapurṇa, *post*. Here the Īśvara S'akti (N.).

[3] A name of Lakṣmī.

[4] See p. 87, note 5.

[5] *Medha*, which means, in particular, the retentive faculty or memory, and in general, intelligence.

[6] For in Her all men have their being. She is as *Ādhāraśakti*, their support (N.).

[7] As the Purāṇas represent them as doing. The verse deals with the attributes of the *ādharaśakti*.

[8] *Gaganam.*

[9] Literally, "headed by," or instances of principal Devas.

[10] Brahmā.

[11] S'iva.

The White-rayed one'[1] Yama,[2] Vāyu,[3] and Ganeśa
Are indeed ignorant,[5]
For can these do anything without Thy power?[6]

6

O Mother! those who do *homa*, with ghee on fire,
With great ceremony in the name of the Devas,
Are of but small intelligence.[8]
If Thou art not *svāhā*,[8] then how can they make sacrifice?
Do they not worship Thee?
If not they are ignorant.[10]

7

In this world Thou art the giver of enjoyment
To things which move and are still.[11]
Thou givest life to all things being as they are parts of Thee.

---

[1] *Subrāmshu*, or the moon.

[2] Lord of Death.

[3] Lord of the Air.

[4] The elephant-headed Deva, son of the Devi as Pārvati and S'iva.

[5] *Vimūdha* (see also Umāsanghitā of S'iva Purāṇā).

[6] *Te vā stuvanti manujā amarān vimudhā,*
Māyā gunaistava caturmukha viṣṇurudrān,
Subrāmshuvahniyamavāyuganeśamukhyān,
Kim tvāmrite janani te prabhavanti kārye.

[7] The sacrifice done with ghee poured into fire.

[8] *Alpadhiyah.*

[9] The mantra used in *homa*.

[10] *Svāhā nacet tamasi te kathamāpuraddhā,*
Tvām eva kim nahi ya janti tato hi mudhah.

[11] Here apparently trees and the like, as contrasted with the animal world. She allots the *karma* (N).

O Mother ! as Thou nourisheth all Thy Suras,[1]
So also dost Thou nourish others.

8

O Mother ! as men who are of good heart,
Never for the mere pleasure thereof
Cut down leafless and bitter (fruited) trees
Which have sprung up in the forest.
Therefore Thou dost even greatly protect the Daityas.[2]

9

Though Thou slayest in the battlefield with Thy arrows the enemies,
Knowing their desire for amorous play with celestial women,[3]
Yet such is Thy nature that even then Thou showest kindness to them.
For Thou so slayest them
That in another body[4] they may obtain fulfilment of their desires.

---

[1] The Devas, Her children.

[2] That is, the Devi does not slay even the Daityas for the mere savage pleasure of killing, and even those whom She slays are slain by Her for the good of the world and their own good, that being slain by Her hand they may go to heaven (see next verse). The Kumārasambhavam says that a man cannot cut down even a poisonous tree if planted by his own hand.

[3] *Devānganāsuratakelimating viditvā.*

[4] That is, a celestial body. For, as Daityas do not perform sacrificial rites, etc., so they cannot gain heaven. But when killed by the hand of the Devi, thither they go to their enjoyment, and Devas are protected.

10

Most wonderful it is that Thou hast assumed body
For the destruction of the Dānavas, [1] famed for their power,
When Thou mightest have slain them by Thy mere will.
The cause of this is Thy play [2] and nothing else, [3]

11

Alas! of a verity unhappy are they
Who when the Kali age, the worst of ages, has come,
Do not worship Thee.
Men cunning and skilled in the Purāṇas
Have made the people devoted to the worship of Hari and S'ankara, [4]
Who are but Thy creatures. [5]

12

Those who worship with devotion Devas,
Though they know that they are distressed, harassed by Asuras, and subject to Thy control,
Are of a surety like unto a man

---

[1] Sons of Danu. Enemies of the Devas.

[1] *Krīḍarasa* that is, *lilā*.

[2] *Krīḍārasastava nachānyatarotraheluh* (*cf.* the Vedantic *sutra okavattulilā kaivalyam*).

[3] Viṣṇu and S'iva.

[4] *Dhūrttaih purāṇa caturairhari śankarāṇām,*
Sevāparāshcha vihitāstava nirmitānām.

Men, the verse says, thus worship the creature instead of the Creatrix.

Who with, the light of a clear lamp in his hands,
Yet falls into some waterless and terrible well. [1]

13

O Mother! Thou art the remover of the pains which arise from birth,
And art known by those desirous of liberation
As the giver of happiness when Thou art *vidyā*,[2]
And of unhappiness when Thou art *avidyā*,[2]
Surely it is only the ignorant who do not worship Thee,
Such as are attached to enjoyment without wisdom.[3]

14

Even Brahmā, Hara, and Hari, as all other Suras,[4]
Ever worship Thy lotus feet, which are our refuge.
But those who are of small intelligence and beset with error
Do not worship Thee.
And so ever repeatedly fall into the ocean of the world.[5]

---

1 *Jnātvā surāmstava vashān asurārddhitāngshcha,*
Yevai bhajanti bhuvi bhāvayuta vimagnāu,
Dhritvā kare suvimalang khalū dīpakangte,
Kupe patanti manujā vijaletighore.

(See also Umāsanghitā.)

2 Knowledge and nescience, the source of *nivritti* and *pravritti*, with the latter's attendant miseries.

3 *Kilamandadhibirnārāditā janani bhogaparaistathājnaih.*

4 Devas.

5 *Tadvai nayelpa matayo manasā bhajanti,*
Bhrāntāh patanti satatam bhavasāgarete.

15

O Caṇḍī ! [1] it is most surely by the favour of the dust on Thy lotus feet
That Brahmā in the beginning of things creates,
Shauri [2] protects, and Hara [3] destroys the whole world.
He is indeed unfortunate
Who in this world does not worship Thee.

16

O Devī ! Thou art the *Devatā* of speech of both Suras and Asuras.
Without power of speech are even the foremost of Devas
When Thou abidest not in them.
If men do speak, it is because they are not deprived of Thee.[4]

17

Hari,[5] when cursed by the greatly angered Bhrigu,[6]

---

[1] Nīlakantha derives the word from *chadi* ("the wrathful one fearful to the whole world"). *S'ruti* says of the Brahman : *Mahadbhayam vajramudhyatam* ("great fear and a ready thunderbolt")

[2] Viṣṇu.

[3] S'iva.

[4] Sarasvatī is She who causes speech. Sound springing from the Mūlādhāra wherein is *Devī* Kuṇḍalinī proceeds from the stage of mere sound (parā), the potentiality of growth in the seed to that of *Paśyantī*, when the latter begins to sprout ; then to *Madhyamā*, when the first two small leaves appear but inseparate, and lastly, as *Vaikharī*, when they separate, remaining united only at their base.

[5] Viṣṇu.

[6] The Ṛṣi of that name.

Became Fish, Tortoise, Boar, and Man-lion,[1] and
Dwarf.[2]
How can those who worship Him
Escape the fire of death?

18

As is well-known, the *linga* of S'ambhu[3] in the forest
Fell on earth in like manner by the curse of Bhrigu.
How can those, O Mother! who on earth worship
Him[4] who holds a skull
Attain to happiness either in this world or the next?

19

They who worship the elephant-faced Lord of
Ganas,[5]
Who was born of Maheśa,
With Him in vain take shelter.
They know Thee not, O Devi! Mother of the
Universe,
Who art easy of worship[6] and the giver of the
fruit of all desires.

---

[1] The Matsya, Kūrma, Varāha, and Nrisingha avatāra of Viṣṇu.

[2] *Chalakrit,* which Nilakantha says = Vāmana Avatāra of Viṣṇu. *Chalakrit*, because Balirāja was deceived by him.

[3] S'iva, who retired into the forest after the death of Sati, and who was powerless to protect even his own *linga*.

[4] S'iva.

[5] Ganeśa, son of S'iva, so powerless.

[6] Devī is (as the Lalitā, verse 133, also says), "easily worshipped" (*sukhā-rādhyā*), without bodily pain by fasting etc., without restrictions on the mode of meditation. In the Kūrma Pr. the Lord describes to Himavat an easy mode of worship if he be unable to meditate on the Supreme Form. The Devī is also "easily pleased" (Lalitā, verse 162, *kṣipraprasādinī*)—that is, even by a little worship as the Saura and S'iva Purāṇas say of the Lord of Umā, with whom the Devī is one.

20

Wonderful it is that through Thy compassion
Even the multitude of enemies slain by Thy sharpened arrows
Have thus been made to reach Heaven.
For had they not been so slain
Calamities and the most painful of painful states would they have suffered
In that hell which is the result of their (evil) *karma*.

21

Even Brahmā, Hara, and Hari
From pride[1] know not Thy power.
How, then, are others able to know it,
Bewildered as they are by Thy (three) *guṇas* of incomparable power?[2]

22

Even *Munis*[3] suffer, who, being ignorant (of Thee).
Do not adore Thy thought-transcending lotus feet,
And are set upon the worship of sun and fire.[4]
By them, even though they read hundreds of *S'ruti*,[5]

---

[1] *Garvabhāvāt*.

[2] Devī is "all-bewildering" (*Sarvamohinī*). In Kūrma Pr., S'iva says: "This *Māyā* is dear to me by which the world is bewildered. I bewilder the whole universe with the Devas, Daityas, and men." The operation of the *tāmasika guṇa* veils from them the truth.

[3] The Mārkaṇḍeya Purāṇa says: "That Divine Devī Mahāmāyā forcibly draws away the minds of even the sages (*Munis*), and leads them into confusion."

[4] Because they are *pratyakṣadevatā*—that is, visible, and She, the supreme ground of them, is beyond vision, mind, and speech.

[5] The reading of much *śruti* (revelation) teaches them nothing, for their ignorance conceals from them its true meaning.

The Supreme object of desire[1] is not known,
which is the essence of all Vedas.

23

Methinks it is Thy (three) *guṇas*,
The power of which is so famed on earth,
Which makes men turn away from devotion (to Thee),
And attaches them to Viṣṇu, Īśa,[2] Bhāskara,[3] Ganeśa,
By (the teaching of) various *Āgamas*[4] of their own devising.[5]

24

O Ambikā! (so great is Thy mercy)
That Thou art not angry with,
But showest kindness to, and maketh greatly prosperous
Even those who, skilful in the *mantra* of delusion,[6]

---

[1] *Paramārthatattva*. S'ankhya says that there are two different kinds of *artha* or object. One is *bhoga* (enjoyment), the second, which is the supreme object (*paramārtha*) is *mokṣa* (liberation). The one exists in the current issuing from Devī (*Avidyā*), the other returns on the other current, which draws to the Devī (*Vidyā*).

[2] S'iva.

[3] The Sun (*Sūrya*).

[4] Here used generally for *S'āstra*, though also used in a special sense as denoting Veda and Tantra, to the latter of which, Nīlakantha perhaps refers. *Nānātantraihmohakaih* ("many deluding Tantras"). The reference is here to the dualistic scriptures.

[5] *Svabuddhirachitairvividhāgamaishcha* ("composed by themselves").

[6] *Mohamantranipunām*

Make the best of men[1] turn away from Thy feet
By Āgamas made by themselves,[2]
Teaching of devotion to Hari and Hara.[3]

25

In the Satya age[4] the *sattva guṇa* [5] was very powerful,
Therefore there were no Asadāgamas.[6]
But in the Kali age learned folk conceal Thee (from the people).
And adore those Devas imagined by them (to be objects of worship).[7]

---

[1] According to Nīlakantha, Brāhmanas.

[2] Literally, "said by themselves" (*svoktāgamaih*)—that is as Nilakantha says, *puruṣapranītāgamaih* (or Āgamas composed by men and not revealed by S'iva).

[3] Viṣṇu and S'iva who are themselves only the children of the Mother, and as much creatures, though of the highest kind, as others are.

[4] The first and best of the four ages : Satya, Tretā, Dvāpara, and Kali, the commonly supposed present age. In the second, virtue (*dharma*) decreased by a quarter, in the third by a half, and in the present or Kali age only a quarter of *dharma* remains.

[5] The *guṇa*, which manifests on the moral plane as goodness.

[6] Literally, "bad Āgama," a name applied by some to the Tantra of the "downward current" (*arddharetas*), but here has a general significance to all *S'āstra*, whether Tantra or otherwise, of a dualistic character (*asachchhāstrāni*).

[7] *Tūrye yuge bhavati chātibalang guṇasya,*
Turyasyatena māthitānyasadāgamāni tvam,
Gopayanti nipunāh kavayah kalauvai
Tatkalpitān suraganā napi sangstuvanti.

"Imagined by them" (*tatkalpitān*). This does not mean that the Devas do not exist. Hari, Hara, Īśa, Ganeśa, Bhāskara, and others have been mentioned in previous verses. The verse is *stutivāda*, in which that which is its direct object, is dealt with to

26

Munis,[1] in whom the *sattva guṇa*[2] is very pure,
Meditate upon Thee,
Who art the giver on earth of the fruit of liberation,
Who art perfect in *yoga*[3] and the supreme knowledge.
Such never again suffer pain in the womb of a mother.[4]
They are only praiseworthy who are absorbed in Thee.

27

Citśakti[5] is in *Paramātmā*,
Therefore also it is manifested[6] in the world,
Wherein it is known as the cause of its creation, maintenance, and destruction.[7]

---

the exclusion of all others. What is meant is that She alone is to be worshipped and not any other. *Kalpanā* is to mistake one thing for another. Thus the world is taken (*kalpitā*) to be real when the Brahman alone is so. And so, too, mother-of-pearl is mistaken for silver (*shuktirajatakalpanā*), or a rope for a snake (*rajjusarpakalpanā*); so people take the Devas to be the ultimate object of worship when it is only the Devī whose manifestations they are, who is such.

1 Sages.

2 See Introduction.

3 *Yogasiddhām.* The manifested Devi as Umā was a great *yoginī.*

4 Are never reborn. According to Hindu ideas the child suffers great pain and misery in the womb of its mother, the remembrance of which is lost on its birth into the world.

5 That is, *caitanya* (Nilakantha). See the Samkṣepaśāriraka.

6 In name and form (*nāmarūpātmaka.*).

7 *Bhavakrityakartā.* Literally, "performer of worldly action"—that is, those stated. For, according to Vedānta and Nyāya, it works therein by its S'akti, though in S'ankhya the Puruṣa is merely an enjoyer, spectator, and witness (*bhoktā, draṣṭā, sākṣī*).

Who else in this world without Thee and of his own power
Is able to create, move and destroy ?[1]

28

O Mother of the world !
Can the *Tattvas*,[2] deprived of *Cit*,[3] create the world ?
They are lifeless things.[4]
O Devī ! can the *indriyas*[5] with their objects and functions,[6]
Bear fruit without Thee ?

29

O Mother ! had you not as *Svāhā*[7] been the cause thereof,
Even the Devas could not have obtained their enjoined own portion,
Offered in sacrificial rites by *Munis*[8].

---

[1] *Cf.* Dakṣinamūrtisamhitā.

[2] The twenty-four beginning with *Mahat*.

[3] *Vide ante*.

[4] *Jarāni*; mere matter but for the informing life of the Goddess.

[5] The so-called "senses" of knowledge (*Jnānendriya*), viz.: *Cakṣu* (eye), *S'rotra* (ear), *ghrāṇa* (smell), *rasanā* (tongue), *tvak* (skin) and of action (*karmendriya*); viz., *Vak* (speech), *pāni* (hand), *pāda* (feet), *pāyu* (anus), *upastha* (genitals).

[6] *Indriyāni guṇakarmayutāni*. Thus, form (*rūpa*) is the *guṇa* or object (*viṣaya*) of the eye, and *darśana* (or seeing), its function (*karma*).

[7] The *Mantra* used in *Agnikriyā* and wife of Agni.

[8] If the Mantra Svāhā, which is the Devi, be not said, then the Devas get nothing from the *homa*. Their S'astric portion they obtain by virtue only of the Devī as *Svāhā*, the cause thereof.

Therefore Thou maintainest the whole world.[1]

30

By Thee all this universe was in the beginning of things created;
Thou protecteth the Regents of the Quarters among whom Hari and Hara are foremost.
At the dissolution of things Thou devourest the whole universe.
That which has been done by Thee from the creation
Even Devas[2] know not.
What, then, shall we say of unfortunate men?

31

O Mother! Thou hast by slaying the greatly formidable Asura,
Who assumed the form of a buffalo,[3]
Protected the Devas.
Even the Vedas know Thee not as Thou really art.[4]
Small of intellect as we are how can we praise Thee?

32

O Mother! Thou hast accomplished a great work
In destroying this wicked foe of ours,
A thorn painful beyond all thought
(In the side of) the whole world.

---

[1] The Devī protects the Devas, and if the Devas are maintained, then the whole world is maintained, as the Devas are Her agents in the maintenance thereof.

[2] *Manujā*, which here, according to Nīlakantha, includes Devas.

[3] The Demon Mahīṣa.

[4] *Gatingtava yathārthatayā na jagmuh.*

Thy fame will spread throughout the whole universe.
Do Thou, whose power is known to be incomparable,
By Thy mercy protect us. [1]

[1] The hymn concluding, Devībhāgavata continues, Vyāsa said: "Devi, thus praised, said in soft, sweet voice, 'Oh, best of Devas, tell Me what other thing most difficult and hard to accomplish you would have Me do?'"

DURGĀ

(MAHĀBHĀRATA VIRĀṬA PARVAN)[1]

SALUTATION to Thee, O giver of blessings,
Dark[2] Virgin,[3] observant of the vow of chastity,[4]
Whose form is beauteous as that of the rising sun,
And Thy face as that of the full moon;
Four-armed and faced art Thou.
Wide-hipped, full-breasted,[5]
Wearing emerald sapphire bangles and armlets;
Thou art resplendent as Padmā, Spouse of Nārāyaṇa,[7]
And rangest the ethereal regions.
Thy form and chastity[8] are of the purest.
Dark art Thou like the blue-black cloud,
Whose face is beauteous as that of Saṁkarṣaṇa.[9]
Long are Thy two arms, as it were bannered poles in honour of Indra.[10]

---

[1] Chap. VI., sung by Yudhiṣthira, when on the way to the City of Virāṭa.

[2] *Kṛṣṇā.*

[3] *Kumāri* (see p. 46, note 3.)

[4] For She observed *brahmacarya.*

[5] *Pinashronipayodhare.*

[6] Lakṣmi.

[7] Viṣṇu.

[8] *Brahmacarya.*

[9] S'iva.

[10] In ancient times a long bamboo surmounted with a flag was set up on the lst of Assar, in honour of Indra to secure rain.

Thou bearest in Thy six other arms
A vessel, lotus, bell, noose, bow, a great discus,[1] and other weapons.
Purest woman art Thou on earth.[2]
Thy well-formed ears are decked with beautiful earrings.
Thy face challenges the moon in beauty.
Wonderful is Thy crown, and beautiful is the braid (of Thy hair).
Thy body is like that of a serpent[3]
Thou glitterest with brilliant girdle round Thy hips,
And shinest like Mount Mandāra encircled by the snake.[4]
With standing peacock feathers on Thy head, Thou art resplendent.
By Thy vow of virginity Thou hast maintained heaven.[5]
It is for this, O slayer of the Asura Mahiṣa,[6]
That Thou art praised and worshipped by the Devas for the protection of the three worlds.[7]
Foremost of Devas, be gracious to me;

---

1 *Cakra.*

2 *Striviśuddhāchayābhuvī.*

3 *Bhujangā bhogavasena*, which Nilakantha says is *Sarpaśarirākārena.*

4 Thus used for the churning of the ocean.

5 *Tridivam* or *svarga*; for there "the Three" shine.

6 The son of Jambāsura, whom the Devī fought for many years before he was slain by Her (see Mārkaṇḍeya Purāṇa). During the great Durgā festival in autumn, the Devī is represented as slaying this formidable Asura, so called as having assumed the form of a buffalo.

7 *Bhuh, Bhuvah, Svah,* the earthly, atmospheric, and celestial spheres.

Show me Thy mercy, and be auspicious.[1]
Both Jayā and Vijayā[2] art Thou.
Thou givest victory in battle;
Give me, too, victory, O Devi!
Give me now a boon.
Thy constant abode is on the Vindhya, the foremost of mountains.
O Kālī! O Kālī! O Mahākālī![3]
Thou delightest in wine, meat, and animal sacrifice,[4]
Bestowing boons, going whithersoever Thou wilt.
Thou art ever followed by Brahmā[5] and other Devas,
By those who call upon Thee to lighten their burdens.
As by those who salute Thee at dawn of day.
Nothing is unattainable either by way of wealth or children
Thou art called Durgā by all because Thou savest men from difficulty.[6]
Whether in dangerous lands or sinking in the great ocean,
Thou art the sole refuge of men.
When assailed by robbers, when crossing streams and seas,
As also in wildernesses and great forests,

---

[1] *S'ivābhava*. S'iva is so called because he is auspicious.

[2] Two Companion Devatās of Durgā.

[3] Spouse of Mahākāla, an aspect of S'iva.

[4] *Siddhumāmsapaśupriye*. *Siddhu* is a spirit distilled from molasses.

[5] *Bhutaih*, which Nīlakaṇṭha says here denotes the oldest beings, Brahmā and other Devas.

[6] Literally, one who rescues from difficulty.

Those who remember Thee, O Mahādevī! are never lost.
Thou art fame, prosperity, constancy, success, and modesty,
Intelligence, knowledge, and man's offspring.
Thou art the two twilights,[1]
Night, the light of sun and moon,
Sleep, beauty, forgiveness, and mercy.
Thou, when worshipped by Thy devotees, destroyest
Ignorance, man's fetters, loss of children and wealth, disease and fear of death.
I who have lost my kingdom seek Thy protection.
I bow to Thee, Sureśvarī, with bended head:
Grant me protection,
Thou whose eyes are like the leaf of the lotus.
O Thou who art truth itself, be true to us.
O Durgā! give me shelter,
Who art merciful to Thy devotees, protect me.[2]

---

1 *Sandhya*, early dawn when the stars are vanishing, and evening as they are about to appear.

2 Thus praised by the son of Pāndu, the Goddess showed Herself to him.

ĀRYĀ[1]

FORM THE HARIVAMSĀ

THOU art liberation,[2] prosperity, life,[3]
Fame, modesty, and learning, reverence and intelligence,
Twilight,[4] night, lustrous day,
Sleep and the night of death,[5]
Āryā, Kātyāyani, Kauśiki,[6]
Observant of *brahmacarya*,[7]
Mother of the leader of the celestial hosts,[8]
Formidable one,[9]
She who undergoes great austerities[10]

---

[1] The sacred hymn as sung in ancient times by *Ṛṣis*, related in chap. lviii of the Harivamśa, a sequel of the Mahābhārata.

[2] *Siddhi* (success,) which here means the supreme *siddhi* or *mukti* (liberation).

[3] That is according to the commentator *jivanam*.

[4] *Sandhyā* or junction-time, morning and evening.

[5] *Kālarātri* which is *pralayarātri*, or the night of the dissolution of all things.

[6] Born in the race of the sage Kuśika.

[7] The virgin state, or the first of the *āśramas*.

[8] Skanda, or Kārtikeya, son of S'iva and the Devi.

[9] *Ugrachāri*, which should be *ugrachārini*, but this is *Arsha* (composed by *Ṛṣis*), to whom the rules of grammar do not apply.

[10] The Devi practised great austerities to gain S'iva as Her husband.

Jayā and Vijayā,[1]
Contentment, nourishment, forgiveness, mercy, eldest sister of Yama,[2] clad in blue silken raiment,
Of various form,[3] without form, having many forms.[4] With red, half-opened eyes.[5]
Large-eyed protectress of Thy votaries.
O Goddess! Thou resideth on the peaks of fearful mountains, by rivers, and in caves, forests, and groves.
Greatly worshipped by the S'avara, Varvara, and Pulinda tribesmen,[6]
Thou traverseth in all directions of the world
With peacock-feathered flags.
Thou livest on the Vindhya mountain,
Surrounded by fowls, goats, sheep, lions, and tigers,
Amidst the constant ringing of bells.[7]
Thou holdest the trident and spear.[8]

---

[1] Companion Devatās of Durgā.

[2] Mrityu, the God of Death.

[3] *Bahurūpā* (see the Lalitā, verse 155). The Devī Bhāg. Pr. says, "She is formless because She is supreme, She has many forms because of Her activity" (see also Devi and Vāmana Purāṇas): "She is also the *S'akti* of the countless Rudras." The term is much commented upon in the Purāṇas, Upapurāṇas, and Tantras.

[4] *Anekavidharūpinī.*

[5] *Virūpākṣī.* S'iva is also called *Virūpākṣa.* His eyes are, either owing to his state of *samādhi*, or consumption of *bhang*, pictured as in a vague, dreamy, half-open state.

[6] *S'avarair varvaraischaiva pulindaischa supūjitā*—a line worthy of remark, for these were savage and non-aryan tribes.

[7] During worship of the image the worshipper rings a bell. There was a constant ringing of bells.

[8] *Pattisha,* a kind of spear with a sharp edge.

Sun and moon are Thy banners.
Thou art the ninth day of the dark half of the month,
And the eleventh day of the light half thereof.[1]
Baladeva's[2] sister art Thou, glorious one,[3]
Fond of warring[4] (with demons),
Abode of all creatures.
Thou art death,[5] and the supreme end[6] of men,
Daughter of the cowherd Nanda,[7]
Unconquered,
Wearing bark and good cloth;
Raudrī,[8] twilight,[9]
With dishevelled hair,[10]
And who art death,
Fond art Thou of offerings of wine and flesh.[11]
Thou art Lakṣmī,[12]
And assumest the form of Alakṣmī[13] for the destruction of Dānavas,[14]

---

[1] Auspicious days. On the ninth (*Navamī*) there is *Caṇḍīpātha* (reading of Caṇḍī), and on the eleventh (*Ekādaśī*) fasting.

[2] Kṛṣṇa's eldest brother.

[3] *Rajanīya* in text is said to be a wrong reading for *mahanīya*.

[4] *Kalahapriyā*. Literally, quarrelsome.

[5] *Niṣṭha*, which according to the commentator, here means *maraṇam*.

[6] That is, *mukti* (Liberation).

[7] Foster-father of Kṛṣṇa.

[8] The dark (*tāmasika*) energy, called Raudrī, is said to be Cāmuṇḍā· There are said to be nine crores of different Cāmuṇḍās. (see Bhāskararāya Comm., Lalitā, verse 155).

[9] *Sandhyā*.

[10] Kāli and Tāra are always so represented (see Karpūrādistotra).

[11] *Surāmāmsabalipriyā*.

[12] Devī of wealth and prosperity.

[13] Devī of misfortune and poverty.

[14] Sons of Danu, enemies of the Devas.

Thou art Sâvitri[1] of the Vedas,
Mother of Mantras.[2]
Thou art the *Dakṣinā*[3] of the *ṛtvik*,[4] and art in the altars of sacrificial rites,
And the religious sense[5] of *Ṛṣis*.
Thou art Aditi of Devas.[6]
Plough of cultivators, earth of all creatures,
The success of merchants who fare in big ships,[7]
The coast of ocean,
And foremost Yakṣi of the Yakṣas,[8]
Surasā of Nāgās,[9]
Virginity[10] of maidens and good fortune of women,
Knower of the knowledge of Brahman,[11]
Initiation and supreme beauty,
Lustre of light, Rohinī[12] of planets.
Lakshmī, most successful art Thou in courts and fortresses,
In the confluence of rivers and in the full moon.
Thou art called Krittivāsa.[13]

---

1 The Gāyatri *mantra*.

2 *Mantraganasya*, or, according to another reading, *bhūtaganasya*.

3 The present offered to the officiating Brāhmaṇa.

4 Priest.

5 *Dharmabuddhi*, a term difficult to translate. A man is said to have *dharmabuddhi* who has great respect for religion and duty.

6 The Devas were children of Aditi, as the Daityas were of Diti.

7 *Sāngyātrikānām* = *potavanijām*.

8 That is, She is the Mother of Kubera, the King of the Yakṣas, a class of *Devayoni*.

9 Mother of the serpent divinities (Nāgās).

10 *Brahmacarya*.

11 *Brahmavādinī*.

12 The name of an asterism.

13 The name of S'iva as clad in tiger-skin.

Thou art Sarasvati in the works of Vālmīki,[1]
Memory in those of Dvaipāyana,[2]
Religious sense of *Ṛṣis* [3] and (perfect) mind of
Devas.[4]
Thou art the Goddess of wine,[5]
Adored art Thou by Thy creatures for Thy deeds.
Thou art the charming look of Indra,
And art the thousand-eyed [6],
Devī of ascetics,
Ārani [7] of Agnihotra Brāhmaṇas,[8]
Hunger of all creatures,
Who satisfieth those in heaven.
Thou art *Svāhā*,[9]
Contentment, patience,
Receptacle of the Vasus,[10] hope of men,
Contentment which comes of work fully done;

---

[1] Author of the Rāmāyana. Tradition says that he obtained a boon from the Goddess of learning and composed that work.

[2] Kṛṣṇa Dvaipāyana, one of the Vyasas, arranger of the Purāṇas, etc., who is said to have had all such *śāstra* by heart.

[3] *Vide ante* (see p. 157, note 5).

[4] *Mānasī*, which the Commentator says = " *Satyasangkalpātmikā chetovritti* " that is, whose will and thought fully realizes itself.

[5] *Surādevi*.

[6] Indra.

[7] *Ārani* are the two sticks of *samid* wood used to kindle sacrificial fire.

[8] Brāhmaṇas who cherish fire in the house and perform *homa* thrice daily.

[9] Wife of Agni, the *mantra* used when making *homa*..

[10] Of whom there are eight: Apa, Dḥruva, Soma, Dhara, Anila, Anala, Pratyusha, Prabhāsa (see Vishnupurāṇa, Book I., chap. xv.)

All the quarters and their opposites,[1]
Flame of fire, lustrous Sakunī,[2]
Pūtanā,[3] the terrible Revatī,[4]
Overpowering sleep of all beings,
Warrior.[5]
Of learning Thou art, *Brahmavidyā*,[6]
Om and *Vaṣat*.[7]
The *Ṛṣis* know Thee as Pārvati amongst women.
As Prajāpati[8] has said, Thou art Arundhati[9]
amongst women, with but one husband.[10]
The difference of disputants.[11]
Famous also art Thou as Indrāṇi[12]
This universe, mobile and immobile, is permeated
by Thee.
Without a doubt Thou art saviour in all battles.
Amidst fires and on the banks of rivers,
Amidst robbers, in forests and caverns,
When in prison or when assailed by enemies,
And in all times and places where life is in peril.

---

1 *e g.*, north and south, east and west, etc.

2 A terrible spirit of that name.

3 A female demon who attempted to destroy, but who was destroyed by the infant Kṛṣṇa.

4 Name of the twenty-seventh constellation, containing thirty-two stars.

5 *Kṣatriyā*.

6 The science of Brahman.

7 The *Mahāmantra* "*om*". *Vaṣat* is a *mantra*. As *Svāhā* is used with *homa*, so *srauṣat*, *vauṣat*, *vaṣat*, and *svadhā* are used in *pitṛkriyā*.

8 Brahmā.

9 Wife of the sage Vaśiṣṭha, famous for her constancy and devotion.

10 *Ekabhartrinām*.

11 *Bhedovivādashilānām*.

12 Spouse of Indra.

My heart, my reason, and mind are devoted to Thee.
Deliver me from all sins. Be gracious to me.
Whoever rising at dawn reads[1] for the space of three months
This sacred hymn to Devī compiled by Vyāsa,
Being himself pure and of controlled mind.
Obtains the desired fruit.
Whoever reads it for six months, to him also
The desired fruit is given. Such as read it for nine months obtain celestial vision, and he who reads it for one year gains all such success[2] as man may desire.
O Devi ! as was said by Dvaipāyana, Thou art the supreme divine Brahman.
Thou destroyest the bonds and the fearful destruction of men,
The loss of children and wealth, fear of death and disease.
Thou art in the form of desire, and dost grant the objects thereof.
Having deluded Kamsa, Thou enjoyest the whole world,
And I also shall live as a cowherd among kine ;
To accomplish my work I shall become a cowherd of Kamsa.[3]

---

1 Here follows the *phala* portion. (see p. 73,note 1).

2 *Siddhi*

3 The tyrant who sought to slay Kṛṣṇa. The Chapter concludes: "Having thus addressed the Devī, the Lord disappeared, and She, too, saluting Him, expressed Her consent by saying, 'So be it'."

DURGĀ[1]

From the MAHĀBHĀRATA[2]

1

I SALUTE Thee, leader of Yogis,[3] one with the
Brahman,[4]
Dweller in the Mandāra forest.
Virgin,[5] Kāli,[6] Spouse of Kāpāla,[7] of tawny hue.[8]
Salutation to Thee, Bhadrakāli.[9]
Reverence to Thee, Mahākāli,[10]

---

1 See p. 120, note 9; p 128, note 1 : p. 81, note 1.

2 Bhishma Parvan, s. 43 (see Muir, O. S. T. iv, 432).

3 *Siddhasenāni*. The *siddhas* are here *yogis* and sages. Nīlakaṇṭha (cited *post* as N.), in his Commentary, says the term means: She who, as leader (literally, commander of an army), gives success in *yoga* and attainment of the supreme abode.

4 *Āryye*. Literally, noble, but here means, as Nīlakaṇṭha says, *prapya-brahmasvarūpa*—the own form of the accessible Brahman, as distinguished from the *nirguṇa Brahman* beyond thought and speech.

5 Kumāri. It also means (N.) that She is very young.

6 See p. 152, note 3.

7 Kāpāli, one of Her forms. Kāpāla is Rudrā, as leader of Kāpālas (Kāpālikas).

8 *Kapilākṛṣṇapingalā*

9 Auspicious Kāli, who gives prosperity to Her devotees.

10 See p. 152, note 3. The great Kāli, Destructress in the form of death.

Caṇḍī,[1] Fearless one.[2] Salutation to Thee,
Saviour[3] imbued with all good fortune.[4]

2

Of the race of Kata[5] greatly worshipful,
Dreadful one,[6] Giver of victory,[7] Victrix,[8]
Who holdeth a peacock's tail for Thy banner,
And art adorned with various jewels,
Bearing formidable spear, sword, and shield (made of skin).
Younger Sister of the chief of cowherds,[9]
Eldest one,[10] born in the family of the cowherd Nanda,[11]
Delighting in the blood of Mahiṣa,[12]

---

1 Spouse of Caṇḍa, or Kālāntaka, or Yama.

2 *Caṇḍā*—bold, daring, brave, courageous.

3 *Tārinī*, for She delivers from calamity.

4 *Varavarninī* (N.), not "beautiful coloured," as it has been translated.

5 Kātyāyanī.

6 *Karālī* = *krure* or cruel (to demons and other ill-doers). *Karālavadanā* (wide-opened mouth) is an epithet of Kālī. "Gaping-mouthed, terrible, four-armed, with dishevelled hair" — *Karālavadanām ghorām, chatur-bhujām,* as the Kālī *dhyāna* runs.

7 *Vijaya*—that is, particular (*viśiṣṭa*) victory (N.).

8 *Jayā*. *Jayā* and *Vijayā* are also the names of two female attendants (*Sakhī*) of Durgā.

9 Gopendra or Kṛṣṇa. In the Harivaṃśa and Caṇḍī it is said that with the view of defeating the designs of Kaṃsa in regard to the destruction of Devakī's offspring, Devī will be born as the ninth chiid of Yaśodā in the same night as Kṛṣṇa was born as the eight child of Devakī, when Kṛṣṇa would be carried to Yaśodā and She to Devakī.

10 *Jyeṣtha* = *śreṣthā*—superior to or best of all.

11 In whose house Kṛṣṇa was reared.

12 The Asura of that name (see Caṇḍī).

Kauśikī,[1] wearing yellow garments.

3

With auspicious smile,
Whose mouth devoured all demons,[2]
Salutation to Thee, delighter in battle.
Umā,[3] giver of *shāka*,[4]
In the form of Maheśvara,[5] and in that of Vāsudeva,[6]
Destructress of Kaitabha,[7]
Golden-eyed, with half-opened eyes [8], grey-eyed,[9]
Veda and *S'ruti*,[10] and most sacred.
Propitious to Brāhmaṇas engaged in the sacrificial rites,
Thou art Jātaveda,[11]
And art ever present in the sacred shrines [12] in the chief cities of Jambudvīpa.[13]

---

1 A name of the Devī, as born in the race of the sage Kuśika.

2 *Kokamukhe*—when in battle with Raktabīja.

3 See Hymn to Annapūrṇa, *post*.

4 *Shākambarī*. *Shāka* is a vegetable food given by Devī at the time of famine (Caṇḍī).

5 *Svetā* (N.), not white, as it has been translated.

6 *Kṛṣṇā* (N.), not black, as it has been translated.

7 A Daitya brother of Madhu (Caṇḍī).

8 *Virūpākṣi* (see p. 155, note 5).

9 *Dhūmrākṣī* (N.) says grey and green, like those of a cat.

10 Here Upaniṣads.

11 *Jātavedasī*. Jataveda is a name of Agni (Fire).

12 *Chaityeshu*. Ordinarily this term is applied to the Buddhist shrine, of which it is commonly said: "One should not enter a Jaina's temple or Buddhist *chaitya*, even if pursued by an elephant" (*Hastinā tādyamānopi na gachchet jaina-mandiram* also *dhaitya mandiram*.) Here the term means *devatālaya*.

13 A Purāṇic island by that name, not as it has been translated; "Who dwellest continually near to mountain precipices and sepulchres."

4

Of Sciences Thou art the knowledge of Brahman,
Thou art the liberation of embodied beings,[1]
Mother of Skanda.[2]
O Bhagavatī[3] Durgā ![4] Thou liveth in inaccessible
regions—
Svāhā,[5] *Svadhā*,[6] *Kalā*, and *Kāṣṭhā*,[7]
Sarasvatī,[8] Savitrī.[9]
Mother of Vedas and Vedānta[10] art Thou called.
I praise Thee from the pure depth of my heart.
By Thy favour let us be victorious in battle.
Ever dost Thou abide in inaccessible regions,
In places full of fear and difficulty ;
In the houses of Thy devotees, and in Pātāla.[11]
In battle Thou conquereth the Dānavas.[12]

---

1 " The great sleep of embodied beings," according to the last translator : But *Mahānidrā* (great sleep) is here *mukti* (liberation), which is the result of the *Brahmavidyā*, spoken of in the preceding line.

2 Kārtikeya. By this it is meant that She is *sarvadevatārūpā*, in the form of all Devas, of whom Skanda is selected as a type(N.).

3 See p. 120, note 5 ; p. 98, note 5.

4 *Kāntāravāsinī* (N.).

5 Mantra used with *homa,* but here it means that all ritual acts are her embodiment (*Sarvakarmarūpā*).

6 *Mantra* used in *pitṛkriyā* (see last note).

7 *Kalā* is a division of time—one minute forty-eight seconds, and *kāṣṭha* is one-thirtieth of that.

8 Devī of speech and learning.

9 She is *sarvavāng-maya-rūpa*(N.).

10 End of the Vedas or Upaniṣad.

11 The nether world.

12 See p. 156, note 14.

Thou art drowsiness[1] and slumber.[2]

5

Thou hast power to show wonderfully the world,[3]
Modesty,[4] and beauty.[5]
Cause of creation and destruction,[6]
Creatrix,[7] Mother,[8] contentment, nourishment, constancy,
Light, Supportress of the sun and moon,
Power[9] of Him who possesses power,[10]
In ecstasy[11] Thou art perceived by Siddhas and Cāranas.[12]

---

[1] *Jambhane* = *tandrā* (N.), not "destroyer" as it has been translated.

[2] *Mohinī* = *Nidrā* (N.).

[3] *Māyā* = *adbhutapradarśanām* (N.).

[4] *Hrī* = *lajjā* representative of, and including all other actions of mind (N.).

[5] *S'rī*, or prosperity, and other attributes of Lakṣmī.

[6] *Sandhyā*. the intervening period when night is going and morn coming. and *vice versa*, applied here to similar junction times in the creation and dissolution of the world (N.).

[7] *Sāvitrī*. She who, by the lustre of Sūrya, reveals (N.).

[8] Because, as a mother, She supports the world and all beings therein.

[9] *Aiśvarya*. The supreme faculties of omnipresence, omnipotence, etc.

[10] *Maheśvara*. She is the greatest wealth of Brahman.

[11] *Sankya* or *Samādhi*, where light appears and the *ātman* is known (N).

[12] Siddhas here mean those who are liberated whilst yet living (*jīvanmukta*), and Cāranas those who are *siddhas* from their birth.

HYMNS TO THE DEVĪ

FROM S'ANKARĀCĀRYA

TRIPURASUNDARĪ

(TRIPURASUNDARĪSTOTRA)

1

I SEEK refuge with Tripurasundarī,[1]
Who wanders in the Kadamba forest ;[2]
The spouse of the Three-eyed One,[3]
Bank of cloud (in the sky of the heart) of numbers of sages,[4]

---

[1] The Devī is so called as the Spouse of S'iva, destroyer of the *tripura*, or cities of the three Asuras—Kamalākṣa, Tarakākṣa, and Vidyun-māli. According to the Kālikā Purāṇa, Paraśiva is Tripura, because he has three *pura* in Him, His body becoming triple upon the manifestation therein of Brahmā, Viṣṇu, and S'iva. The Devī is then the S'akti of Paramaśiva.

[2] The Kadamba (*Nauclea cadamba*) is a tree with orange fragrant blossom whereunder Kṛṣṇa played (see *Ādyākālīsvarūpaśtotra* in Mahānirvāṇa Tantra). *Kadamba* also denotes number (multitude), and in this sense the *Kadamba* forest is the universe which the Devī permeates.

[3] S'iva with the central eye of wisdom. S'iva is also *Tryambaka*, because He is the father of the three Devas, Brahmā, Viṣṇu, and Rudra (Tarkālangkāra Commentary, Mahānirvāṇa Tantra). The Ṛgvidhāna uses it as equivalent of Mahādeva.

[4] *Muni*. As the bank of cloud gives water, so She quenches the spiritual thirst of *munis*.

Whose hips defeat the mountain by their greatness.[1]
Who is served by celestial women,
Whose eyes are like the newly blown lotus,
And who is dark as the colour of a freshly formed
rain-cloud.[2]

2

I seek refuge with Tripurasundari,
The Spouse of the Three-eyed One,
Who dwells in the Kadamba forest,
And who is ever wandering ;
The Large-eyed One who holds a golden *vinā*,[3]
Wearing a necklace of priceless gems,
Whose face is glowing with wine,[4]
And who of Her mercy grants prosperity to Her
devotees.

3

Ever are we protected by Her whose abode is the
Kadamba forest,
The weight of whose breasts are garlanded with
glittering gems,
Whose breasts are rising,[5]

---

[1] *Nitambajitabhudaram*. *Nitamba* literally means buttocks, which, however, here reads rather absurdly in English, the side or hips being *pārśa*, *kakṣa*, or *shroni* (*cf.* tenth śloka of the *Karpurākhyastava* " *Samantādāpīnastana-jaghanadhrikyauvanavatī* ") .

[2] That is, of the dark blue colour seen when the blue of the sky appears through a freshly-formed black rain-cloud.

[3] A stringed musical instrument of that name.

[4] *Mukhasamullasattvārunim*. *Vāruni* is wine made from rice. Here and in following verses the divine ambrosia (*amṛta*) is referred to.

[5] "Rising" (*cf. Durgādhyāna* in "Devī Purāṇa") *pīnonnata payodharām*. As to weight and greatness, see *Annapūrṇādhyāna*, *Bhuvaneśvaristotra*, " *āpīvarastanatating tanuvrittamadhyām*, " and Introduction.

And excel the mountain in greatness;
Whose cheeks are flushed with wine,[1]
Ever singing sweet songs; the playful one,[2] dark
as a cloud,
Ever compassionate to all.

4

I seek refuge with Tripurasundarī,
The Spouse of the Three-eyed One,
Who stays in the Kadamba forest,
Who is seated in the golden circle and dwells in
the six lotuses,[3]
Ever revealing like lightning the great power (of
devotees),[4]
Whose beauty is like that of the *Jaba* flower,[5]
And whose brow is adorned with the full moon.

5

I take refuge with Her, the sweet speaker,
Daughter of the sage Matanga,[6]

---

[1] *Madārunakapolaya* (see n. 4, p. 170).

[2] *Līlayā*. Play (*līlā*) is the mark of a Deva, and the Devī's substance is play (*līlāmayī*). The Devī is Lalitā ("She who plays"): Padma Purāṇa says: "Having passed beyond the world She plays, hence She is called Lalitā." But the Creation is also Her play.

[3] *Ṣaḍāmbhu*—that is, the six *cakra* or centres in the human body: the *mulādhāra, svādihsṭhāna, manipūra, anāhata, viśuddha,* and *ājnāpadmas* (see the translation of the Ṣatcakra Nirūpaṇa from the Sanskrit, *The Serpent Power*). The Devī exists as Kuṇḍalinī in these *cakra*.

[4] *Satatasiddhisaudaminim*. *Siddhi* (power so called), which lies latent, is instantly brought to light by Her.

[5] Scarlet hibiscus, the Tāntrik flower sacred to the Devī.

[6] *Ṛṣi*.

Whose breast is adorned with the *vinā*.[1]
And whose head is beauteous with locks of curling hair ;
Who dwells in the lotus ;[2]
The destroyer of the wicked,
Whose eyes are reddened with wine ;[3]
The charmer of the enemy of the God of Love.[4]

6

I take refuge with Tripurasundarī,
The Spouse of the Three-eyed One,
Who should be meditated upon as in the first flush of Her nubile youth,[5]
Her blue garment stained with drops of blood.[6]
Holding the wine-cup,[7]
Her eyes rolling with wine ;[8]

---

1 The musical instrument which She holds and which rests on Her breast.

2 For she is also Kamalā or Lakṣmī.

3 *Madārunāvilochanam*(see p. 170. note 4).

4 That is, charmer of S'iva who destroyed Kāmadeva with the fire from His eyes when the latter sought to distract him by thought of passion from the *yoga* in which he was engaged.

5 *Smaretprathama puṣpinīm,* literally "as having the first 'flower'" which is used in the same symbolical sense as in English. The *puṣpotsava* is the religious festival held on its first appearance at puberty.

6 *Rudhiravindunīlambaram*—that is, stained with the *puṣpa* ("flower"). As this first shows itself when woman is ready to bear, so in the blue sky, which is the Devi's garment, signs are seen which herald Her creation.

7 *Grihītamadhupānikam.*

8 *Madhuvighurnanetranchalam* (see p. 170, n. 4).

With heavy, high, and close-set breasts,[1]
Dark of colour, and with dishevelled hair.[2]

9

At time of recitation I remember the Mother,
Lustrous as the scarlet hibiscus,[3]
Her body pasted with saffron and sandal,
Her hair kissed by musk ;[4]
The Mother with smiling eyes,[5]
With red garland, ornaments, and raiment,
Who holds the arrow, bow, noose, and goad ;[6]
The charmer[7] of countless men.

---

[1] *Ghanastana bharonnatām* :" heavy " (*cf. Annapūrṇadhyāna Annapradāna-niratām stanabhāranamrām* "); " high " (*cf. Durgādhyana, ante* Introduction); " close," so that, as it is said in the Kumarāsambhavam (chap. i.) of Kalidāsa : " Even the filament of a lotus could not be passed between them " (" *mrinālasūtrāntaramapyalabhyam* ").

[2] *Galitachikurām.* The Devi in this and other forms, as Kāli, Tārā and Chinnamastā is so represented. The epithet is a common one in Tantra (*cf. Karpūrādistotra*, verse 3).

[3] *Jaba, v. ante.* So also the Lalitā (verse 147), " whose body is like the China rose."

[4] See the *Ādyākālisvarūpa Stotra* in the Mahānirvāṇa Tantra.

[5] The Devī is, according to the Lalitā Sahasranāma (verse 59) *chāruhāsa* (with beautiful smile), indicating a certain state of consciousness (*prabodha*) of highest bliss.

[6] These are Her weapons. The Tantrarāja (Vāsana chap.) says : " Mind is the bow of sugar-cane, desire the noose, anger the goad, and the five subtle sources of the elements (*tanmātra*) the five arrows of flowers." But the Yoginīhridaya says : " The noose is *Iccāśakti*, and goad *Jnānāśakti*, and the bow and arrows *Kriyāśakti*."

[7] She deludes men with her *māyā* ; hence the Lalitā (verse 137) calls Her " all-bewildering " (*sarvamohinī*). The Kurma Purāṇā says : " This *māyā* is dear to me by which the world is bewildered. I bewilder the whole universe with the Devas, Daityas, and men."

8

I worship the World-Mother
Who is served by celestial women,
The Spouse of Indra,
Skilful in plaiting hair ;[1]
The devoted Spouse of Brahmā,
Anointed with sandal paste ;
The Spouse of Viṣṇu,
Adorned with pleasing ornaments.

---

[1] *Cikurabandhasairindhrikām* : for Her hair, which is in some of Her aspects dishevelled, is in others beautifully arranged.

GANGĀ

(GANGĀṢṬAKAM)

1

O Bhagavatī Gangā ! [1]
Thou art the playful garland on the head of Hara ;[2]
Such as but touch a drop of the spray of Thy waters
Recline on the lap of the fan-holding women of the
city of the immortals, [3]
Freed of the fear arising from the sinful Kali age. [4]

2

(O Devī Gangā !) may you purify us,
Thou who separateth the earth from Heaven, [5]
Gladdening the creeper-like matted hair on the
head of Hara, [6]
Descending from the region of heaven,
Oozing from out the cave of the golden mountain, [7]
Falling upon the surface of the earth,

---

[1] The River Ganges, in whom the Devī manifests.

[2] S'iva. The Ganges in its descent from heaven at the call of Bhagīratha was caught in the matted hair of S'iva.

[3] *Amarāvatī*. The city of Indra.

[4] Kaliyuga. The fourth, and, according to orthodox views, the present age, marked by the prevalence of sin.

[5] By the celestial Ganges called Mandākinī.

[6] See note 2 *ante*.

[7] Sumeru.

Purifier (as the River Mandākinī) of the city of the Devas,
Who art the powerful Destructress of the multitude of men's sins.

3

The trunks of elephants and their young make play with Thy waters,
Fragrant with ichor-maddened swarms of bees,
Trickling from the temples of elephants bathing therein.
Thy stream is browned with the sandal paste
Dropping from the breasts of Siddha women [1] who bathe therein.
And nigh the river bank Thy water is strewn with *Kuśa* [2] grass and flowers,
There thrown by sages [3] at morn and even. [4]
May the water of the Ganges protect us!

4

This divine sin-destroying Bhāgirathī [5] now on earth
Was in the beginning water in the vessel [6] of the Primeval Grandfather. [7]
Then it was pure water from the feet of the Lord (Viṣṇu),

---

1 Siddhas are celestial spirit (*devayoni*) of great purity.

2 A species of grass used in worship.

3 *Munis*.

4 The flower and grass is thrown by them when they worship the Ganges in the morning and evening.

5 Gangā is called Bhagirathi, because She was brought down from heaven by the prayer of Bhagiratha, son of the solar race, in order to secure heavenly bliss for his kinsmen.

6 *Kamaṇḍalu*, a gourd-shaped vessel used by ascetics.

7 *Pitāmaha*. Brahma is so called.

Who sleeps on the serpent.[1]
Again it was the gem adorning the matted hair of
S'iva,[2]
And, lastly, the daughter of the great sage Jahnu.[3]

5

May the entrancing[4] Gangā falling on the matted
hair[5] of Hara,[6]
Descending from the Lord of Mountains,
Moving sinuously like a serpent to the ocean,
Flowing by the city of Kāśī,[7]
Dispeller of countless worldly fears,[8]
Saviour of those who bathe in Her waters,
Be ever victorious.

6

How can he who has seen Thy wave be bound by
illusion ?

---

[1] The thousand-headed serpent Ananta Deva (see Viṣṇu Purāṇā).

[2] *Ante* p. 175, n. 2.

[3] Hence the river is called Jāhnavī. The verse speaks of the stages of the descent of the heavenly stream. *Ṛṣi* Jāhnu swallowed the Ganges, and then, at the prayer of Bhagiratha, he let it issue from his thigh. The Ganges is called his daughter as She issued from him.

[4] *Manohāriṇī* ("mind stealer").

[5] S'iva, like the ascetics, wears a coil of matted hair (*Jaṭa*)

[6] S'iva.

[7] Benares, through which the Ganges flows.

[8] Fearlessness is the special gift of the Devī. The Mārkandeya Purāṇā says: "When You are remembered in times of difficulty, You take away all fear of all beings." She is *Bhayāpahā* (remover of fear); for S'ruti says ("Tai Up." ii. 9, 1): "By knowing the bliss of that Brahman none fear anything."

To him who has drunk of Thy water thou givest a dwelling in the city of the yellow-clad Deva.[1]
O Gangā! what time the bodies of those who assume body[2] fall on Thy lap,[3]
For such, O Mother,[4] even Shatakrita's[5] grandeur[6] is but a small thing.

7

O Bhagavatī![7] on Thy bank I drink Thy water only.
I worship Kṛṣṇa, all thirst for worldly enjoyment having gone.
Destroyer of all sin, Whose companionship is the stairway to Heaven,[8]
O Devī! Gangā of lightsome, tremulous wave,
Be gracious to me.

8

O Mother! O Spouse of S'ambhu![9]
Who art ever associated with S'ambhu
At death, upon Thy banks, with my hands folded upon my head,

---

1 That is, Viṣṇu, who is clad in yellow, and whose city is His heaven (*Vaikuṇṭha*).

2 Men.

3 That is, when on death, they are thrown into the Ganges.

4 The Devī is the Holy Mother (*S'rīmātā*), the first of Her names.

5 Indra, King of the celestials.

6 *Pada* or portion.

7 Feminine of Bhagavan, a term applied to God, and which means He who possesses *Bhaga*.

8 *Svarga*.

9 S'iva.

Remembering Thy name and the feet of Nārāyaṇa,[1]
May my devotion to Hara and Hari[2] ever endure
At the time of the festival of life's departure![3]
He who of pure mind reads this sacred eight-versed
hymn to Gangā
Will be wholly released of all sin
And will go the region of Viṣṇu.[4]

---

1 Viṣṇu.

2 Viṣṇu and S'iva.

3 Death (*prāṇaprayāṇotsava*), for it is the entrance to heavenly bliss.

4 *Vaikuṇṭha* (see p. 178. n. 1).

WAVES OF BLISS

(ĀNANDALAHARĪ)

1

O BHAVĀNĪ,[1] the four-headed Lord of creatures,[2] is
not able to worship Thee,
Nor even the five-headed destroyer of the Tripura,[3]
Nor the six-headed commander of the celestial
hosts,[4]
Nor even the thousand-headed Lord of serpents.[5]
If, then, they cannot, tell me who else is able so to
do?

2

O Devī! how can we speak of Thy qualities,
Which are not to be described by any *Nigama*,[6]
As the sweetness of ghee,[7] milk, the grape, and
honey

---

[1] Bhava is S'iva, and is His name in the watery form of the *aṣṭamūrti* (eight forms). The Vāyu Purāṇa says that He is called Bhava because all things come from Him and subsist in water. The Devi is Bhavāni as the Spouse and giver of life to Bhava.

[2] Brahmā.

[3] S'iva.

[4] Kārtikeya, son of S'iva.

[5] Ananta on whom Viṣṇu reposes.

[6] Generally S'āstra and in special technical sense Tantra in which the Devī is the Guru.

[7] Clarified butter.

Cannot be distinguished and described by words,
But may be perceived by the tongue only;
In like manner Thy beauty can be seen only by
the eyes of Parameśvara.[1]

3

We ever pray to Thee, O Gauri![2]
Youthful daughter of the Lord of mountains.
Beautiful is the betel[3] in Thy mouth
And the collyrium on Thy eyes;
Beautiful, too, are the saffron on Thy forehead,
The necklet of pearls on Thy throat,
Thy silken garment and the glittering gold waist-
ornament on Thy large hips.[4]

4

May Bhagavatī,[5] Satī,[6] whose lotus eyes sparkle,[7]
Spouse of S'ambhu,[8] on the slope of whose breasts
Rests a beautiful garland of the flowers of the
Mandāra tree,[9]
Whose earring is the pleasing sound from the *vinā*,[10]

---

[1] The supreme Lord.

[2] See p. 30, note 3.

[3] *Tāmbūla*, or pan, which is chewed.

[4] *Prithukatitate*.

[5] Feminine of Bhagavan.

[6] Devi as daughter of Dakṣa (see Introduction).

[7] *Ambhoruhacatulacakṣu*. Literally, the lotus eye is ever moving, now glancing here, now there. Motionless eyes in women are not considered beautiful.

[8] S'iva.

[9] One of the five heavenly trees in the garden and city (*Amarāvati*) of Indra—viz., Mandāra, Pārijāta, Santāna, Kalpavrikṣa, Harichandana.

[10] The stringed instrument of that name borne by the Devi as Sarasvatī.

Who stoops (from the weight of her breasts),[1]
Whose beautiful swaying gait is that of the female elephant[2]—
May that Bhagavatī be ever victorious!

5

O beauteous Aparṇā![3]
Bestow the fulness of happiness on me,
Thou whose limbs art covered
With ornaments of gold and gems glittering like the newly risen sun,
Whose eyes are beautiful as those of a doe,
Of whom S'iva is a part,[4]
Who is of the golden colour of lightning,
Beauteous in yellow garments and tinkling anklets.

6

Shines forth does the Devī born in the snowy mountains.[5]

---

[1] *Nātangī*. So also the Annapūrṇā *dhyāna* represents the Devī as giver of food "stooping from the weight of Her great breasts" (*annapradāna niratāmstanabhāranamrām*, and see verse 6 *post*).

[2] *Mātangīrucirāgati bhangī bhagavatī*.

[3] Name of the Devī. According to the Kālikā, and Brahma Purāṇas the Devī, as the daughter of Himavat, renounced even leaves as food (*a-parṇā* = without leaf); hence she is called by Devas Aparṇā. According to another derivation, the name comes from *apa* (removing), *rina* (debt). So Bhāskararāya, who gives it, says in his *Devīstava*; "When you have not discharged your debt to me, though I respect your name, O S'ivé why are you not ashamed to bear the name of Aparṇā?" (discharger of debt)? According to the Nirukta, *parna* = falling. *Aparṇa* = free from falling.

[4] That is, it is by Her favour that S'iva forms part of Her.

[5] *Himādrehsambhūtā*—that is, the Himālaya, hence She is also called *Girijā* (mountain-born).

Her beautiful hands are like a red leaf.[1]
She is adorned with beautiful flowers and pearls.
Her head, by its weight of hair, seems covered by a swarm of bees.[2]
It is She with whom Śiva seeks shelter,
Who stoops from the weight of Her breasts,[3]
Whose words are sweet,
The Destructress of ills,[4]
Ever and in all places pervading,[5]
Tender creeper[6] of Intelligence and Bliss.[7]

7

Others worship with reverence the plant with leaves and particular qualities,
But I know that Aparṇā alone in this world should be worshipped.[8]
Then the old Śiva garmented with space

---

1 Either from their natural colour or because dyed with lac.

2 The bee goes to the lotus ; the bees (her hair) settle upon her (lotus) face.

3 *Kucābharanatā* (see note 1, p. 182).

4 Disease (*rujānghantrī*).

5 Literally, one who goes (*gantrī*).

6 *Latikā*. Dim. of *latā* creeper to which woman is compared, for she clings to her husband as the creeper to the tree. Hence worship with woman in the Tāntrik *Pancatattva* is called *latāsādhana*.

7 *Cidānanda* which, with *sat* (being), constitutes the nature of the Supreme Being (Parabrahman).

8 That is, some worship a particular Devatā to gain a particular result—*e.g.*, Sarasvatī for learning, Lakṣmī for wealth etc.; but Śankarācārya worships the supreme Aparṇā, whom the Devas worship, who is without qualities, and does so only to give Her honour.

Surely grants to Thy worshipper the fruit of full liberation.[1]

8

Thou art the Mother of all Vedas,
The regulator of all *dharmas* [2]
And the root of all wealth—
Thou whose lotus feet are worshipped even by the wealth-giver.[3]
O Mother! Thou art the primal cause of all desires.
Victrix of Kandarpa,[4] Thou art the seed of liberation for the good.[5]
Thou art the Spouse of the Parabrahman.[6]

9

Although my mind be fickle and wanting in great devotion to Thee,
Yet by Thy mercy Thou should look auspiciously upon me.
The cloud gives sweet water to the mouth of the *Cātaka*[7] bird.

---

[1] Full *kaivalya mokṣa*, liberation above the various *pāda*, *sālokya*, etc. (see p. 59, note 1), for *muktī* is of various kinds.

[2] Law of religion, duty, etc.

[3] That is Kubera, Deva of wealth.

[4] A name of Kāma, God of Love (see p. 40, note 1).

[5] *Satām.* She gives liberation to them.

[6] The Supreme Being, for it preceded S'aktī, as *S'ruti* says, "*Sa aikshata,*" etc. As the S'āradā Tilaka (chap. i.) says: "*Saccidānanda vibhavāt sakalat parameshvarāt, āsichchaktistītonādonād-bindusadmudbhavah.*

[7] A bird (cuculus melanolcucus) which is said to live on raindrops.

I know not by what (good) fate my mind is
directed.[1]

10

O virtuous One, from the corner of Thine eyes
Cast now a glance of kindness upon me;
Neglect so to do is not proper on Thy part,
Seeing that I have reached the refuge of Thy
initiation.
Alas! the creeper of desire,[2] whose very name
shows that it gives desire,
Yet cannot give that which is desired,
What difference is there between it and any other
common creeper?

11

I, though I have sought refuge with other Devatās,
Have yet placed full trust in Thy lotus feet.
If, nevertheless, your heart is not timely set on me,
Then with whom shall I in my helplessness seek
shelter,
O Mother of the big-bellied one![3]

12

As iron touched by the touchstone becomes at once
gold,

[1] That is, just as the *cātaka* is given something, though it does not and cannot pray for it, so what the writer of the hymn receives must, since his devotion (*bhakti*) is so small and lacking in the force of prayer, be due to some undisclosed merit acquired as the result of past *karma*.

[2] *Kalpalatikā*—that is, a creeper which, like the *kalpa* tree, grants all desires that may be asked of it.

[3] Ganeśa.

As the water of the roadway mixed with that of the Ganges becomes pure,
In like maner will not my heart,
Greatly soiled though it be by my great sins [1]
Become pure if attached with devotion to Thee?

13

O Īśāni,[2] as the old Lotus-Born [3] and others have said,
The rule is that if others than Thyself art worshipped,
Only the particular fruit desired is gained;
But Thou giveth more even than is asked for.
Make me, then, ever attached to Thee by day and night.

14

O Spouse of the great Lord of the three worlds![4]
Most pleasant is Thy abode,
The walls whereof glitter with various gems and crystals,
Whereon Thy image is reflected.
On the summit of Thy abode the quivering light waves of the moon (are shed).
Therein dwell Mukunda,[5] Brahmā, and other Devas.
It is ever victorious.

---

[1] *Tattatpāpaih*. Literally, "those particular sins"—the sins of the hymnist who knows what they are.

[2] Feminine of Īśa (Lord).

[3] Brahmā.

[4] See p. 151, note 7.

[5] Giver of liberation—that is, Viṣṇu.

15

Thy dwelling is in Mount Kailāsa.[1]
Thy worshippers are Brahmā, Indra, and other Devas.
All are subservient to Thee in the three regions.[2]
The number of *siddhis* [3] join their palms (in adoration before Thee.).
S'iva is Thy lover;
Therefore, O Daughter of the Lord of mountains[4]
Nothing is equal to Thy fortune.

16

The old bull is (S'iva's) carrier.
Poison is his food;[5] space is his dwelling;
The cremation ground is his playground;[6]
Serpents are his ornaments.

---

[1] See *Introduction to Tantra S'āstra*.

[2] See p. 151, note 7.

[3] Great powers, such as *aṇimā*, *laghimā*, etc., the power of becoming extremely light or heavy, of entering into things, etc., which, in their fulness, constitute the *aiśvarya* of the Lord (Īśvara), and in a lesser degree of those who approach His nature.

[4] Himālaya, for Devī was the daughter of the Mountain-King Himavat.

[5] See p. 16, note 2.

[6] Dakṣa, in the Bhāgavata Purāṇa, reproaching S'iva, says: "He roams about in dreadful cemeteries, attended by hosts of ghosts and spirits, like a madman, naked, with dishevelled hair, wearing a garland of dead men's skulls and ornaments of human bone, pretending to be S'iva (auspicious), but in reality Aśiva (inauspicious), insane, beloved by the insane, the Lord of Bhūtas (ghosts and spirits), beings whose nature is essentially darkness" (Muir, O.S.T., iv. 738). The cremation ground is His abode, for there the passions are burnt away.

All things in the world are known to the enemy
of Smara ;[1]
But the wealth of all this is due to the greatness of
Thy fortune,
O Mother !

17

The Lord of *Paśus*,[2] besmeared with ashes, sits in
the cremation ground.
From his nature arises the force which destroys
the world.
Out of compassion for the whole world, He held
the poison in his throat.[3]
O Kalyāṇi ![4] in all this I see the fruit of his companionship with Thee.

18

O Daughter of the mountain,[5]
When Gangā had seen Thy great beauty,
She was afraid,[6] and turned to water ;
Then S'iva, seeing her sad, lotus-like face,
In his mercy made a dwelling for Her on his own
head.[7]

---

[1] God of Love, whom S'iva consumed.

[2] *Paśupati :* a name of S'iva : as to *Paśu* (see *Introduction to Tantra S'āstra*). Here the equivalent of Lord of men.

[3] See p. 16, note 2.

[4] Beneficent one. According to the Padma Purāṇa Devī is worshipped as Kalyāṇi in the Malaya mountain, to which reference is made in verse 20.

[5] See p. 187, note 4.

[6] *Bhītaivāsīt*, or may be abashed.

[7] Jāhnavī, whence Gangā is called Jāhnavī. When Gangā fell from Heaven, S'iva first held Her in the locks of his hair, until Her anger at being called down by Bhagīratha had abated. She

19

O Bhagavati,[1] the Creator having with his own
hands taken Thy bathing water
Mingled with liquid sandal, musk, saffron, and
flowers,
And the dust of Thy moving feet,
Created therewith the lotus-eyed women of the
city of the Devas.[2]

20

If one but contemplates Thee, in play with Thy
maidens,
In pleasing springtide with its flowers and creepers
Upon the lake, beautiful with many a blossoming
lotus and flocks of geese,
The waters of which are rippled by the breeze
from the Malaya mountain,[3]
From such an one all fevered ills[4] pass away.

---

then fell into the Bindu lake, whence issue the seven sacred streams. One branch followed Bhagīratha wherever he went, and on the way flooded the sacrificial flame of the *muni* Jāhnu. In his anger he drank up its waters. Bhagīratha's work seemed to be fruitless. But after intercession, the *muni* allowed the waters to flow from him, and as so, issuing from him, the Ganges is called his daughter Jāhnavī.

[1] See p. 178, note 7.

[2] *Amarāvati*, the city of Indra.

[3] See note to verse 17.

[4] Literally, fever-produced disease (*jvarajanitapīdāpasarati*).

YAMUNA[1]

(YAMUNĀṢṬAKAM)

1

MAY the daughter of Kalinda[2] ever cleanse my
mind of its impurity,
She whose waters, beauteous as the black body of
the enemy[3] of Mura,[4]
Cleanse the overgrowth of plants[5] and shrubs
which line its pleasant banks.
Indra's heaven compared with Thy waters is but
a thing of straw.
Destructress of the sorrow of the three worlds—
Dhunotu me manomalam Kalindanandinī sadā.[6]

2

May the daughter of Kalinda ever cleanse my
mind of its impurity,
She whose stream is highly adorned with over-
flowing water
Destructress of sin, dark as night, like unto nectar,

---

[1] The river sacred in particular for its memories of S'rī Kṛṣṇa, who on its banks sported with the cowherd women (*Gopis*).

[2] Yamunā.

[3] S'rī Kṛṣṇa.

[4] A Daitya slain by S'rī Kṛṣṇa.

[5] *Kunjapunja.*

[6] The refrain is translated in the first line.

Greatly powerful for the destruction of all great sins,
Beneficent One who is black of colour,
Through company with the body of the good son of Nanda [1]
Dhunotu me manomalam Kalindanandinī sadā.

3

May the daughter of Kalinda ever cleanse my mind of its impurity,
The touch of whose shining waves washes away the sins of multitudes of beings.
Devoted to Thee is the *Cātaka* bird, [2] receptacle that Thou art of freshness and sweetness. [3]
Giver of desire,
On the borders of whose banks swans ever dwell,
Dhunotu me manomalam Kalindanandinī sadā.

4

May the daughter of Kalinda ever cleanse my mind of its impurity.
The gentle breeze on Her banks dispels the lassitude
Of those who have rambled and played [4] thereon.
The beauty of Her waters is beyond the power of words;
It is, indeed, the consortment with Her current,

[1] The cowherd who brought up S'rīkṛṣṇa, when his life was threatened by Kamsa.

[2] As to which see p. 184, note 7.

[3] Literally, "who are slaves to Her by reason of their inhabitancy of Her banks"

[4] After the *rāsalīlā* S'rikṛṣṇa and the *Gopīs* are tired by their dance and play, and are refreshed by repose upon Her banks where gentle breezes blow.

Which purifies all rivers, male and
female,[1] on the earth.
Dhunotu me manomalam Kalindanandinī sadā,

5

May the daughter of Kalinda ever cleanse my
mind of its impurity,
Destroyed by (the whiteness of) Her sandy banks
laved by Her waters;
She who is ever white,[2]
Adorned with blossoms beauteous as the rays of
the autumn moon.[3]
May She then purify me by Her waters,
Most excellent that they are for the worship of
Bhava,[4]
(By her white splendour),[5] Destructress of the
darkness of night[6]—
Dhunotu me manomalam Kalindanandinī sadā.

6

May the daughter of Kalinda ever cleanse my mind
of its impurity.
The paste and unguents of the beauteous Rādhikā[7]
Colours Her waters in which Rādhikā plays.

---

[1] Rivers are either male (*nada*) or female (*nadī*). Of the former class are the Sone, Sindu, etc., and of the latter Gangā. Narmadā, Gandakī, etc.

[2] Her sandy banks are so.

[3] Of a soft and silvery white.

[4] For use in the ritual worship of S'iva.

[5] *Malam* (*manomalam*). Impurity is a thing which is dark. The river by the white splendour of its white banks and blossoms is therewith contrasted.

[6] For luminously white is She like the moon.

[7] The beloved of S'rīkṛṣṇa.

Possessor is She of the body of the husband [1] of
Rādhikā,
Which by none other may be possessed.
Skilled is She in making Her way through the
seven sleeping oceans,
And in filling them with waters [2]—
Dhunotu me manomalam Kalindanandinī sadā.

7

May the daughter of Kalinda ever cleanse my
mind of its impurity!
Her stream is beauteous with the women of the
cowherds,[3]
Made passionate [4] by the scent of the paste and
unguent,
Dropped therein from off the body of Acyuta,[5]
Garlanded is She with clusters of Champak flowers,

---

[1] S'rikṛṣṇa; for He too bathes in her stream, which possesses also His dark colour.

[2] Alluding to the destruction of the Asuras, called Kālakeya. These excluded the Devas from *svarga*. On their chiefs being slain by Indra, they betook themselves to the depths of the ocean, whence they issued at night to destroy the *Ṛṣis*. The latter asked the aid of Viṣṇu, who told them to go to Agastya. He at one sip swallowed all the oceans, which thus disappeared (therefore "sleeping oceans" of text) until the River Ganges was brought down by Bhagīratha when they were again filled with Her waters. This incident is attributed to the Yamunā, both rivers being manifestations of the same Devī.

[3] Literally, *Ali*, which, according to the Amarakośa = *Sakhi*; female friend, referring to the *Gopis* who loved Krishna.

[4] *Lampata*; Whose senses were roused by the scent of the pastes which had fallen from the scented body of Kṛṣṇa.

[5] Kṛṣṇa ("imperishable one").

Set in the flowing[1] hair of Rādhikā.
Of all such as come to bathe in Her waters
Neither is one the servant nor the other master.[2]
Dhunotu me manomalam Kalindanandinī sadā.

8

May the daughter of Kalinda ever cleanse my mind of its impurity!
Pleasant always is She with groves,
Where Nandanandi[3] ever played.[4]
Bright is She with the ripened blossom
Of the *kadamba*[5] and *mallika*[6] flowers upon Her banks.
It is She who safely carries across the ocean of the world[7]
All such men as bathe in Her stream.
Dhunotu me manomalam Kalindanandinī sadā.

---

[1] *Vilola.* Her hair is dishevelled and moving in the movements of breeze and play.

[2] Literally, "In the case of those who come down to bathe in Her waters She ever destroys all righteousness of master and servant"—that is, all are equal in Her waters which purify all without distinction.

[3] The text has *Nandinandana,* but this has no meaning. *Nandanandi* is He who pleases Nanda or Kṛṣṇa, whose foster-father Nanda the cowherd was.

[4] With the *Gopi* women.

[5] A beautiful flowering tree with yellow blooms under, and on which (as when he stole the garments of the bathing *Gopis*) Kṛṣṇa played (See p. 169, note 2).

[6] A kind of Jasmine.

[7] See p. 16, note 1.

"MAY THE DEVI GRANT ME PARDON"

(DEVI APARĀDA KṢAMĀPANA STOTRA)

1

ALAS ! I know not either Thy *mantra* [1] or *yantra*,[2]
Nor how to welcome Thee,[3]
Or how to meditate upon, nor words of prayer to
Thee,
Nor do I know Thy *mudrā*,[4]

---

[1] *S'abda* is Brahman, and *mantra* the manifestation thereof. From *manana* arises realization of the monistic truth. *Man* of *mantra* comes from the first syllable of *manana*, and *tra* from *trāna*, or liberation from the bondage of the *samsāra*. That is called *mantra* which calls forth (*āmantrana*) the *caturvarga*, and which is the *svarūpa* of Devatā. (See *Introduction to Tantra S'āstra* and the Chapter on Mantra Tattva in *Principles of Tantra*.

[2] *Ibid.*, The Tāntrik diagram which is worshipped in lieu of the image (*pratimā*). The Gāyatrī *Yantra* is figured on the cover of this work. *Mantra* is *Devatā*, and *yantra* is mantra, in that it is the body of the *Devatā*, who is *mantra*.

Yantram mantramayam proktam mantrātmā devataivahi
Dehātmanoryathā bhedo yantradevatayostathā (Kaulavaliya Tantra).

"The substance of *yantra* is *mantra*. *Devatā* is *mantra*. As there is a distinction between body and *ātmā*, so there is between *yantra* and *Devatā*."

[3] By the *āvāhana mantra*, always said in worship of the *pratimā*.

[4] Ritual gesture, it being said ; *Devānām modadā mudrā tasmāttām yatnātścaret* (see *Introduction to Tantra S'āstra*)"—" *Mudrā* is giver of pleasure to Devas, therefore it should be done with care."

Or how to lay before Thee my griefs;
But this I know, O Mother!
That to follow Thee is to remove all my pain.

2

By my ignorance of Thy commands.
By my poverty[1] and sloth,
I had not the power to do that which I should have done,
Hence my omission to worship Thy feet.
But, O Mother! auspicious Deliverer of all.
All this should be forgiven,
For a bad son may sometimes be born, but a bad mother never.[2]

3

O Mother! Thou hast many worthy sons on earth,
But I, your son, am of no worth;
Yet it is not meet that Thou should'st abandon me,
For a bad son may sometimes be born, but a bad mother never.

4

O Mother of the world, O Mother!
I have not worshipped Thy feet,
Nor have I given abundant wealth to Thee;
Yet the affection which Thou bestoweth on me is without compare,
For a bad son may sometimes be born, but a bad mother never.

5

I have abandoned the worship of other Devas

[1] Want of means to perform the proper worship.

[2] A celebrated line; *Kuputtro jāyetā kvacidapi kumātā nabhavati.*

Because of the variety and confusion of the
injunctions relating to their worship.
I am no more than eighty-five years of age, [1]
If Thou will not bestow Thy kindness on me,
What shelter have I without Thy support,
O Mother of the big-bellied Deva ! [2]

6

Prayer, sweet as the sweet melon
Makes even a dog-eater [3] perfect ;
Even a beggar walks without fear
With crores [4] of gold pieces.
O Aparṇā ! [5] this is the fruit of Thy *mantra* entering
their ears.
Who can say, O Mother !
The fruit which is born of the recitation [6] of Thy
mantra ?

7

He who is besmeared with the ashes of the funeral
pyre,[7]
He who swallowed poison,[8]

---

[1] How is this stated if the hymn be the work of S'ankarācārya, to whom it is attributed, for he is said to have died at the early age of thirty-two ?

[2] *Lambodarajananī*. The Deva is the elephant-headed Ganeśa.

[3] That is, a low caste such as the *Caṇḍāla*, who eats any filth.

[4] A crore is 100 lakhs ; a lakh is 100,000.

[5] See p. 182, note 3.

[6] That is, *japa*, which is only recitation (in English) in its lowest form, the highest form being mental (*mānasa*) only. *Japa*, which is defined as *vidhānenā mantroccāraṇam*, is either *vācaka*, *upāmshu*, or *mānasā* (see Tantrasāra, 75 *et seq.*).

[7] S'iva, to whom the rest of the attributes in this verse refer.

[8] See p. 16, note 2.

Who is clothed with space,[1]
With matted hair, garlanded with the Lord of Serpents,
The Lord of men,[2]
The Lord of Ghosts[3] holding a skull in His hands.
Owes his great states as Lord of the World
To his acceptance of Thee as His Spouse, O Bhavānī![4]

8

No desire have I for liberation,
Nor have I desire for wealth,
Nor wish for knowledge,
O Moon-faced One! neither have I wish for happiness!
But this only I beg of Thee,
That my life may pass in the recitation of these words:
Mridānī,[5] Rudrānī,[6] S'ivā, S'ivé, Bhavānī.[4]

9

I have not according to the injunctions laid down therefor

---

[1] S'iva is represented naked, as the Yogins, of whom He is the Master, ever are.

[2] *Paśupati*. *Paśu* literally means animal, but men are also *paśu*.

[3] *Bhūteśa*., S'iva is surrounded by hosts of spirits.

[4] See p. 180, note 1.

[5] Mrida is a title of the *sāttvika* S'iva. She is His Spouse.

[6] Devī is the Spouse of the countless S'ivas called Rudras, in whom the *tamoguna* prevails. The dark (*tamas*) energy, called Raudrī, is said to be Cāmuṇḍā.

Worshipped Thee with the various articles [1] of
    worship.
What is there which I have not wrongly done or
    omitted in my meditations on the Brahman?
O Dark One! [2] it will be but fitting on Thy part
If Thou bestoweth not kindness on me, helpless
    though I am.

10

O Durgā, [3] our Lady! O Ocean of mercy!
When overwhelmed by danger [4] I remember Thee.
Think not, however, this to be deceit on my part,
For children afflicted by hunger and thirst ever
    remember their mother.

11

O Mother of the world! [5]

---

[1] *Upacāra.* There are sixteen such, called the *shoḍaśa pūjā
upacāra*—viz., (1) *āsanam* (seat); (2) *svāgatam* (welcome); (3)
pādyam (water for feet) (4) *Argyam* (offering of water, *durva* grass,
rice, etc.); (5) and (6) *ācamanīyam*; (water for sipping; twice);
(7) *madhuparka* (honey, ghee, milk); (8) *snānam* (bathing); (9)
vasanam (cloth); (10) *ābharaṇam* (jewels); (11) *gandha* (scent, sandal
paste, etc.); (12) *puṣpa* (flowers); (13) *dūpa* (incense), (14) *dīpa*
(lights); (15) *naivedyam* (food); (16) *vandanam* or *namaskāra*
(prayer).

[2] *S'yāmā.*

[3] A great name of the Devī. The Devi Purāṇa says that
She is so called because the Devas were delivered from fear in
difficulty and battle; hence She is deliverer (Durgā). The Mār-
kaṇḍeya Purāṇa and the Lakṣmī Tantra in the Pancarātra says:
"In this place I shall kill a great Daitya (Titan) named Durgama.
Hence my name shall be Durgā."

[4] The Mārkaṇḍeya Purāṇa says: When Thou art remembered
in times of difficulty, Thou takest away all fear of all things."

[5] *Jagadambā.*

It is nothing wonderful if Thou art full of
compassion for me ;
A mother does not abandon her son
Even if he have an hundred faults.

12

There is no such great sinner like me,
There is no such destroyer of sin as Thou.
Now, Mahadevi, you have heard what I have to say,
It remains for Thee to do what may seem fitting
to Thee.

MAṆIKARṆIKĀ

(MAṆIKARṆIKĀSTOTRA)

1

It was on Thy bank, O Maṇikarṇikā ! [1]
That Hari and Hara, givers of *sāyujya mukti*, [2]
Disputed together at the departure festival [3] of a
certain one.
Hari [4] said, "Let Him be like unto me ;"
Whereon forthwith from within the body
Came forth S'iva mounted on Garuda, [5]

---

[1] Is the name of a celebrated *ghat* at Benares, where the bodies of the dead are burnt, and at which the gem of the ear ornament of the Devī fell. The Kāśipancakastotra of S'ankara says that where there is *nivṛtti* of *manas*, there is the great peace. That peace is the foremost of *tīrthas* (here rivers) and Maṇikarṇikā (*Manonivṛtti paramopaśāntih sā tīrthavaryā maṇikarṇikāca*).

[2] One of the forms of qualified *mukti* (liberation); the four muktis are *Sālokya* (remaining in the same region with the Deva), *Sāmipya* (remaining near the Deva), *Sārupya* (receiving the same form as the Deva), and *Sayujya* (becoming one with the Deva).

[3] *Prayāṇotsava*—that is, death.

[4] Viṣṇu

[5] The Bird King, who is the vehicle (*vāhana*) of Viṣṇu, son of Kaśyapa by his wife Vinetā, elder brother of Aruṇa.

In yellow garment,[1] with the mark of Bhrigu's foot
on His breast.[2]

2

Indra and the Thirty,[3] at the close of their period
of enjoyment,[4]
Descend to earth again,[5]
And are reborn as men, or even as beast, bird, or
worm ;
But those, O Mother Maṇikarṇikā ! who plunge
into thy waters,
Are freed from sins, and indeed in *Sāyujya*[6] man
becomes
Nārāyaṇa[7] himself, with crown and *Kaustubha gem.*[8]

---

[1] The colour of Viṣṇu's robes. The verse is intended to show the unity of both Viṣṇu and S'iva.

[2] *The Ṛṣis* once disputed amongst themselves as to the relative merits of Brahmā, Viṣṇu, and S'iva, and the *Ṛṣi* Bhrigu was sent to test them. The first and last on being purposely slighted by Bhrigu showed the weakness of resentment. Finding Viṣṇu lying down with Lakṣmi in the daytime he upbraided him for this and planted with force his foot on his chest. Viṣṇu not only took all this in good part, but rubbing the foot of Bhrigu expressed the hope that the latter had not hurt it by his action. On this exhibition of divine quality the palm was adjudged to Viṣṇu, who thereafter bore the mark of Bhrigu's foot on his breast.

[3] *Tridaśah,* a collective name for the other Devas. The thirty-three (three being understood) *gaṇas* of Devas, of which the Devi is Tridaśeśvari.

[4] In heaven (*Svarga*).

[5] For the enjoyment in *Svarga,* which is part of the worlds of birth and rebirth, is not eternal, but on fruition the *jivātmā* again descends to earth to work out its unexhausted *karma.*

[6] *Sāyujyepi.* As to *sāyujya,* see *ante,* p. 201, note 2.

[7] Viṣṇu.

[8] A great and brilliant gem worn by Viṣṇu.

3

Kāśi[1] is of all cities the most praiseworthy,
For it is the city of *vimukti*[2] adorned with Gangā.
There Maṇikarṇikā is the giver of happiness,
And *Mukti* itself is Her servant.[3]
When Brahmā weighed Heaven with its Devas against Kāśi,
Kāśi, as the heavier, remained on earth,
But Heaven, the lighter, rose to the skies.

4

Nought is better than any part of the banks of Gangā,
But there, where Kāśi is, is the best,
And Maṇikarṇikā, where Īśvara gives *mukti*, is the best of all.
This place, inaccessible even to Devas,
Destroys a mass of sins.
Through many virtues acquired in previous births
Alone may it be attained, and by the pure only.

5

The multitude of being is immersed in the ocean of pain,
How may they gain release?
It was with this knowledge that Brahmā constructed the city of Vārānaśī,[4] which gives all bliss.

---

[1] Benares.

[2] *Nirvāṇāmokṣa*, the highest form of *Mukti* (liberation). As the saying goes: "Ayodhyā, Mathurā, Gayā, Kāśi, Kānci, Avantikā, Purī, these seven *tīrthas* (places of pilgrimage) give *mukti*, but Kāśi (Benares) gives *nirvāṇa mukti*."

[3] As the servant awaits the orders of his mistress, so *mukti* (liberation) awaits the command of Maṇikarṇikā.

[4] Benares.

Men seek the happiness of Heaven.
But in so doing they but show small desire,
Since from Heaven they must fall again to earth
At the close of their appointed time of happiness.[1]
But Kāśī is the city of liberation,[2]
Ever beneficent, giving *dharma*, *artha*, *kāma*, and
mokṣa. [3]

6

He who holds the bamboo flute,[4] upholder of the
mountain,[5]
Who bears on his breast the *S'rivatsa* [6] mark,
And S'iva, with venom in His throat, [7]
Who bears Gangā upon his head, [8]
And the husband of Lakṣmi, [9]
Are one and the same. [10]
Many of such, O Mother Maṇikarṇikā!
As bathe in Thy waters become Rudras and Haris. [11]

---

[1] See p. 202, note 5.

[2] *Mukti* (see p. 203, note 2).

[3] Piety, wealth, fulfilment of desire, and liberation.

[4] Kṛṣṇa, who is often so figured.

[5] Mount Govardhana, which Kṛṣṇa, by his might, upheld.

[6] Curls of hair on the breast of Viṣṇu.

[7] At the churning of the ocean, poison issued which, to save the world, S'iva swallowed. It coloured His throat blue; hence he is called Nīlakaṇṭha.

[8] The River Ganges (see p. 188, note 7).

[9] Viṣṇu.

[10] They with Brahmā; for as the Rudrayāmala says: "Though three they are one" (*Ekam murtistrayo deva*). All the Devas and Devīs are but manifestations, with the apparent limitations incident thereto, of the Supreme Unity—the Brahman.

[11] S'iva and Viṣṇu.

How, then, can there be any difference between
them ?[1]

7

Death upon Thy Banks, which is the giver of
happiness,
Is praised even by the Devas.
On him who thus dies S'akra[2] ever looks with His
thousand eyes.
Sāvitrī[3] of a thousand rays welcomes Him as He
ascends (to the heavens).
Such a pure one, mounted on a Bull or on Garuda,[4]
May go to whatsoever abode he will.

8

Even the four-headed Deva,[5]
The *Guru* who initiates into the meaning of the Veda,
Is unable even in an hundred of his[6] years
To describe the purity which arises upon bathing
at midday in Maṇikarṇikā.
But the Deva who bears the moon upon his
forehead,[7]
By the power of his *yoga* knows Thy purity.
S'iva makes that man who dies on Thy Bank
Either Himself or Nārāyaṇa.

---

[1] That is, they cease to differ from one another, having become Hari and Hara, who are themselves one.

[2] Indra, king of the celestials.

[3] The sun (Sūrya).

[4] The first is the vehicle (*Vāhana*) of S'iva. The second, the carrier of Viṣṇu.

[5] Brahmā.

[6] Not human years.

[7] S'iva.

9

All such sin-destroying fruit as is earned by millions of troublesome horse-sacrifices [1]
Exists in the purity which comes from bathing in Maṇikarṇikā.
He, who having bathed therein,
Reads this hymn, goes to the abode of the light of Brahman,
Having crossed the great ocean of this world
As if it were but some little pool.

[1] The Vaidika Aśvamedha.

GANGĀ[1]

(GANGĀSTOTRA)

1

O Devī Sureśvarī ![2] O Bhagavatī Gangā !
Saviour of the three worlds of restless waves,
Clear is Thy water circling upon the head of S'iva[3],
May my mind ever repose at Thy lotus feet.

2

Mother Bhāgirathi ![4] giver of happiness,
Renowned in Nigama[5] is the greatness of Thy water ;
Thy greatness is more than I can know,
Protect me, O merciful one, ignorant that I am.

---

[1] This hymn to the Devi Ganges, which is in the sweet *pajjhatika* metre, is also rhymed thus :

Devī Sureśvarī Bhagavatī Gange,
Tribhuvanatārinī taralatarange,
S'ankaramaulī vihārinī vimale,
Mamamatirāstām tavapada kamale.

[2] Īśvarī (feminine of Īśvara or Lord) of the Suras or Devas.

[3] See p. 188, note 7.

[4] So called because called down from Heaven by Bhagīratha of the solar race.

[5] Tantra.

3

O Gangā! sprung from the feet of Viṣṇu,[1]
Whose waves are white as snow as moon and pearl,
Remove from me my weight of sin;
Help me to cross the ocean of the world.

4

They say that him, O Gangā! who is devoted to
Thee
Yama[2] can never behold.
He who has drunk of Thy clear water
Attains of a surety the supreme Abode.

5

O Jāhnavi! O Gangā! deliverer of the fallen,[3]
Whose waves are beautiful,
Claving the foremost of mountains,[4]
Mother of Bhiṣma,[5] daughter of the foremost of
munis.[6]
Protectress of the fallen; praised in the three
worlds.[7]

6

O Gangā! who goeth to the ocean,
Ever free of sadness is he who salutes Thee.

---

[1] Gangā was born at the feet of Viṣṇu. So it is said in the *mantra* used when bathing in the Ganges: "*Viṣṇupādābja sambhūte Gange bhuvanatārini dharma draviti*" (the Ganges is *dharma* in liquid form) "*vikhyāte pāpam me hara Jāhnavi.*"

[2] Deva of Death.

[3] Into sin.

[4] The Himālaya.

[5] Son of Santanu by Gangā.

[6] See p. 188, note 7.

[7] See p. 151, note 7.

Giver of fruit like unto the *kalpa* tree,[1]
By thy favour the woman who looked coldly
Now casts her loving glances.[2]

7

He who bathes in Thy current, O Mother!
Is never again reborn in woman's womb
O Protectress from hell! O Jāhnavi! O Gangā!
O Destructress of sins! lofty art Thou by Thy greatness.

8

O Thou who art eternal! O wave of purity!
May Thou, bestower of bliss, refuge of Thy worshippers!
From whose eyes come glances of compassion.
Whose feet the lustre of gems on Indra's crown adorn,
Be ever victorious!

9

O Bhāgirathi![3] dispel my illness, melancholy, and pain,
As also my sins and all my many follies;
Essence of the three regions, necklace (on the breast) of Earth,[4]
Of a surety Thou art my refuge in the world.

---

[1] The tree in the paradise of Indra which granted all desires.

[2] *Vimukhavanitākritataralāpānge.*

[3] So called after Bhagiratha, who called her down to earth (see p. 188, note 7).

[4] *Vasudhāhāra*—that is, as a necklace adorns a woman, so the Devi by the flowing lines of Her stream, adorns the Earth.

10

O Alakanandā![1] O supreme Bliss![2]
O worshipful by those who despair!
Be Thou merciful.
He whose abode is by Thy Banks
Of a verity dwells in *Vaikuṇṭha*.[3]

11

Better were it to be a fish or tortoise in thy waters,
Or a feeble lizard upon Thy banks, or a poor dog-eater[4]
Within two *kos*[5] of Thy stream,
Than to be a noble king and yet far away from Thee.

12

O Bhuvaneśvarī![6] pure one, praised of all,
Devī in liquid form,[7] daughter of the foremost of *Munis*,[8]
He who daily reads this hymn to Gangā
Is of a surety ever victorious.

13

They who with devotion in their heart to Gangā (Recite) this hymn
Composed in the sweet, pleasant, charming *pajjhatika* metre,

---

[1] A river flowing from the Himālaya into the Ganges.

[2] *Paramānandā*, as is the Supreme, whose manifestation She is.

[3] The heaven of Viṣṇu

[4] That is, a *caṇḍāla*, one of the lowest and most unclean castes.

[5] A *kos* is two miles.

[6] *Īśvarī*, of the world.

[7] For the Ganges is the manifestation of the Supreme in the form of the sacred river.

[8] Jahnu (see p. 188, note 7).

Which gives the highest happiness,
Gain the eternal bliss of liberation.

14

A worldly [1] man shall read [2] this hymn to Gangā
Which [3] is the essence of the world, the giver of desired fruit,
The essence of all pure things enjoined.[4]
Composed by S'ankara,[5] the worshipper of S'ankara.[6]
This hymn is ended.

---

[1] *Viṣaya,* which also in a bad sense means a sensua list o materialist.

[2] *Paṭhati.* Literally, "reads," but used for the *vidhiling* tense *paṭhet.* Thus in Caṇḍi it is said : *Paṭhet stotram samāhitah,*' and in the Vatukastotra, "*Paṭhetvāpāṭhayetvāpi*" ("should read or have read to him").

[3] That is, the hymn.

[4] *i.e.,* forms of worship (*pūjā*), sacrifice (*yajna*), etc.

[5] That is, S'ankarācārya.

[6] S'iva.

NARMADĀ

(NARMADĀṢṬAKASTOTRAM)

1

O DEVĪ NARMADĀ ![1] I salute thy lotus-like feet,
Beauteous with the breakers of the heaving waves of ocean,
With which the drops of Thy waters mingle.[2]
O giver of prosperity ! I salute Thy feet bathed in water,
Which destroys rebirth, the cause of which is sin,[3]
As also all fear at the coming of the messenger of death.[1]
Tvadīya pāda pankajam namāmi devi narmadé.

2

O Devi Narmadā ! I salute Thy lotus feet
Giver of celestial (blessing) to the lowly fish in Thy waters,
Foremost of all sacred rivers.[6]

---

[1] One of the sacred rivers of India, and a form of the Devi.

[2] The ocean is the husband of all rivers.

[3] Rebirth is caused by *karma*.

[4] When a man is about to die, a messenger is sent by Yama to take his life.

[5] The refrain is translated in the first line.

[6] The is *stuti* (praise). In all sanskrit works the particular Devatā who is the subject of hymn, meditation or prayer is spoken

Destructress of the heavy weight of sin of the Kaliyuga,[1]
Giver of welfare to multitude of fine fish, tortoise, alligators, and ruddy geese.[2]
Tvadīya pāda pankajam namāmi devi narmadé.

3

O Devi Narmadā! I salute Thy lotus-like feet.
The overflow from Thy depths washes away the sins of the world.
Thou destroyest all great sins and the mountain[3] of calamities.
O giver of happiness to the son of Mṛkaṇḍu,[4]
At the fearful moment of the world's dissolution.
Tvadīya pāda pankajam namāmi devi narmadé.

4

O Devi Narmadā! I salute Thy lotus-like feet,
And Thy waters worshipped by the son of Mṛkaṇḍu, S'aunaka, and other enemies of the Asuras.

---

of as the greatest of all. *Tīrtha* is not only a place of pilgrimage such as a shrine and the like, but also, according to the Amarakośa, a sacred river.

[1] The present or fourth age, marked by the predominance of sin, each of the preceding eras (Dvāpara, Tretā, Satya) being more virtuous than the other. In the Kaliyuga era time works evilly.

[2] The *cakravāka* bird (by some said to be the Brahmini duck) celebrated in sanskrit poetry for its devotion to its mate. During the night-time the male and female birds call to each other from opposite banks of the stream, as I have heard them do on the reaches of the lonely Malia River in Northern Orissa.

[3] *Dāritāpadacalam.*

[4] The *Mahāmuni* Mārkaṇḍeya.

Destructress of rebirth in the ocean of the world,[1]
Portectress from all worldly pains,[2]
Tvadiya pāda pankajam namāmi devi narmadé.

5

O Devi Narmadā ! I salute thy lotus-like feet,
Worshipped by countless lakhs[3] of immortals,[4]
Asuras,[5] Kinnaras,[6] and others,
Whose banks resound with the fearless song of many lakhs of birds.[7]
Giver of happiness to Vaśiṣṭa, Pipala, Karddama,[8] and other sages,[9]
Tvadiya pāda pankajam namāmi devi narmadé.

6

O Devi Narmadā ! I salute Thy lotus-like feet,
Held in the minds of the bees,[10] Sanatkumāra, Naciketa,[11] Kaśyapa,

---

[1] The edition used has *punarbhavābdhi janmajam*, but this seems meaningless, and it is read as *janmaghnam*.

[2] *Bhavābdhi dukhha barmadé*. Literally, "armour given to the pain of the world."

[3] A lakh is 100,000.

[4] *Amara—i.e.*, Devas.

[5] Demonic spirits, opponents of the Devas or Suras.

[6] A class of spirits (*Devayoni*).

[7] *Dhira*—that is because they are undisturbed by men who have become enemies to their brother creation.

[8] *Ṛsis* and *munis* of that name.

[9] *S'iṣṭa*, which means a gentle and learned man who governs himself by his own wisdom, and is not governed by external restraints.

[10] The bee hovers on the lotus seeking honey. The sages gather round the feet of the Devi seeking the wisdom of which She is the embodiment.

[11] *Munis* and *ṛṣis*.

And by the bees, Atri, Nārada and other sages.
Thou who blesseth the work of sun, moon, Rantideva, and Devarāja,[1]
Tvadiya pādapankajam namāmi devi narmadé.

7

O Devi Narmadā; I salute Thy lotus-like feet,
Weapon against lakhs of sins known and unknown,
The Giver of enjoyment and liberation to all beings and animals,[2]
And of happiness to the abode of Virinci,[3] Viṣṇu, and S'iva,
Tvadīya pāda pankajam namāmi devi narmadé.

8

O Devi, Narmadā, ! I salute Thy lotus feet.
How sweet is the sound heard on the banks of Her who has sprung from the hair of S'iva [4].
Destroyer of pain and sin of hunter, and singer [5] of the learned and the fool,
And of the heat of the submarine fire,[6]

---

[1] Indra.

[2] Both enjoyment and liberation is given to men: to animals enjoyment (*bhukti*), though they, too, by merit acquired in present birth may attain future birth in human form.

[3] Brahmā.

[4] *Maheśakeśajatate.* As to Gangā, see p. 188, note 7. It is the same and only Devi who manifests both as Gangā and Narmadā, and all other rivers and things.

[5] Hunting is sinful. The singers are a mixed caste.

[6] *Kirātasūtavādaveṣu pandita śathe.* When the *Dakṣayajna* was destroyed by S'iva, it changed into a mare (*Vadavā*). S'iva followed, and it plunged into ocean. Fire is produced by it. The *S'loka* says that Her water is so great aud pure that it is unaffected by this fire. As regards the rest of this somewhat obscure verse, it means that the Devi is the remover of the sin of all whoever they may be.

Giver of happiness to all being.
Tvadiya pāda pankajam namāmi devi narmadė.

9

Who ever reads but thrice daily this hymn to
Narmadā
Will never fall into misfortune,
He will never see Raurava,[1]
He will never be reborn,
But will reach the glorious abode of Śiva,
So difficult to attain, by this body so easily gained.[2]

---

[1] One of the great hells.

[2] *Sulabhya dehadurlabham.* Not that it is easy to attain human birth. On the contrary, it is said: "*Naratvam durlabham loke* and *vidyātatra sudurlabhā,*" etc. ("The state of a man is difficult to attain, and still more so that of a wise one," cited in Sahitya Darpaṇam, chap. i, by Viśvanātha Kavirāja). What is apparently meant is that, compared with the difficulty of attaining to Śiva, the state of humanity is easily attainable.

ANNAPŪRṆĀ

(ANNAPŪRṆASTOTRA)

1

O Mother Annapūrṇā ![1]
Īśvarī,[2] who ever bestoweth happiness,
Granting gifts and dispelling fear.
O mine of gems of beauty,
Who washeth away all sin,
Who giveth purity to Thy devotees,
Who purifieth the mountain range,[3]
Which is undestroyed even at the time of dissolution,[4]
Presiding Deity of Kāśī,[5]
Maheśvarī[6] in every truth,
O vessel of mercy! grant me aid.

2

O Thou who hast clothed Thyself in cloth of gold,

[1] The name of the Devi, the "bountiful Lady" who gives food and presides over Kāśī, the Holy City of Benares.

[2] Feminine of Īśvara or Lord.

[3] The Himālaya purified by the presence of the Devi, who there incarnated as Pārvatī, daughter of Himavat, the Mountain-King.

[4] *Pralaya*, the destruction of the world.

[5] Benares (see note 1.)

[6] Great Īśvarī (see note 2).

Decked with ornaments made of many and varied gems,
Whose breasts rounded like a water-jar,
Are resplendent with their necklace of pearls,
Whose beauty is enhanced by the fragrance of the Kashmir aloe.
O Devi! who presidest over the city of Kāśī,[1]
O Mother Annapūrṇā Īśvarī,[2]
O vessel of mercy, grant me aid!

3

O giver of the bliss of *Yoga*,[3]
Destructress of enemies,[4]
Inspirer of devotion to *dharma* and *artha*,[5]
Who art lustrous as the light waves of sun, moon, and fire,
Protectress of the three worlds[6]
Giver of all dominion[7] and all desires,
Presiding Devi over the city of Kāśī,
O vessel of mercy, grant me aid!

---

1 Benares.

2 Feminine of Īśvara or Lord.

3 Union of the human (*jīvātmā*) with the supreme (*paramātmā*) soul effected through the practice of *Yoga*.

4 That is, sin.

5 Two of the fourfold aims (*Caturvarga*) of sentient being—viz., *dharma* (religion, duty, etc.), *artha* (wealth, wherewith life is sustained and religious sacrifices are effected), *Kāma* (desire which prompts great achievements and fulfilment), and *mokṣa* or liberation.

6 That is, *Bhuh*, *Bhuvah*, *Svah*, the terrestrial atmospheric and the heavenly spheres.

7 *Aiśvarya* (lordship).

4

Thou who maketh Thy dwelling in the cave of Mount Kailāsa,[1]
Who art Gaurī,[2] Umā,[3] and S'ankarī,[4] Kaumārī,[5]
Who giveth us power to understand the meaning of *Nigama*,[6]

---

[1] The sacred mount and paradise of S'iva; esoterically the Sahasrāra whereto as Kuṇḍalinī She repairs.

[2] The daughter of Guru, the King of mountains (see p. 187, note 4). Gaurī also means "fair".

[3] A name of the Devī. When of the age of sixteen she practised great austerities that She might be the Spouse of S'iva, upon which Her mother, endeavouring to persuade Her, said, U ("Oh"), Mā ("not"). As it is said by Kālidāsa in the first Canto of the Kumārasambhavam; "*Umeti mātrā tapaso niṣiddhā paschā dumākhyāng sumukhījagāma.*" ("By the words U, Mā, She was thus forbidden by Her mother to practise austerity, thereafter the pure Umā obtained Her name.") Umā is Kumārī, who has renounced all attachment, and is devoted to Her Lord. A *sūtra* runs, "*Icchāśaktih Umā kumārī*" (The energy of will is Umā the unmarried). The Commentary on this *sūtra*, cited by Bhāskararāya, says: "The eternal state is his whose mind has ascended the degrees of *yoga* called *vismaya*, and who realizes the supreme Bhairavata (an aspect of S'iva). That *Yogi* obtains at length the *Icchāśakti* called the Supreme Queen (*Parābhaṭṭārika*) known also as Kumārī."

[4] Name of the Devī as Spouse of S'ankara, the benefactor.

[5] Name of the Devī as one of the *aṣṭanāyikā* and Spouse of Deva Kārtikeya.

[6] This term, applied to the Veda generally, means particularly the Tantra in the form in which the Devī is *guru* and S'iva, *śiṣya*. As it is said:

Nirgato girijā vaktrāt,
Gatāscha girija śrutim,
Matascha vāsudevasya,
Nigamā parikathyate.

In the Lalitā the Devi is addressed *as nijājnarūpā nigamā* (the *nigama* are the expressions of Thy commands).

Thou art the letters of the *bija*[1] Om[2],
Opener of the panels of the door of liberation,[3]
Presiding Devī over the City of Kāśī,
O vessel of mercy, grant me aid!

5

Thou supporteth all beings visible and invisible,
Whose belly is the vessel which contains the universe.[4]
Thou discloseth the subject of the drama of Thy own play,
And art the fount of the light of wisdom,
Pleasing the mind of the Lord of the universe,
Presiding Devī over the City of Kāśī,
O vessel of mercy, grant me aid!

6

Īśvarī of all men on earth,
The waves of Thy blue-black hair look (beautiful) like plaits.
Īśvarī who ever giveth food,
Bestower of happiness to all, who advanceth all people,

---

[1] The Tāntrik ("seed") *mantras*, such as *Hrīm*, *Hūm*, *Klīm*, etc. *Mantras* are classified according to the syllables they contain.

[2] The Mahāmantra *Om*, composed of A + u + m, coalesced by *sandhi* into Om. The three *varṇas* signify the three members of the *Trimurti*, Brahmā, Viṣṇu, and S'iva, who, as the Rudrayāmala says, are born of the Praṇava (Om), and though in appearance three, are yet one (*ekamūrtistrayo devāh*). From the *Praṇava* all Devas, Vedas, sun, moon, and all being comes by the power of Devī, the supreme S'akti.

[3] *Mokṣā*, or unity with the supreme, and therefore liberation from rebirth in the phenomenal world.

[4] *Brahmāṇḍabhāṇḍodarī*. The *Brahmāṇḍa* (universe) is the "mundane egg" of Brahmā.

Presiding Devī over the City of Kāśi,
O vessel of mercy, grant me aid !

7

Thou givest all instruction onwards from the time of initiation,[1]
And art the cause of the threefold manifestation of S'ambhu.[2]
Scented with the Kashmir aloe, Thou art the Īśvarī of the three regions.[3]
Thou art triple waved,[4]
And the night of dissolution.
Thou art the cause of all lastings things,
And fulfiller of the desires of those who desire.
It is Thou who maketh the greatness of peoples.
Presiding Devī over the City of Kāśi,
O vessel of mercy, grant me aid !

8

Thou, Devī, art adorned with all various kinds of gems,
Daughter of Dakṣa,[5]

---

[1] *Dīkṣā,* through which each Hindu passes, by reception of his *mantra.* It is said sometimes that initiation is the third birth, the first being that from the mother, the second is *upanayana* (investiture with sacred thread), and the third is initiation. The Tantras speak of thirty-two *Dīkṣās,* from *Sudhavidyā* to *Anuttara.*

[2] That is, as creator, maintainer, and destroyer.

[3] Bhuh, Bhuvah, Svah (see p. 151, note 7)

[4] For She flows in the form of the three sacred rivers: Gangā, Yamunā, and Sarasvati.

[5] The father of Sati, a manifestation of Devī, who, dying at the *Dakṣayajna* reappeared as Pārvatī.

Beautiful, pleasing the world
With the sweet milk of Thy left breast.[1]
Thou art Maheśvarī, for Thou givest prosperity to all,
For Thou givest welfare,
And fulfillest the desires of your devotees.
Presiding Devī over the City of Benares,
O vessel of mercy, grant me aid!

9

Thou art She who shinest with the brilliance of millions of suns, moons, and fires.
Whose earrings are brilliant as the sun, moon, and fire,
Who art the cause of the colour of both sun and moon,
Who holdeth a rosary,[2] a book,[3] a noose, and a goad.[4]
Presiding Devī over the City of Benares,
O vessel of mercy, grant me aid!

10

Protectress of Kṣatriyas,[5]
Great dispeller of all fear,
Mother, who art an ocean of mercy,
In very truth the ever auspicious giver of salvation,
The cause of the beauty of Viśveśvara,[6]

---

[1] Because Ganeśa and Kārtikeya, Her children, suck Her right breast.

[2] *Mālā*.

[3] *Pustaka,* which is also known as the *Vidyāmudrā*.

[4] See p. 173, note 6.

[5] The warrior caste.

[6] Lord of the universe.

It was Thou who made Dakṣa to weep.[1]
Remover of all ills,
Presiding Devī over the City of Benares,
O vessel of mercy, grant me aid !

11

O Annapūrṇā ! who art ever full (of bounty),
Who art dear to the life of S'ankara,[2]
O Pārvatī, give me aid !

12

My mother is Devī Pārvatī,
My father is Deva Maheśvara,[3]
My friends and relatives are those who are devoted
to S'iva,
And the three regions [4] are my fatherland.

---

[1] When his *yajna* was destroyed by Her husband S'iva. There are two Dakṣas—Prajāpati, and a human king, an incarnation of the former. Though S'iva destroyed the sacrifice, Devī was the instrument. The Lalitā, verse 120, addresses the Devī both as *Dākṣāyanī* (daughter of Dakṣa) and *Dakṣayajna vināsinī* (destroyer of the sacrifice of Dakṣa).

[2] S'iva.

[3] *Ibid.*

[4] See p. 151, note 7.

GANGĀ

(GANGĀSTOTRA)

By Vālmīki[1]

1

O Mother Gangā! co-wife[2] with the daughter of
Himālaya,
Thou art the necklace on the dress of the Earth,[3]
And the banner staff whereby one ascends to
Heaven.
O Bhāgīrathī![4] I pray to Thee.
May my body perish after it has lived on Thy banks,
After it has drunk Thy pure water
And swung on Thy waves.
And has remembered Thy name and cast looks on
Thee.

2

O Mother Gangā! O deliverer from Hell!

---

[1] From the Brihatstotraratnākara, edited by Jagannātha Mehta (Benares).

[2] *Sapatnī*. Pārvatī, the daughter of Himālaya, is one wife and Gangā the other.

[3] The stream is compared to a necklace of pearls on the dress of a man or woman.

[4] So named as having been called down by Bhagīratha. *Vide ante*, p. 188, note 7.

Even a bird living in the hollow of a tree growing
on Thy bank,
Even a fish or a tortoise living in Thy waters
Are greater than a King worshipped by his
enemies' wives,
Made afraid by the sound of the bells on the necks
of his maddened elephants.[1]

3

Not even a bull or a bird or a horse,
Nor a serpent nor an elephant,
Suffer the pains of rebirth and redeath
If they live at Kāśi[2] on Thy holy banks.
Better off are they than even a Rājā living elsewhere,
Fanned though he be with the *couris*[3] of courtezans,[4]
Whose ever moving golden wristlets sweetly tinkle.

4

O our Supreme Lady Bhāgirathi![5]
O wanderer in the three regions![6]
When shall it be that I shall be fanned
By the hands of heavenly women[7] with their
beautiful *couris*?
When, too, shall I be happy enough to see my body
Pecked by crows, devoured by dogs, drawn along
the earth by jackals.

---

[1] When the bells are rubbed against the necks of the elephants. The picture is one of victory, pomp, and beauty.

[2] Benares.

[3] Whisks made of yak tails.

[4] *Vārastrī*.

[5] See p. 188, note 7.

[6] See p. 151, note 7.

[7] *Divyastrī*.

Carried by Thy currents, tossed upon Thy banks,
And borne by Thy waters to and fro!

5

May the daughter of Jahnu[1] be ever victorious and protect us,
She who is like the fresh fibrous stem of the lotus-like feet of Viṣṇu,[2]
Like a garland of jasmine[3] flowers on the head of S'iva,
Like the banner of victory of Lakṣmi presiding over liberation,
She[4] who cleanses us of the stain of sin arising from the Kaliyuga.[5]

6

May Thy sacred water be pure for my daily bathing,
Thy water covered with leaves of palm and *tamāla*,[6]
Of *Sāla*[7] and pine, with all their creepers
On which play no rays of the Sun.[7]
White and brilliant, like the conch, the Moon, and the water-lily,
Stirred by the rising breasts of the wives of the Gandharvas,

---

[1] See p. 188, note 7.

[2] Gangā was born from the feet of Viṣṇu.

[3] *Mālati*. Gangā, on Her fall from Heaven, touched the head of S'iva. There Her white encircling stream is compared to a wreath.

[4] That is, Gangā.

[5] The fourth and worst of the ages.

[6] Names of trees. The reference to pine and palm show the descent of the stream from the Himālaya to the plains of Bengal.

[7] In the caverns of the Himālaya.

Devas, Siddhas, and Kinnaras,[1]
What time they bathe therein.

7

May the water of Gangā, who ever charms, sanctify us;
She who has fallen from the feet of the enemy of Mura,[2]
Who wanders upon the head of the enemy of Tripura,[3]
The Destructress of sins.

8

May the auspicious water of Gangā ever purify us;
The Destructress of sins, the great enemy of sins,
Adorned with waves, wandering in the mountains,
Piercing through the caverns of the Lord of mountains[4]
With roaring sounds.
Stealer of the dust from the feet of Lord Hari.[5]

9

Whosoever at early dawn,
Having cleansed his body
And purified his mind

---

1 Classes of minor divinities or *Devayoni*.

2 That is, S'rīkṛṣṇa (Viṣṇu), who slew the Daitya Mura.

3 That is, S'iva, who conquered the three cities made of gold, silver, and iron of the three Asuras Kamalākṣa, Tārakakṣa, and Vidyunmāli respectively.

4 Himālaya.

5 Viṣṇu, from whose feet She was born.

Of all uncleanliness arising from the sinful
Kaliyuga,[1]
Reads this hymn to Gangā composed of eight verses,
Shall never fall into the ocean of the world again,
But shall attain liberation.

[1] *Vide ante*, p. 163, note 6,

Of all uncleanliness arising from the sinful
Kaliyuga,[1]
Reads this hymn to Gangā composed of eight verses,
Shall never fall into the ocean of the world again,
But shall attain liberation.

[1] *Vide ante*, p. 163, note 6,

3

Giver of boons art Thou to all;
Formidable terror to the wicked;
Remover of all pain and sorrow.
O Devi! salutation to Thee.

4

O Devi Mahālakṣmi!
Thou art the giver of intelligence and success,
And of both worldly enjoyment and liberation.
Thou art the self of *Mantra*.[1]
O Mahālakṣmi! obeisance to Thee.

5

Thou art without beginning or end.
O Supreme Devi Mahālakṣmi!
Thou art the primeval power,
And art born of *yoga*.
O Mahālakṣmi! salutation to Thee.

6

Thou art both gross and subtle,[2]
Thou art terrible and a great power,
Great-bellied art Thou.[3]
Thou removeth all great sins.
O Mahālakṣmi! obeisance to Thee.

---

[1] *Mantrātmikā* (see Introduction).

[2] See Introduction.

[3] *Mahodari*, for all things are in Her.

7

O Devī Mahālakṣmi !
Thou art the supreme Brahman,
The ever-pervading *Ātman*.
Thou art the great Lord [1]
And Mother of the world.
O Mahālakṣmi ! Salutation to Thee.

8

O Devi clad in white raiment,[2]
Adorned with varied gems.
Mother and upholder of the world art Thou.
O Mahālakṣmi ! obeisance to Thee.

9

The *Sādhaka* [3] who ever reads [4] this hymn to Mahālaksmi.
Composed of eight verses,
Attains a kingdom and all success.

10

Whosoever reads this hymn once a day
Is freed from sin,
He who reads it twice a day
Has ever abundance of paddy [5] and wealth.

---

[1] Maheśvarī.

[2] Lakṣmī is generally clad in red and Sarasvati in white, but the Supreme S'akti has all the attributes and qualities of the rest.

[3] Worshipper. See *Introduction to Tantra S'āstra*.

[4] Here follows the *phala* portion of the *stotra*.

[5] When *pūjā* is done to Lakṣmi, the *Mūrti* (*Lakṣmirkānta*) is placed on paddy, which is kept in the Thakurghar for a whole year, and then thrown into the Ganges.

11

Whosoever reads this hymn thrice a day,
All his great enemies perish ;
Mahālakṣmi ever bestows Her grace on him,
Grants him all boons,
And does him all good.

HYMN TO KALI

(KARPŪRĀDI-STOTRA)

PREFACE

THIS celebrated Kaula *Stotra*, which is now translated from the Sanskrit for the first time, is attributed to Mahākāla Himself. The Text used is that of the edition published at Calcutta in 1899 by the Sanskrit Press Depository, with a commentary in Sanskrit by the late Mahāmahopādhyāya Kṛṣṇanātha Nyāya-Pañcānana, who was both very learned in Tantra-S'āstra and faithful to his Dharma. He thus refused the offer of a good Government post made to him personally by a former Lieutenant-Governor on the ground that he would not accept money for imparting knowledge.

Some variants in reading are supplied by this commentator. I am indebted to him for the Notes, or substance of the notes, marked K. B. To these I have added others, both in English and Sanskrit explaining matters and allusions familiar doubtless to those for whom the original was designed, but not so to the English or even ordinary Indian reader. I have also referred to the edition of the *Stotra* published by the Gaṇeśa-Candra-Ghoṣa at Calcutta in 1891, with a translation in Bengali by Gurunātha Vidyānidhi, and a commentary by Durgārāma-Siddhāntavāgiśa Bhattācārya. I publish for the first time Vimalānanda-Svāmī's Commentary to which I again refer later. When in this Introduction or in the Commentary I have not mentioned these two works my authorities are the

Tantras or Tāntrik works which I cite, or the information I have gathered from those whom I have consulted.

One of the chief features of this *Stotra* is that it gives the *mantroddhāra* of the Dakṣiṇā-Kālikā. It not only gives us the *Dhyāna*, *Yantra*, *Sādhana* and *Svarūpa-varṇanā* of the Mahādevi, but it also contains the chief Mantras of Dakṣiṇākālikā. The adjective "*Tava manu-samuddharaṇajanu*" qualifying "*idam stotram*" in S'loka 21 expressly states this fact.

Among the various Mantras of Dakṣiṇā Kālikā the greatest is the "*Vidyā-rājñī*" consisting of 22 syllables (*Dvāviṁsākṣarī*). The mantra gives the fullest and the truest symbol of the Svarūpa of Her. This *mantra* is contained in the first five S'lokas.

The first	S'loka	contains	*Krīṁ, Krīṁ, Krīṁ*	(3 *akṣaras*)
2nd	,,	,,	*Hūṁ, Hūṁ*	(2 ,,)
3rd	,,	,,	*Hrīṁ, Hrīṁ*	(2 ,,)
4th	,,	,,	*Dakṣiṇe Kālike*	(6 ,,)
5th	,,	,,	*Krīṁ, Krīṁ, Krīṁ, Hūṁ, Hūṁ, Hrīṁ, Hrīṁ, Svāhā*	(9 *akṣaras*)

So the first five S'lokas give us altogether 22 *akṣaras* *i.e.* the full *Vidyārājñī*.

In Vimalānanda-Svāmī's *Tīkā* of the 5th S'loka in the revised Sanskrit text he has proved by quotations from the 9th paṭala of S'āktānanda-taraṅgiṇī that this 22-syllabled *mantra* is the full and true representation of the Svarūpa of the Mahādevi. See the quotation which begins with

"*Krīm-kāro mastakaṁ devi Krīm-kāraśca lalāṭakaṁ*"

and ends with

"*S'vā-śabdena pada-dvandvam hā-kāreṇa nakhaṁ tathā*"

The words "*Svarūpaṁ*" (5th sl.) and "*Sakalaṁ*" (6th sl.) point to this *Vidyārājñī*. After the full *Vidyārājñī* has been given in the first five S'lokas, the 6th S'loka gives the various other Mantras of less importance and significance—ranging from one syllabled to nine-syllabled, 15-syllabled, 21-syllabled and so forth.

This Mantroddhāra has been made following the authority of Kālikā-śruti, Niruttara-Tantra and other Tantras. Many commentators, however, have apparently in the view of Vimalānanda failed to consult the above authorities and have thus fallen into errors and have given a different *Mantroddhāra*. Some take the 1st S'loka to give a one-syllabled *mantra*, the 2nd sloka as also the 3rd, two two-syllabled *mantras*, the 5th a nine-syllabled one and so on : a view which it is contended is opposite to such passages as "*atha hainaṁ brahmarandhre brahma-svarūpinim āpnoti........bṛhad-bhānu-jāyāṁ uccaret*" in the 1st Sūkta of Kālikopaniṣad ; or passages in Niruttara-Tantra (Ch. II) beginning with "*Atha vaksye Kuleśāni Dakṣiṇā-kālikā-manuṁ*" and ending with "*Sarva-mantra-mayi vidyā sṛṣṭi-sthityanta-kāriṇi.*" The Svāmī further refers me to the end of the Kālikopaniṣad where dealing with the various Mantras of the Dakṣiṇā-Kālikā it is said "*Atha sarvām vidyām prathamaṁ ekaṁ dvayaṁ vā trayaṁ vā nāmatrayaputitaṁ vā kṛtvā japet.*" The great Tāntrik Pūrṇānanda Giri explaining the passage says "*Sarvām vidyām-iti pūrvoktadvāvimśatyakṣaryāh prathama bījaṁ vā bījadvayaṁ vā* etc. (*vide* S'yāmā-rahasyaṁ, Rasikamohan's edition, p. 36.)

From the above consideration, it is clear that at the very beginning in the first 5 S'lokas the 22-syllabled *Mantra* is given and then the others. It may be added here that the fact of Mahākāla's composing the Hymn in 22 S'lokas not more nor less—is also an indication of the correctness of the Svāmī's view, who, in further support of it cites 5 S'lokas dealing with the *Mantroddhāra* from the *Krama-stava* of the Dakṣiṇā-Kālikā under the first 5 Slokas of the Karpūrādi, which will be found in the printed text.

In course of revising his *Vyākhyā* Vimalānanda-Svāmī has in the first six S'lokas given good grounds to prove that the *Stotra* not only contains the *Mantroddhāra* and the *Sādhana* of S'rī-S'rī-Dakṣiṇā-Kālikā but also in it are given the *Mantras* and *Rahasyapūja* of S'rī-S'rī-Tāra and S'rī-S'rī-Tripura-sundari.

In addition to the Mantroddhāra the following matters are contained in the *Stotra*.

		No. of Slokas
Dhyāna	.. ..	1, 2, 3, 4, 5, 6, 7, 8, 11
Yantra	.. ..	18
Sādhana	.. ..	10, 11, 15, 16, 17, 18, 19, 20
Madya	.. ..	13
Māṁsa	.. ..	19
Maithuna	.. ..	10
Phala-śruti	.. ..	21, 22

The Slokas 9, 12, 14 contain *stuti* only.

S'lokas 10, 15-18, 20 refer to the Tāntrik *vīrācāra-sādhana*. *Vīrācāra* is for the class of *sādhaka* who are *vīra-bhāva* and *abhiṣikta*. To those who follow *paśvācāra* this ritual is strictly forbidden. The nature of the *rahasya-pūjā* is indicated in the text, to which I have added an explanatory commentary in English.

To the *Paśu*, *sādhana* by night is prohibited, for it connotes in S'ākta-sādhana, worship with the *Pañcatattva*. The *Paśu* is still bound by the *pāśa* (bonds) of desire, etc., and he is, therefore, not *adhikārī*, for that which, if undertaken by the unfit, will only make these bonds stronger. For him, on the contrary, there are severe restrictions in this matter, for, as the S'āktakrama cited by the commentator says *Maithunaṁ tatkathālāpaṁ tadgoṣṭhiṁ parivarjayet.*" (The *Paśu* should avoid *maithuna*, conversation on the subject, and the like.) The *Paśu* should avoid the eight forms of *maithuna* known as *aṣṭāṅga maithuna*— viz., *smaraṇaṁ* (thinking upon it), *kīrtanam* (talking of it), *kelih* (play with women), *prekṣaṇam* (looking upon women), *guhyabhāṣaṇaṁ* (talk in private with women), *saṁkalpa* (wish or resolve for *maithuna*), *adhyavasāyah* (determination towards it), as well as *kriyāniṣpattih* (actual accomplishment). The Nityā Tantra, which the commentator cites, says: "*Rātrau naiva yajed devīṁ sandhyāyāṁ vā'parāhnake*"—"He (the *Paśu*) should never worship the Devī during the latter part of the day or in the evening or at night." To this, from amongst many other authorities, I may add the Svatantra, which says that the Paśubhāva Sādhaka should do one lakh of *japa* in day time and that a *Vīra* devoted to his own Ācāra should do one lakh of *japa* at night :

Paśubhāvarato mantrī divā lakṣa-japaṁ caret.
Svācāranirato vīro rātrau lakṣa-japaṁ caret.

In connection with this verse I must observe that in the notes to verse 20 it is said that the first half of the 20th S'loka is meant for "*Paśusādhakas*" and that the 2nd half refers to the "*pūrṇābhiṣiktavīrasādhaka,*" as also that the word "*paraṁ*" (afterwards) means and refers to the time when the '*Paśu*' having received *abhiṣeka* enters *vīrācāra* and is *adhikārī* for the midnight *puraścaraṇa*. Vimalānanda tells me that this is wrong and that the whole S'loka has reference to the *vīra* or *divya-sādhaka* and that no portion of it refers to the *Paśu-sādhaka*.

The quotation just made from the Svatantra-Tantra no doubt seems to lend support to the view that the first part of the S'loka refers to the Paśu, but he informs me and I fully accept the correction that he and other followers of the Sāstra knew the passage to bear a meaning which is consonant with his view, that is, it means this :—*Mantrī* means the *vīrasādhaka*; the *mantrī* should perform *lakṣa-japa* in the day time following the *ācāra* of the *paśu* (*paśu-bhāvaratah*). The *vīra-sādhaka* should perform *lakṣa-japa* in the night following his own *ācāra* (*svācāra-niratah*). The word "*svācāra*" (own *ācāra*) points to his interpretation being correct.

In support of his view the Svāmi cites the following Verses which all say the same thing namely that the initiate should be Brahmacārī during day and at night worship according to Kulācācāra. Kaulāvalī says:

Naktaṁ-bhojī hāviṣyānnaṁ japed vidyām divā śucih.
Dvivāsāh sarvathā vīro brahmacārī bhavet sadā.
Rātrau saṁpūjāyed devīṁ kulācāra-krameṇa tu
Dvijanmanāṁ tu sarveṣām dvidhā vidhi-rihocyate.

Again, Kālikopaniṣad says:

S'āṁbhava-dīksāsu ratah śākteṣu vā divā brahmacārī rātrau nagnah sadā maithunāsaktamānasah Japa-pūjādiniyamaṁ kuryād iti.

Kaulāvalī again says:

Unmukhyāh Kālikāyāśca viśeṣah kathyate' dhunā
Divase brahmacaryeṇa sviyasaṁkhyājapaṁ caret.
Rātrau māṁsāsavairmatsyairmudrābhir maithunodbhavaih.

The reason of the *vīrasādhaka* being instructed to adopt the *ācāra* of *brahmacārī* in the day-time is the necessity for the concealment of the *vīrācāra* from the public which Tantra so often insists upon. S'iva says that *virācāra* cannot be understood aright by the common people and therefore must be concealed, as closely as a man should conceal his own mother's sin " *gopayet mātṛ-jāra-vat.*"

Moreover, the worship of Kālī in "*paśvācāra*" is totally forbidden by S'iva. The *Paśu* is precluded by Tantra from the worship of Kālī. For example, the Niruttara-Tantra says:

Divya-bhāvaṁ vīra-bhāvaṁ vinā Kālīṁ prapūjayet.
Pūjane narakaṁ yāti tasya duhkhaṁ pade pade.
Paṣubhāva-rato devi yadi Kālīṁ prapūjayet.
Rauravaṁ narakaṁ yāti yāvad ābhūta-saṁplavaṁ.

(By the worship of Kālī without *Divyabhāva* and *Vīrabhāva* the worshipper suffers pain at every step and goes to hell. If a man who is of the *Paśubhāva* worships Kālī then he goes to the *Raurava* Hell until the time of final dissolution).

Vimalānanda-S'vāmi says: The worship of Kālī without the use of wine, though seen in many places, is Paurāṇik and not Tāntrik (*i.e.* sanctioned by the Tantra.)

Verses 1-8, 11, the first part of verse 20, and 21 (except at midnight) deal with *japa* of the *mantra* of, and *dhyāna* upon, the Devī, which, of course, may be done by the *Paśu*. Verses 9, 12, 13 and 14 are *stuti*, and 22 is the usual *phalaśloka*, which states the reward to be gained by the reading of the *Stotra*.

Verses 10, 15-18, and the second portion of verse 20 deal with *Latāsādhana*. The *śakti* of this *sādhana* is ordinarily the own wife of the *sādhaka*, married according to the Vaidik injunctions; the *svaśakti* or *ādyāśakti*, as she is technically called in Tantra. One's own wife is *Ādyā*-S'akti and *Sādhana* should be done with her aid (*Adyā-śaktiḥ svadārāḥ syāt tāmevāśṛtya sādhayet*). With her is practised that *śaktisādhana*, the aim of which is the acquirement of self-control, which, checking the outward-going current, places the *sādhaka* upon the path of *nivṛtti*. Indeed, the Kaulikārcanadipikā says, "Without *ādyā śakti* worship is but evil magic". (*Ādyāśaktiṁ vinā pūjā abhicārāya kalpate*). It is only the *siddha*, which term is here used in the special sense of one who has obtained complete control over his passions, to whom is permitted another *śakti* (*paraśakti*). So the Prāṇatoṣinī quotes, "a man shall obtain *siddhi* with his own *śakti*, and afterwards (that is, when he is *siddha*) he should make *japa* with *paraśakti*" (*Svaśaktau siddhim āpnuyāt paraśaktau tadā japet*). And similarly Niruttara Tantra says, that the *sādhaka* who is *siddha* in Kulācārā may worship "another" woman. (*Siddhamantrī kulācāre parayoṣām prapūjayet*). In both these cases *paraśakti* has a double meaning *viz*., "another" woman that is corporeal woman, or "Supreme" that is the Supreme Woman who in the body is Kuṇḍalinī-S'akti. This latter appears to be the sense in the quotation which speaks of the *siddhamantrī*. It has been said also, as in the Mahānirvāṇa Tantra, that *paraśakti* must (if unmarried) be married either by Vaidika or S'aiva rites, or (if married and the husband is dead) according to the latter rite. Further, that which determines the moral character of an act is the intention with which it is done. As the Kaulāvalīya says, when a man's intention is bad then his act is so, otherwise there is no fault :

Ata eva yadā yasya vāsanā kutsitā bhavet.
Tadā doṣāya bhavati nānyathā dūṣaṇaṁ kvacit.

As an example of the same act and varying intention, it is aptly said: "A wife is kissed with one feeling and a daughter's face with another". (*Bhāvena cumbitā kāntā bhāvena duhitrānanam*). A *Mantrin* who is given over to lust, for the subjugation of which the *sādhana* is prescribed, goes, as is said in the Tantrasāra, to the Hell called Raurava. (*Lingayonirato mantri raurakam narakam brajet*). In the words of the Āhārabheda-Tantra—*Vāmācāro bhavet tatra vāmā bhūtvā yajet parām.* "One may be a *Vāmācāri* if one can worship *Vāmā* being oneself a woman." This is on the principle that a worshipper should always be like the object of his worship. Woman is *Devatā*, and the embodiment of the Supreme S'akti, and is as such honoured and worshipped, and is, when *pūjyā śakti* never the subject of enjoyment.

Verses 15 and 16, as sufficiently appears from their context, refer to the *sādhana* of those who are not *siddha.*

Verses 10, 17 and 18 apply to both *sādhaka* and *siddha*; as to verse 20, see pp. 238, 239 *ante*.

By such *sādhana* the last vestiges of the most powerful of such bonds is sought to be destroyed, and with such destruction the seed of *karma* and rebirth. He, like S'iva, becomes destroyer of Smara, and S'iva Himself. Verses 4, 18 and 20 refer directly to this fruit of *sādhana*. Others indicate the material and intellectual greatness on earth of the *sādhaka*, who devoutly worships the Devi. To him is given mastery over all persons and things of the world, which on death, if *siddha*, he leaves for the dwelling by the Supreme Feet (verse 17), or Nirvāṇa. As S'iva says in the Kālīvilāsa-Tantra "I have told you, my beloved, all about the five Tattvas, Sādhana in the cremation ground and with the funeral pyre; now listen to the doctrine of the Siddha-vīra."

Madyaṁ matsyaṁ tathā māṁsaṁ mudrāṁ maithunam eva ca
Śmaśānasādhanaṁ bhadre citāsādhanam eva ca.
Etat te kathitaṁ sarvaṁ siddhavīramataṁ śṛṇu.

It is the *sādhana* of the cremation-ground on which all passion is burnt away. There are two kinds of cremation-ground, of which the one is the funeral pyre (*citā*), and the other *yonirūpā mahākālī*. As the first Chapter of the Niruttara-Tantra says there are two cremation grounds namely that which is the funeral pyre and *yoni* which, in its *sūkṣma* sense, is the Devī, the *śmaśāna* being in the same sense dissolution or *pralaya*. (*Śmaśānaṁ dvividhaṁ devi citā yoni prakīrtitā*). In even the *sthūla* sense the *sādhaka* must be *susādhaka*, for union without right disposition—*japa*, *dhyāna* etc.—is the animal *maithuna* of a *paśu*.

Sloka 19 refers to animal and human sacrifice to Kālī. Reference to this sacrifice is also made in the Kālikā-Purāṇa, and the Tantrasāra speaks of a substitute in the figure of a man made of the paste of cereals. The latter work also says that by the sacrifice of a man one acquires great prosperity, and the eight *siddhis*. (*Naradatte maharddhih syād aṣṭasiddhir-anuttamā*). But it adds that this is not for all. For the Brāhmaṇa may not make such a sacrifice. (*Brāhmaṇānāṁ narabalidāne nādhikārah*). And if he does so, he goes to Hell. Moreover according to K. B., who cites as his authority the Yāmala quoted in the Kālikalpalatā, the King alone can make such a sacrifice.

This leads one to point out that the Hymn has other than these gross (*Sthūla*) meanings. In Brāhmanism everything has three aspects—Supreme (*Para*),

Subtle (*Sūkṣma*) and Gross (*Sthūla*). Thus the nineteenth S'loka when referring to the sacrifice of various animals and of man himself intends according to the subtle sense the six great sins for which they stand, ranging from Lust (goat) to Pride (man). It is these which must be sacrificed by the knowers who are worshippers of the Mother, the age of material sacrifice, so universal throughout the world, having passed away. So again the word Paraśakti may refer to the Supreme S'akti or may be used in the sense of a S'akti other than the *svaśakti* or Sādhaka's wife who, may, in the case of the competent (*adhikārī*), be an associate in the worship on the principle stated in the Guhyakālīkhaṇḍa of the Mahākāla-Saṁhitā.

" As is the competency of the Sādhaka, so must be that of the Sādhika. In this way only is success attained and not otherwise even in ten million years ".

Yādṛśah sādhakah proktah Sādhikā'pi ca tādṛśah
Tatah siddhim-avāpnoti nānyathā varṣa-kotibhih.

This principle rests on the fact that man and woman together make one whole and can only co-operate in the rites where the attainments or *Adhikāra* of each is the same. But this does not necessarily mean that such co-operation is by *Maithuna* in its sexual sense; quite the contrary. In the same way in the Vaidik ritual the wife is *Sahadharmiṇi*. But such ritual is only for the competent within the bounds of S'āstric injunction for, as the S'aktisaṅgama Tantra (Part IV) says,— " Though a man be a knower of the three times, past, present and future and though he be a controller of the three worlds, even then he should not transgress the rules of conduct for men in the world were it only in his mind ".

Yadyapyasti trikālajñas-trailokyāvarṣaṇakṣamāh.
Tathā'pi laukikācāram manasā'pi na laṅghayet.

But *Paraśakti* again may mean no woman at all, but Supreme S'akti or the Mother Herself whose forms they are and in such sense the union of the Sādhaka is with the "Woman" within himself—the Kuṇḍalinī S'akti who in Yoga unites with Her Supreme Husband Paramaśiva. (See *The Serpent Power*). The context must be known as in the misunderstood saying "*Maithunena mahāyogī mama tulyo na saṁśayah*," which does not mean, as a recent English work on Hinduism suggests, that by sexual connection (*Maithuna*) the *Mahāyogī* becomes without doubt the equal of S'iva or God. This is on its face absurd and had it not been that such criticism is clouded with prejudice the absurdity would be recognised. How can sexual connection make any one God or His equal? The person spoken of is a *Mahāyogī* who. as such, has no connection physical or otherwise with women. *Maithuna* means "action and reaction" and "coupling" and sexual intercourse is only *one form* of such coupling. Thus when Mantra is said there is a coupling or *Maithuna* of the lips. In Yoga there is a coupling (*Maithuna*) of the active and changeless Principles of the Universe. The saying means that the *Mahāyogī* who unites Kuṇḍali-S'akti in his body with Paramaśiva becomes himself S'iva.

So again it is said in an apparently alarming verse quoted by Tarkālaṁkāra, in his commentary on the Mahānirvāṇa.

Mātṛ-yonau kṣipet lingam bhaginyāh-stanamardanaṁ
Guror-mūrdhni padaṁ dattvā punarjanma na vidyate.

This verse in its literal sense means that if any one commits incest with his mother and sister and places his foot on the head of his Guru he is liberated and is never again reborn. But of course that is not the meaning. The first half of the line refers to the placing of the *Jīvātmā* in the triangle situated in the *Mūlādhāra* centre with the *Svayaṁbhuliṅga* in it which triangle is called *Mātṛ-yoni*. The *Liṅga* is the *Jīvātmā*. From this point upwards, after union with Kuṇḍalinī, the *Jīvātmā* is to be led. The union of *Jīvātmā* with Kuṇḍalinī is spoken of in the second half of the first line. Kuṇḍalinī is the sister of the *Jīvātmā* both being in the same body. The meaning of the last line is as follows:—after union of Kuṇḍalinī and *Jīvātmā* the united couple are led up to the *Sahasrāra* or thousand-petalled lotus in the head which is situated above the twelve-petalled lotus which again is the abode of the Guru. When the Yogī is above the twelve-petalled lotus his feet may be described as being on the head of the Guru. Moreover it is said that at this point the relationship of Guru and disciple ceases. *Mātṛ-yoni* is also the term given to those sections of the fingers between the joints on which count of the Japa or recital of the mantra is *not* to be done. If *Mātṛ-yonim* suggests incest, then this verse is a prohibition of it—*Mātṛ-yonim parityajya viharet sarva-yoniṣu*. There are many other technical terms in Tantra-Śāstra which it is advisable to know before criticising it. One of the tests to which an intending disciple may be put consists in being questioned as to such passages. If he is a gross-minded or stupid man his answer will show it.

In order therefore that the Hymn may be understood in its various aspects I have given in the notes explanations of or in respect of its *Sthūla* or gross meaning. This is followed by the valuable commentary given to me, some years ago and now first published, by Vimalānanda-Svāmī which is called *Svarūpavyākhyā*; that is, it gives the subtle (*Sūkṣma*) or, as we should say in English, the inner sense or esoteric meaning according to the teaching of his own Guru Mahāmahopādhyāya - Rāmānandasvāmī - Siddhānta-pañcānana. The text books and Commentary are preceded by an admirable little essay of Svāmī Vimalānanda by way of Introduction to the *Vimalānandadāyinī svarūpa-vyākhyā* on his "Lord of Hymns" which is commonly known as the Karpūrādi Stotra chanted by Mahākāla to, and in honour of, Dakṣiṇā-Kālikā. It, as also the inner-sense Commentary, is written for those liberation-seeking Sādhakas who, worshipping S'rīvidyā, meditate not on the gross form (*Sthūlamūrti*) but on the *Svarūpa-tattva* of Brahma-vidyā Kālikā. As such many will be glad, as I was, to read it and will derive benefit therefrom.

I may note here that the Svāmī while revising the Vyākhyā, has given a new interpretation of the line "*te Lakṣmī-lāsya-līlā-kamala-dala-dṛśah vāma - rūpāh bhavanti*" in the 5th S'loka and of "*rati-rasamahā-nanda-niratām*" in the 13th S'loka.

On the attainment of *siddhi*, ritual ceases. There is neither sacrifice nor worship, nor *yoga*, *puraścaraṇa*, *vrata*, *japa*, or other *karma*. For all *sādhana* ceases when it has borne its fruit in *Siddhi*. The Siddha - Kaula is beyond all rules.

For the meaning of these and other terms, the reader is referred to the Author's Principles of Tantra, (Tantra-tattva)," "S'akti and S'ākta," "The Serpent Power" and "Garland of Letters" which is a study on the Mantra - S'āstra; and for other Hymns to the Devi, his and Ellen Avalon's "Hymns to the

Goddess," translated from the Sanskrit of the Tantra, Purāṇa, and the Devi-stotra of Śaṁkarācārya, which gives other specimens of the Hindu Hymnal, of which that now published is but one and a special type.

Puri JOHN WOODROFFE

30 May, 1922

---

* HYMNS TO THE GODDESS and HYMN TO KALI are now published together in this book. (PUBLISHERS' NOTE).

INVOCATION

AIM

I make obeisance to the Lord Guru, the wish granting Tree of Suras, eternal Consciousness and Bliss Itself, the highest of the highest, Brahman, Śiva Himself. I make obeisance to Her who by Her Śakti of three Guṇas creates, maintains, and at the end of the Kalpa withdraws, the world and then alone is. Devoutly I call to mind Her, the Mother of the whole universe, Śivé Herself.

OM

Obeisance to the Supreme Devatā

Here follows an Introduction to the Vimalānandadāyini Commentary on that Lord of Hymns called the Karpūrādi-Stotra to Śrimad Dakṣiṇa-Kālikā.

All-good and all-powerful Parameśvara is without beginning or end. Though in Himself Nirguṇa He is the Ādhāra of the three Guṇas. Though Himself formless He creates, preserves and withdraws the world of extended matter (Prapañca) by means of the Āvaraṇa and Vikṣepa-Śaktis of His own Māyā which can make that possible which seems impossible. The Śvetāśvatara-Upaniṣad says that by meditation was seen the Sva-śakti of the Deva, who is the abode of all causes, associated with Kālatattva. In the Niruttara-Tantra Śiva peaks of the three-eyed corpse-like One,

Nirguṇa but also seat of Guṇas associated with S'akti. Though Himself without beginning, middle or end, He creates and is the material Cause of the world which has a beginning, middle, and end. For this reason the Tantras and other S'astras call Him Ādinātha, Mahākāla, Paramaśiva and Paramabrahman. It is this unlimited, undivided, beginningless, and endless Mahākāla who is imagined to be limited by the Sun, moon and Planets, and, as such, is called by the names of Kāla, Kāṣṭhā, Muhūrta, Yāma, Day, Night, Pakṣa, Month, Season, Half-year, Year, Yuga, Kalpa and so forth. It is He who divides Time into Kāla, Kāṣṭhā and so forth, and as Vyaṣṭi is called by the name Kāla, and the rest. He is named Paramaśiva Mahākāla when creating, preserving and withdrawing the millions of worlds.

Apart from individual name and form, He exists as the Samaṣṭi of them and the Endless Supreme Greatness (Paramomahān). Viṣṇu-Purāṇā says that Bhagavān Kāla is without beginning or end. From him appears the limited in creation. Atharvaveda says that Kāla created beings (Prajā); He is Prajāpati. From Kāla was self-born Kaśyapa and Tapas. Mahākāla is omniscient since He is all-pervading, dependent on none, and the Ātmā of all. Kūrma-Purāṇa also says that he is the Supreme, imperishable, without beginning or end, all-pervading, independent, the Ātmā of all who fascinates (Manohara) all minds by His greatness. Kālamādhava cites Viṣṇu-dharmottara as saying that He is called Kāla because of his dissolving (Kalanāt) all beings, and He is Parameśvara because He is Himself without beginning or end. Mahākāla is Himself Nirguṇa and Niṣkriya, but his S'akti makes the Sun and other heavenly lights rise, stay and set.

It is by the Power of the S'akti of Kāla that men
and other Jīvas are conceived in the womb, are born,
attain childhood, boyhood, middle and old age and
leave the world on death. In the S'āntiparva of Mahābhārata, Vedavyāsa says that it is through Kāla that
women bear, that birth and death occur, winter, sum-
mer and rains come, and the seed germinates. Even
Brahmā, Viṣṇu and Rudra appear, stay and disappear
through the S'akti of Kāla. None can escape Its operation. Viṣṇu-Saṁhitā says that even those Devas who
create and withdraw the world are themselves with-
drawn by Kāla. Kāla or time is certainly then the
stronger. Mahākāla is called Mahākālī because He is
one and the same and not different from His eternal
S'akti. It is She who is Mahāvidyā, Mahādevī, Mahāmāyā, and Parabrahmarūpiṇī. As Ādinātha Mahākāla is the first creator of the world so the S'akti of
Mahākāla, the merciful Mahākālī is the Ādiguru of
the world. Yoginī Tantra says that Mahākālī is the
Mother of the world. and one with Mahākāla, as is
shown in the Ardhanārīśvara Mūrti.

It was this Brahmavidyā who (Yoginī-Tantra, 10th
Paṭala) at the beginning of this Kalpa was heard as a
bodiless voice from the sky by Brahmā, Viṣṇu, and
Maheśvara, who were then told to perform Tapasyā
for the acquisition of creative and other S'aktis. It
was this Aniruddha-saraśvatī who in the Satyayuga
appeared in the Heavens before Indra and other proud
Devatās in the form of a brilliant Yakṣa, and crushing
the pride of the Devas Agni and Vāyu, in the form of
all-beautiful Umā, taught Brahmatattva to Indra, the
King of the Devas (See Kenopaniṣad 11, 12).

This Kālī again who is Parameṣṭiguru and grants
Kaivalya, compassionating the sensuous and short-

lived Jīvas of the terrible Kaliyuga revealed the S'āṁbhavī-Vidyā. This, which was taught in the form of conversations between Devī and Īśvara, had been during the three preceding ages kept as concealed as a lady of high family from public gaze. It contained three sets of sixty-four Āgamas each, which revealed the path of Liberation for these Jīvas. Though She is Herself eternal and Saccidānandarūpiṇī, She at times out of compassion for Sādhakas assumes forms fitted for their Sādhanā. Similarly the Veda, Āgama and the rest though everlasting portions of the S'abda-brahmarūpiṇī are only revealed to Sādhakas at different times in the several Yugas.

When the Mahādevī who is Consciousness (Cinmayī) at the beginning of the Kalpa was pleased by the Tapasyā of Deva Rudra, floating on the Causal Waters, She assumed the Virāt aspect and became thus visible to Him. At that time by the command of Mahādevī the Deva Rudra saw in the Suṣumnā millions of universes (Brahmāṇḍa) and millions of Brahmās, Viṣṇus and Maheśvaras in them. The Deva, greatly wondering in the Heart-Lotus of Mahādevī, there saw the Mūrti of S'abdabrahman consisting of Āgamas, Nigamas, and other S'āstras (See Yoginī-Tantra, 9th Paṭala). He saw that of that Mūrti, Āgama was the Paramātmā, the four Vedas with their Angas were the Jīvātmā, the six systems of philosophy (Darśana) were the senses, the Mahāpurāṇas and Upapurāṇas were the gross body, the S'mṛtis were the hands and other limbs, and all other S'āstras were the hairs of that great Body. He also saw the fifty Mātṛkā (Letters) resplendent with Tejas on the edges and petals of Her Heart-Lotus. Within the pericarp of the Lotus of the Virātrūpiṇī He saw the Āgamas, brilliant as millions of suns and moons, replete with all Dharma and Brahmajñāna, powerful to destroy all Māyā, full of all Siddhis and Brahmanirvāṇa. By the grace of Mahākāli he fully mastered the Veda, Vedānta, Purāṇas, Smṛiti and all other S'astra. Later, Brahmā and Viṣṇu received this knowledge of Āgama and Nigama from Him.

In the Satyayuga Brahmā revealed the Smṛtis, Purāṇas and other S'āstra to the Devarṣis. In this way Brahmavidyā was promulgated to the world. This therefore is authority to show, that just as Brahman is everlasting, so are the Āgamas and Nigamas which tell of Brahman. Just as in the Satya and other Yugas, only the three twice-born castes, wearing the sacred thread, but not the S'ūdra and other low castes were entitled to worship according to the Veda, so in those three Yugas only Devarṣis, Brahmarṣis and Rājarṣis, who had conquered their passions and knew Advaita doctrine and Brahman, were entitled to the Āgama S'āstra which destroys all sense of difference caused by ignorance and grants knowledge of Advaitatattva.

By S'iva's command they kept it as secret in their heart as they would a knowledge of their own mother's illicit love. By Upāsanā they became liberated whilst yet living (Jivanmukta) and attained to Brahmanirvāṇa. At that time the Upāsanā of the Āgama was unknown to Sādhakas devoted to Karma. For this reason many people nowadays think the Tantra-śāstra to be of recent origin. Probably all know that in the first three Yugas Brāhmaṇa boys, after investiture with the sacred thread, used to learn the Karmakāṇḍa and Jñānakāṇḍa of the Veda orally from thir preceptors. The Veda was not then classified or reduced to writing.

Towards the close of the Dvāparayuga, Śrikṛṣṇa-dvaipāyana Maharṣi Vedavyāsa divided the Veda into four parts and reduced it to writing. This however does not show that the Veda is a recent production. The Supreme Science (Para vidyā) which is contained in the Āgama was also handed down from generation to generation of Gurus in the first three Yugas and is being now similarly transmitted. Towards the end of the Dvāparayuga, and at the beginning of the Kali age, merciful Śiva impelled by compassion for humanity bound in the toils of ignorance, divided the Tantraśāstra, which is unlimited knowledge, into three sets of sixty-four parts each, according to the necessity of different Adhikāris, and then told them to Gaṇapati and Kārtikeya the two beloved sons of Pārvati. They repeated these Tantras to Ṛṣis of Siddhāśramas, and these last, in their turn, told them to their own disciples. Of the Ṛṣis who knew Āgama the chief was Dattātreya, an incarnation of Viṣṇu. At the beginning of the Kalpa the ancient Brahmavidyā contained in the Āgama appeared from out the Parameṣṭi-guru who is Mahābrahmavidyā and exists in man's heart unlimited and imperishable. If Sādhanā is done according to the instructions of a Sadguru it becomes visible in the Sādhaka's heart. Upāsanā, in the Vaidik form, predominated in the Satyayuga. In those days Brāhmaṇas, and other twice-born castes, impelled by a desire for wealth, progeny and so forth used to worship Indra, Agni, Vāyu, Sūrya, Soma, Varuṇa and other Devas presiding over particular Śaktis of Parameśvara in whom all Śaktis reside. But desire-free Brahmarṣis and Maharṣis did Sādhanā of Brahmavidyā the full and perfect Śakti. And so we see in the tenth Maṇḍala of the Ṛgveda-Saṁhitā that Mahādevī appeared in the heart of the daughter of Maharṣi Āmbhṛṇī and so told the true nature of Brahmavidyā to Ṛṣis. This is the Devīsūkta full of Advaitatattva, the Hymn telling of the true nature of Brahma-vidyā in the Veda. In the Tretā and other Yugas the Brāhmaṇas and other twice-born devoted to the Karmakāṇḍa used to perform Yajñas and so forth, according to the Smṛtiśāstras of Manu and others. But Brahmarṣi Vaśiṣṭha (in Cīnācāra), Rājarṣi Viśvāmitra (see Gandharva-Tantra, First Paṭala), Videharāja Janaka, Bhṛgurāma the son of Jamadagni (see Kālīkulasarvasva), S'rī Rāmacandra and other high-souled men were worshippers of Brahmavidyā, the full and perfect S'akti. Again in the Dvāparayuga, despite the existence of Vaidik and Smārta cults, the Agnihotra Yajña and other rites used to be performed according to the Purāṇas. But high-souled S'rīkṛṣṇa the son of Vāsudeva (see Rādha Tantra, Devī Bhāgavata and Mahābhārata, Anuśāsana Parva, Ch. 14), the five Pāndavas namely Yudhiṣṭhira and others (Virāṭa Parva, Ch. 6), the high-souled Rājarṣi Bhiṣma, the great Muni Vedavyāsa, high-souled S'ukadeva, Asita, Devala and Brahmarṣis such as Durvāsā were worshippers of Mahāvidya the perfect S'akti. Of this the Mahābhārata and other books provide particular proofs. In the present Kaliyuga also the ten S'aṁskāras such as marriage and so forth of the twice-born, and the obsequial ceremonies such as S'rāddha are performed according to Vaidik ritual. Smṛti governs Cāndrāyana and other matters relating to Āśrama and legal affairs such as inheritance. The autumnal Durgāpūjā and other Vratas are performed according to the Purāṅas. But initiation, Upāsanā of Brahman with S'akti and various practices of Yoga are done according to the ritual of the Āgama S'āstra.

This latter is of three kinds according to the prevalence of the Guṇas namely Tantra, Yāmala and Dāmara. There are in all 192 Āgamas current, namely 64 each in Aśvakrāntā, Rathakrāntā, and Viṣṇukrāntā. Many Tantras were lost in Buddhist and Mahommedan times and the few which still remain with Sādhakas in different parts of the country are not shown by them to any but to their disciples, so that these also are about to be lost. The late Rasika-Mohana-Chattopādhyāya, with great effort and cost, saved some of these and the Englishman Sir John Woodroffe has done the same and I hope yet others will in future be rescued by him.

In the Yoginī-Tantra, Īśvara says to Devi that the difference between Vedas and Āgamas is like that between Jīva and Ātmā, that is between Jīva covered with Avidyā and Īśvara who is full of Vidyā. Indra and other Devas who used to be worshipped as Īśvaras in Yajñas held under the Karma-kāṇḍa or Saṁhitā of the Vedas are, in Tantra-śāstra, worshipped as the Presiding Devatās of the Dikpālinī S'akti of Her who is all S'aktis (Sarvaśakti-svarūpiṇī). The three Īśvaras Brahmā, Viṣṇu and Rudra of the Vedas and Purāṇas are in Tantra-śāstra the presiding Devatās of the creative, preservative, and dissolving S'aktis of Mahādevī. As such they are worshipped as the supports of the couch of the Mahādevī. She in the Devīgītā says that ' Brahmā, Viṣṇu, Rudra, Īśvara, Sadāśiva are the Mahāpreta at my Feet. They are constituted of the five Bhūtas and represent the five different elements of matter.' ' I however ' She says ' am unmanifested consciousness (Cit) and in every way beyond them.'

Again the Veda says 'All this is verily Brahman.' Despite this Mahāvākya, various distinctions are made, such as those of caste, Adhikāra of men and women and so forth. So a male Brāhmaṇa may say Vaidik Mantras but not Brāhmaṇa women. Distinction was again made between objects as between the water of the Ganges and a well. All such distinctions are wholly opposed to the Spirit of the Great Word (Mahāvākya). The Tantra-śāstra says that the supreme Brahman is both subtle and gross. In dependence on the truth of this Mahāvākya Tāntrik Sādhakas purify wine which is 'not to be taken and drunk' according to Veda. Considering it to be as holy as nectar, they offer it into the mouth of Kulakuṇḍalinī who is Consciousness itself (Citsvarūpini). Again, in accordance with Veda, the Tantra holds food to be sacred and knowing that food is Brahman ordains the offering of it to Mahādevī. This offered food is Mahāprasāda and very holy and rare even for Devas, and whether it be brought by a Caṇḍāla, or even fallen from the mouth of a dog. The Vedas and Smṛti say that the Caṇḍāla and other low castes are untouchable. On touching them one must bathe, do Aghamarṣana and so forth. But the Tantra-S'āstra says that even a Caṇḍālā, who has a knowledge of Kula doctrine and Brahman, is superior to a Brāhmaṇa who does not know Brahman. The Tantra-S'āstra again says that during the Cakra all castes are equal. Since all are children of the one Mother of the World, no distinctions should be made at the time of worshipping Her. It is on this Tāntrik authority that no caste distinctions are observed in the matter of eating and so forth in the Virajākṣetra of S'rī S'rī Vimalā Devī. The Veda again prohibits the performance of Yajña or worship after the taking of food. Tantra-S'āstra however says that one should not worship Kālika whilst suffering from hunger or thirst; otherwise She becomes angry. That is since S'iva and Jīva are really one it is futile to worship the Paramātmā saying 'I offer Naivedya' when the Jīva, who is one with It, is in want of food and drink. Smṛti again, which explains Veda ordains that the S'ālagrama stone which represents Nārāyaṇa should not be touched or worshipped by any but Brāhmaṇas. On the other hand, the Tantra-S'āstra ordains that the Bāṇaliṅga representation of the Brahman may be touched and worshipped not only by Brāhmaṇas but by S'ūdras, Caṇḍālas and women. In fact the Karmakāṇḍa of Veda contains many such ordinances opposed to Brahman-knowledge. For this reason Bhagavān S'rikṛṣṇa has said in the Gītā that the Vedas are concerned with objects constituted of the three Guṇas (Triguṇaviṣaya) and bids Arjuna to free himself of the Guṇas. He says the Veda contains the Karmakāṇḍa but that he who seeks the Brahman-state above the Guṇas should abandon the Karmakāṇḍa and perform Sādhanā according to S'āstra by which Liberation is gained. In spite however of differences in worship and practice both Veda and Tantra S'āstras are one in holding that there can be no Liberation without Tattvajñāna. In the Nirvāṇa-Tantra S'iva says 'Oh Devī, there is no Liberation without Tattvajñāna.' According to Veda, a Sādhaka, in order to become fit for Nirvāṇa, must have first accomplished the fourfold Sādhanā. He must have acquired the faith that Brahman is alone everlasting, and have no desire for happiness either on earth or in heaven. He must possess the six virtues, S'ama, Dama and so forth, and must long for Liberation. He then discusses (Vicāra) and ponders on the Mahāvākya 'That thou art' (Tat tvam asi), and thus realizing the unity of Paramātmā and Jīvātmā, attains the knowledge 'He I am' (So'ham).

In Tāntrik Upāsanā the Jñānakāṇḍa is mingled with the Karmakāṇḍa. The Āgama teaches the ignorant Paśu, steeped in dualism, Vīrabhāva Sādhanā in which dualism and nondualism are mingled. It thus endeavours to raise them to the divine state of Jīvanmuktas, the state of pure Monism. Manu says 'Know dualists to be Paśus. Non-dualists are Brāhmaṇas.' Rudrayāmala says that Vīrabhāva is revealed for the development of Jñāna. After perfecting Jñāna and attainment of Brahmasiddhi, the Sādhaka becomes Devatā in a pure state of Sattva. The Vedānta and philosophic S'āstras are replete with instructions and arguments touching non-dualism. But they do not indicate the path by which one can be in actual practice non-dualistic. For this reason we see Vedāntic Pandits deeming it unclean to touch a low caste man such as a S'ūdra. They also observe endless distinctions as to what should or should not be eaten, and what should and should not be offered to Devatā. Tantra - S'āstra however says that non-dualistic Bhāva (Bhāvādvaita) should be accompanied by non-dualistic action (Kriyādvaita). The Yogavāsiṣṭha (Rāmāyaṇa) says that to the Muni who realizes non-dualism (Advaita) in Bhāva, in Kriyā, and in objects (Dravya), in all these three matters, the world seems but a dream.

According to the instruction of Tantra-S'āstra the Sādhaka rises in the early hours of the morning, and sitting on his bed, meditates as follows: 'I am the Devi and none other. I am that Brahman who knows not grief. I am a form of Being-Consciousness-Bliss, Whose true nature is eternal Liberation.' Again at noon sitting at worship he does Bhūtaśuddhi, and therein merging the 24 Tattvas beginning with earth in Paramātmā and thinking of the Paramātmā and Jīvātmā as one he meditates: 'He I am.' Gandharva-Tantra says that, after due obeisance to the Guru, the wise Sādhaka should think 'He I am' and thus unite Jīvātmā and Paramātmā. In all Sthūla-Dhyāna of Mahāvidyās, forming part of daily worship, Tantra-S'āstra everywhere enjoins meditation on the Mahādevī as not different from, but one with, the Sādhaka's Ātmā. The Kālī-Tantra says that, after meditating as enjoined, the Sādhaka should worship the Devī as Ātmā. 'He I am' (So'ham). Kubjika-Tantra says that the Sādhaka should think of his Ātmā as one with Her. Nīla-Tantra in the Dhyāna of Tārā says that meditation should be done on one's own Ātmā as one with the Saviour-goddess (Tārinī). In Gandharva-Tantra Mahādevī says, as regards the Dhyāna of Tripura-sundarī that the Man who meditates on the unattached, attributeless, and pure Ātmā which is Tripurā as one with, and not different from, his own Ātmā becomes himself Her (Tanmaya). One should become Her by ever thinking 'She I am' (Sā'ham). Again in the Kālikula-sarvasva S'iva says that whoever meditates on the Guru and recites the Hymn of the spouse of S'iva and thinks of Kālikā's Ātmā as one with his own Ātmā is S'rī Sadāsiva. Similarly Kulārṇava Tantra says 'The body is the temple of Devatā and the Jiva is Deva Sadaśiva.' Let the Sādhaka give up his ignorance as the offering (Nirmālya, which is thrown away) and worship with the thought and feeling 'He I am.' It is not only at times of worship and so forth that the Sādhaka is enjoined to meditate on Her who is Paramātmā as one with his own Ātmā S'iva teaches that our thought and feeling should be non-dualistic in all that we do, in eating, in walking and so forth. Hence in the Gandharva-Tantra Sīva says 'I am both the Deva and the food offered to Him, the flower and perfume and all else. I am the Deva. There is none other than Me. It is I who worship the Deva and I am also Deva of Devas.' Again it is ordained that at the time of taking Kāraṇa (wine) and the rest they should be offered to the Fire of Consciousness in one's own heart, uttering the Mantra, and thinking that Kula-Kuṇḍalinī extends to the tip of his tongue, let the Sādhaka say: 'The liquid shines. I am the Light. I am Brahman. She I am. I offer Āhuti to my own Self Svāhā.' He who does Sādhanā of the Mahāvidyā in Vīrācāra with such Advaitabhāva attains by Her Grace to Divyabhāva, and with the thought 'I am Brahman' becomes liberated whilst living, and on death is one with Mahādevī. In the Devīgītā S'rī S'rī Devī says 'He becomes Myself because both are one.' Again the Mahānirvāṇa-Tantra enjoins a similar non-dualistic feeling in the Mantra to be said when taking the Dravya (wine). The ladle is Brahman, the offering is Brahman, the fire is Brahman, the offering is made by Brahman and to Brahman he goes who places all his actions in Brahman.'

Saccidānanda Mahāvidyā, in undistinguishable union of S'iva and S'akti, can alone be worshipped with such non-dualism of feeling. Although Tāntrik worshippers are divided into five communities namely S'ākta, S'aiva, Vaiṣṇava, Gāṇapatya and Saura the first alone are all Dvijas since all worshippers of Sāvitrī (Gāyatrī) the Mother of the Veda belong to the S'ākta community. The Mātṛkābheda-Tantra says 'Sāvitrī the Mother of the Veda was born of the sweat of Kālī's body. That Devī grants the threefold fruit and is S'akti of Brahman.' Sādhakas belonging to the other four communities worship their respective male Devatās associating with them their S'aktis. Thus the S'aivas worship S'iva under the names Umā-Maheśvara, S'iva-Durgā, Kālī S'aṁkara, Arddhanārīśvara and so forth. The Vaiṣṇavas worship Viṣṇu under the names, Rādhā-Kṛṣṇa, Lakṣmī-Nārāyaṇa, Sītā-Rāma, S'rī-Hari and so forth. In the Nirvāṇa-Tantra S'rī Kṛṣṇa says 'To those who do Japa of Rādhā first and then Kṛṣṇa to such I, of a surety, grant a happy lot even now and here.' By uttering the name Sītā-Rāma (Sītā coming first) one utters the Tāra of Mahādevī, and for this reason it is also called Tāraka-Brahma. The Sauras perform their worship with the Mantra 'Obeisance to S'rī Sūrya accompanied by the S'akti who reveals.' Moreover the Māyā Bīja (Hrīm), which is the praṇava of Devī, is added to the Mūlamantra by every sect. This clearly shows that all these five sects are directly or indirectly worshippers of the Brahman who is S'iva-S'akti (S'ivaśaktyātmaka) both in his Nirguṇa and Saguṇa aspects. Kaivalyopaniṣad says 'By meditation on the three-eyed, blue-throated serene Lord (Prabhu) Parameśvara, who is without beginning, middle and end, who is one and pervades all things, who is wonderful, Cidānanda Itself, accompanied by Umā, the Muni goes to the Source of all being (Bhūtayoni) to the Witness of all, who is beyond all darkness.' Hence in the Tantra-S'āstra, S'iva has said that the S'iva-śakti-Tattva is the cause of Tattvajñāna and therefore Japa should be done by a Mantra in which they are united. That is one attains Tattvajñāna, which is liberation, by worshipping Brahman as Mother and Father. All Mantras being composed of S'iva and S'akti one should meditate on S'iva-S'akti as being one. In the Tantra S'āstra also S'iva has said that there is no difference between them who are inseparably connected (Avinābhāvasaṁbandha).

He who is S'iva is also S'akti and She who is S'akti is also S'iva. Fatherhood and Motherhood are merely distinctions of name. In reality they stand for one and the same thing. The Tantra S'āstra again says that S'akti, Maheśvara, Brahman all denote the same Being. Male, female, neuter are verbal and not real distinctions. S'akti, Maheśvara, Brahman; all three denote the one eternal Mahāvidyā who is Saccidānanda. Although the Mahāvidyā is in truth Nirguṇa and eternal, She assumes various Māyik forms, varying according to the Guṇas, for the fruition of the desires of Sādhakas. It is said in Candi that She ever appears to fulfil the purposes of Devas, and at such times She, who is Truth eternal, is commonly said to be generated. In the Devyāgama it is said; 'Mahāmāyā who is Cidrūpā and Parabrahmasvarūpiṇi assumes by Her grace towards Sādhakas various forms.' We may meditate on Mahādevi as either female or male, for these terms may be attributed to any gross body. They cannot however be attributed to Her in so far as She is Saccidānanda. Sādhakas of S'akti worship Brahman as Mother, for in the world the mother-aspect alone of Her who is Brahman is fully manifested. In the Yāmala, S'iva says:—'Devi may, My Beloved, be thought of as female or male, or the Saccidānandarūpiṇi may be thought of as Niṣkala-Brahman. But in truth She is neither a female, male, neuter being, nor an inanimate thing. But like the term Kalpavalli (a word in feminine gender denoting tree) feminine terms are attributed to Her.'

In fact the main cause of the birth and nourishment of men and animals is their respective mothers. Their fathers are merely helpers (Sahakāri). Every Jiva on issuing from his mother's womb, lives on her milk, and receives his first initiation with the Mantra 'Mā' (Mother). The first preceptor (Ādiguru) of every man is his mother. She is his visible Devatā. His first lessons are learnt of her. It is the mark also of the Earth to generate and nourish all Jīvas, like a mother, by producing for them all kinds of fruits and grains and holding them in her bosom. Hence we are not wrong in saying that the world is full of the Mother.

In mathematics zero has no value and is merely an empty formless (Nirākāra) thing, indicative of infinity until it is joined to an integer. But when joined to the figure 1 it converts it into 10. Similarly when She who is formless Brahman is joined to Her own Prakṛti, consisting of the three Guṇas, spoken of in S'ruti as 'the unborn one, red, black, and white,' then She assumes for the fruition of the Sādhaka's desires ten different forms (Daśamahāvidyā) whose variety is due to difference in the proportions of the three Guṇas. There are the ten Mahāvidyās who are S'iva S'akti (S'ivaśaktimayī). These ten forms are Kālī and Tārā, the Mahāvidyā Ṣodaśī, Bhuvaneśvarī, Bhairavī, Cinnamastā, Dhūmāvatī, the Vidyā Bagalā, the Siddhavidyā Mātaṅgī, and Kamalā. Some Tantras mention eighteen Mahāvidyās, but these are forms of the ten with slight variations. Of the ten Mahāvidyās, Kālī is S'uddha-sattva-guṇa-pradhānā, Nirvikara, Nirguṇa-brahma-svarūpa-prakāśikā. It is this primordial form which alone directly gives Kaivalya. In Yoginī-Tantra Devī says 'Now see my form (Rūpa) which is Brahmānanda and supreme. Listen, this form is the supreme state (Paramadhāma) in the form of Kālī. There is no Brahman-form higher than this.' In Kāmadhenu-Tantra S'iva says 'In the void is Kālī who grants Kaivalya'. Tārā is Sattva-guṇātmikā and Tattva-vidyādāyinī; Ṣodaśī (Mahātripurasundarī),

Bhuvaneśvarī and Cinnamastā are Rajahpradhānā and Sattva-guṇātmikā and hence they grant Gauṇamukti in the form of Heaven (Svarga), Aiśvarya and so forth. The forms of Dhūmāvatī, Bagalā, Mātaṅgī and Kamalā are Tamah-pradhāna and hence their Sādhanā is done in Ṣatkarma, such as causing death to others and so forth. In short all the forms of Mahādevī give Enjoyment and Liberation directly or indirectly.

The forms of the Mahāvidya are divided into two groups namely the Kālīkula and S'rīkula. So Niruttara-Tantra says that 'Kālī, Tārā, Raktakālī, Bhuvanā, Mardinī, Triputā, Tvaritā, Durgā and Vidyā Pratyaṅgirā belong to the Kālīkula. And to the S'rīkula belong Sundarī, Bhairavī, Bālā, Bagalā, Kamalā, Dhūmāvatī, Mātaṅgī, Vidyā, Svapnāvatī and Mahāvidyā Madhumatī. Of all the Siddhavidyās Dakṣinā is, O my beloved, the Cause (Prakṛti).'

Kālī-kula is for the worship of Jñānis in Divya and Vīrabhāva, and S'rī-kula is for the worship of Karmins in Divya, Vīra and Paśu-Bhāvas. The Tantra-S'āstra gives an account of the Mantras, Yantras, mode of worship and so forth for all the ten or eighteen Mahāvidyās. But almost all Tāntrik writings hymn the greatness of, and give the highest place to, Kālikā the first Mahāvidyā for the others are but different forms of Brahmarūpiṇī Kālikā. The Nigama-Kalpataru says 'Of all castes the Brāhmaṇa is the highest. Amongst all Sādhakas the S'ākta is the highest. Of S'āktas he is the chief who does Japa of the Kālīmantra.' Picchilā-Tantra also says 'of all the Mantras of the Devas that of Kālikā is the best. Even the vilest can become Jīvanmukta simply through this Mantra.' In Yoginī-Tantra, S'iva says 'This Vidyā Kālikā is Mahā-Brahma

Vidyā, through whom even the worst may attain Nirvāṇa. Even Brahmā, Viṣṇu, and Maheśvara are her worshippers. She who is Kālī the supreme Vidyā, is Tārā also. The notion of a difference between them has given rise to various Mantras.' Again the Kāmākhyā-Tantra says 'Oh Parameśvari, seven lakhs of Mahāvidyās remain hidden. Of them all Ṣodaśī is said to be the most sublime. But Oh Devi, the Mother of the world, Kālikā is the mother even of Her.' Niruttara Tantra says 'Without knowledge of S'akti, Oh Devi, there is no nirvāṇa. That S'akti is Dakṣiṇa Kālī who is the own form of all Vidyās (Sarvavidyārūpiṇī).' The Yāmala again says 'As is Kālī so is Tārā and so are Cinnā and Kullukā. Oh Devi, thou, who art the supreme Kālikā, art also the Mūrti which is composed of these four. In the Vaidik system Sāgnika (fire-maintaining) Brāhmaṇas achieved their ends by the offering of oblations to the seven lolling tongues of fire named Kālī, Karālī, Manojavā, Sulohitā, Sudhūmravarṇā, Sphuliṅginī and Devī Viśvarucī' (1st Saptaka, 2nd Khaṇḍa, 4th Sūtra).[1]

Another important characteristic of the Tantra-S'āstra remains to be mentioned. Although this Scripture is very liberal in matters of practice and worship and does not recognize distinctions of caste and so forth, it has yet repeatedly, enjoined Sādhakas to keep this Ācāra hidden from ignorant Paśus. Of Kaulas it says that 'they are at heart S'āktas, outwardly S'aivas, and in gatherings Vaiṣṇavas.' It also contains injunctions such as that the teaching should be kept as secret as one would the knowledge of one's mother's illicit love, and that if it is given out the Sādhaka's purpose is frustrated and so forth. In the Gandharva-Tantra,

[1] See *Muṇḍakopaniṣad, 1-2-4.*

S'iva says that only such men as are without dualism, have controlled their passions and are devoted to Brahman are entitled to this S'āstra. 'He alone is entitled, who is a believer, pure, self-controlled, without dualism who lives in Brahman, speaks of Brahman, is devoted to Brahman, takes refuge in Brahman, who is free from all feeling of enmity against others, and who is ever engaged in doing good to all beings. Others are not true Sādhakas (Brahmasādhaka). It should not be told to Paśus, to those who are insincere, or to men of shallow knowledge.' For this reason S'iva has used symbols in the teaching of all Dhyānas, Mantras, Yantras, and modes of Sādhanā of Devas and Devis. The meaning of these symbols is not known to any but the Sadguru. Hence the secret mysteries are unintelligible even to the learned without the grace of the Guru. In the Kulārṇava-Tantra, S'iva says 'There are many Gurus who know the Veda, the S'āstras and so forth. But, Oh Devi, rare is the Guru who knows the meaning of the supreme Tattva.' Hence in order to know the true meaning of the Dhyānas and so forth, there is no other means than to seek refuge with the Guru who knows the meaning of all Āgamas.

It is owing to ignorance of the true nature of Devatā that even Brahmavidyā, who is subtler than the most subtle and Consciousness Itself, seems to be a gross thing. Even learned men do not shrink from saying that this Brahmamayī, whose desires are fully realized (Pūrṇakāmā) is fond of offerings of blood, flesh and so forth. In the Jñānasaṁkalinī-Tantra, S'iva says, 'Agni is the Deva of the twice-born. The Devatā of Munis is in their hearts. Men of small intelligence worship images. To the wise, Devatā is everywhere.' That is Karmin Brāhmaṇas worship

Agni as Iśvara, Yogis see the Devatā in their own hearts, men of small intelligence (that is compared with the others) worship the Devatā in images, and high-souled seers of the Tattva see Brahman everywhere. In fact much as a teacher shows his little students, small globes and maps, in order to make them understand the nature of the great earth, so Gurus counsel Sādhakas of no great intelligence and of inferior Adhikāra to meditate on Sthūla forms in images and pictures so that their wandering minds may be rested, and they may learn the true aspects of Devatā. Unfortunately however, ignorant men consider the Sthūla form to be the true aspect of the Devatā. In the Kulārṇava-Tantra, S'iva says that some meditate on the Sthūla to still the mind, which, when so stilled, can fix itself on the Sūkṣma. The Sādhaka should first learn from the Guru what quality or action each limb of the image represents, and should then practise meditation on the subtle, otherwise the gross form will itself, become for him mere earth or stone. In Kubjikā-Tantra S'iva says 'Oh Lady of Maheśa. One should meditate on the Formless (here used in the sense as opposed to forms of images, etc.) along with the form. It is by constant practice, Oh Devī, that one realizes the formless.'

Hence Sādhakas who desire Liberation should always think of the Svarūpatāttva of Brahmavidyā-Kālikā. Of this Svarūpa the Devī says in Mahābhāgavata: 'Those who long for Liberation should, in order to gain freedom from the bonds of the body, meditate on that aspect (Rūpa) of Mine which is the supreme Light (Jyotih), Sūkṣma, and Niṣkala, Nirguṇa, the all-pervading, unbeginning, non-dual sole Cause which is Saccidānanda Itself. This is the Svarūpa of the Devī which is beyond all mind and speech.'

The Mārkaṇḍeya-Purāṇa says, 'The Mahāmāyā is Niṣkalā, Nirguṇā, endless, undecaying, unthinkable, formless and both eternal (Nityā) and transient (Anityā)'; that is, Mahāmāyā Kālikā is free from Kalā (Māyā) and free from Guṇas, without end, imperishable, eternal, and not transient as is the world (Jagat), formless, and hence, as such, is not the object of meditation. In the Kūrma-Purāṇa, Viṣṇu in the form of a tortoise says that the Supreme Devī is Nirguṇā, pure, white, stainless, free from all duality and realizable by the Ātmā only. This state of Hers is attainable only by Jñāna. In the Kāmadā-Tantra S'iva says 'That eternal Kālī who is supreme Brahman is one without a second either male or female. She has neither form, Ādhāra, or Upādhi. She is sinless and imperishable Saccidānanda, the Great Brahman.' She who is eternal Brahman has neither appearance (Āvirbhāva), nor disappearance (Tirobhāva), and being all-pervading, She cannot be said, like other Devas and Devīs, to reside in any particular Loka. Thus Brahmā resides in Brahmaloka, Viṣṇu in Viṣṇuloka, Rudra in Kailasa and S'rī Kṛṣṇa in Goloka, but Mahādevī is always and everywhere equally present; though for the fulfilment of the desires of Sādhakas, She appears in particular forms in their minds and hearts. It is clear therefore that her Sthūla aspect is Māyā-made (Māyāmaya) and transient (Anitya). For this reason S'iva, in the Gandharva-Tantra, says, 'That aspect (Rūpa) of the Devī which is the Supreme Bliss and the Great Cause of the worlds neither appears nor disappears'. In the Kulārṇava-Tantra, S'iva says 'It neither rises nor sets, nor grows nor decays; It shines

Itself and makes others shine without any help. This aspect is without condition (Anavasthā) and is being only (Sattāmātrā) and unknowable to the senses (Agocara).' That is, the Svarūpa aspect of the Mahādevī who is Supreme Bliss is the root-cause of this world of three Guṇas. This aspect has no appearance or disappearance and no growth or decay. 'It is self-manifest and manifests all other objects. It is beyond the states of waking, dreams, and sleep. It is unattainable by speech and mind and is Being itself.'

In fact just as fire which, though pervading all objects, does not show its power of burning and lighting, and cannot be put to use for cooking and so forth, until it has been generated by the friction of two objects, so although the Cinmayī is all-pervading, She does not become visible nor does She grant one's desire without the action of Sādhanā. Again just as the Sun, itself motionless in the distant Heavens, by its rays draws moisture from the earth, so the Mahādevi, who is the abode of all S'aktis, though in Herself changeless (Nirvikārā) creates (and the like) the world by means of the eight S'aktis, Brahmāṇi, Vaiṣṇavi, Māheśvarī and other Devatās, presiding as her creative and other S'aktis. For this reason in the Yantra of Mahādevī Kālikā (see Kālikopaniṣad) the Sādhaka worships the fifteen S'aktis, Kālī and others in the fifteen corners, the eight S'aktis Brāhmī and others on the eight petals, the eight Bhairavas and Vatukas Asitānga and the rest at the edges of the eight petals, the four Devatās, Viṣṇu and others, at the four corners of the Yantra, and the ten Dikpālas, Indra and others, in the ten directions as being the rays of Kālikā who is Herself a mass of pure light (Tejoghaṇa). The Mahādevī is worshipped as the

Mūrti consisting of S'iva-S'akti (Sivaśaktimaya) in the Bindu at the centre of the Yantra.

Although the Āgama-S'āstra, which grants Advaitabhāva and educes Tattva jñāna, has been revealed by all-merciful S'rī S'rī Bhairava and Bhairavī, it is still unknown to a mass of people. Many in fact to-day despise the Tantra because it contains Vīrācāra and Kulācāra, and some even refuse to admit that it is a Dharmaśāstra at all. If they had read the Tantra-S'āstra intelligently and learned its principles from S'ādhakas truly versed in it, they would have realized how mistaken were their notions of it and, instead of despising it, would certainly have admitted that this S'āstra is the only means of Liberation for the undisciplined, weakminded and short-lived. Seeing that wine, flesh, fish are consumed and sexual intercourse takes place in the world at large I am myself unable to understand why many people should shudder at the Sādhanā of Pañca-makāra to be found in the Tantra-S'āstra. Do these acts become blameable only if made a part of worship (Upāsanā)?

All know that ghee which nourishes and promotes longevity causes serious stomach-disease and even death if taken in too large quantities, whilst snake-poison, which kills, will yet cure and lengthen the life of a dying delirious man, if it be purified and given under suitable conditions with a cold bath, a diet of whey, and so forth. Similarly the Great Physician (Vaidyanātha) Himself has prescribed the Mantra of Ādyāśakti possessed of all S'aktis, and the invigorating Pañcamakāra as Sādhanā suitable for the cure of the malady of Existence (Bhavaroga) of the sinful Jīvas of this dark Kali age, and as a means whereby they may attain the supreme state full of eternal bliss, imperishable and immortal. All classes of physicians prescribe the use of wine, fish and flesh in measured quantities for the acquisition of strength by patients who are weak and have a low vitality. On that account the medical science does not deserve to be hated. Similarly the Tantra-S'āstra does not deserve to be blamed for prescribing the Pancha-makāra for the Liberation of Jīvas suffering from the disease of worldly existence. S'iva has nowhere said that Sādhakas of S'akti should always drink wine, always slaughter animals and eat their flesh and always enjoy woman, and that thus they will attain Liberation. On the contrary, He has counselled various means for checking excesses in these matters, and He has in particular controlled licence by making these acts part of the worship of Īśvara. It is the degraded conduct of a number of great Paśus who pretend to be Sādhakas which is the cause of the public dislike for, and hatred of, the Tantra-S'āstra. In the Mahānirvāṇa-Tantra S'rī Sadāśiva says 'Wine is Tārā the Saviour in liquid form (Dravamayi). It saves Jivas, destroying dangers and disease, and grants both Enjoyment and Liberation. But wine if drunk in contravention of rule (Vidhi), destroys the intelligence, reputation, wealth and life of men. Even a Kaula who has received Abhiṣeka an hundred times is to be deemed a Paśu and without the pale of Kuladharma if he is addicted to excessive drinking.' In the Kulārṇava, S'iva says 'Oh My Beloved, he who kills animals for self-satisfaction in contravention of S'āstric ordinance (Avidhānena) will dwell in a terrible Hell for as many days as there are hairs on the body of the animal.' These utterances of S'iva clearly show that He has nowhere ordained the free use of Pāñca-makāra by people in general. He has ordained Vīrācāra or Kulācāra only for Sādhakas of the Nivṛtti path who long for Liberation. Such Sādhakas, free from duality (Nirvikalpa) as they are, wish to see the Saccidānanda aspect of the Mahādevi, and S'iva has prescribed the Pañca-makāra to enable them to realize the Ānanda aspect. Just as a man who knows not sweetness is given sugar or honey to eat, so the Sādhaka is made to taste the fleeting objective (Viṣaya) bliss (Ānanda) of Pañca-makāra so that, thus controlling his six enemies for the time being, he may have a notion of the Eternal Brahman-bliss (Brahmānanda). This momentary taste of eternal Brahman-bliss makes the Liberation-desiring Sādhaka eager for and industrious to gain it. But after the attainment of this natural (Sahaja) Brahma-bliss he no more longs for the five Makāras and becomes gradually devoted to Divyācāra. If a Sādhaka takes wine in a limited way, after purification, the out-going of his senses is weakened, and the mind or inner sense is stilled so that he is thus fitted for Sūkṣma-Dhyāna. For this reason wine is called cause (Kāraṇa). In the Kulārṇava-Tantra, S'iva says, 'Ānanda is the Self (Rūpa) of Brahman and that exists in the body. Wine is its revealer and is hence drunk by Yogis. Wine and flesh are taken with Brahma-jñāna for the satisfaction of all Devas, and whoever partakes of them for self-gratification is a sinner.' That is Sādhakas do Sādhanā with Pañca-makāra for the satisfaction of the Devatās whom they worship and the development of Brahmajñāna in their hearts; but whoever takes them for his own enjoyment is doomed to a terrible hell as a great sinner. S'iva has also said in the Kulārṇava, 'One reaches heaven by the very things which may lead to Hell.' The fifth Makāra, that is, sexual intercourse, is the root-cause of the creation of the world of Jīvas. All

Jīvas, be they Devatạ̄s, men, beasts, birds, fish, insects or flies, are produced by the sexual union of their respective parents. In this world every male is an individualised (Vyaṣṭibhūta) aspect of S'iva, the Ādipuruṣa, and Caṇḍī says, 'all females in all the worlds' are part of the Mahāśakti. The Kūrma Purāṇa says, 'The Mahādevī is Herself One, present in many parts or divisions (Anekavibhāgastha), beyond Māyā, absolutely pure, Mahāmāyā, Īśvarī, eternal, stainless (Nirañjana), ancient, consciousness (Cinmayī, the First Puruṣa (Ādipuruṣa) of all Puruṣas.' The Gandharva-Tantra says, 'The male form (Puṁso rūpam) the female form, and any other good form—all this is undoubtedly Her supreme form (Paramam rūpam).' One Brahman, becoming dual appears as S'iva and S'akti, and that aspect in which there is union of S'iva and S'akti is the true aspect of Saccidānanda Brahman. It is from this aspect of Blissful (Ānandamaya) union that the world is created, and for that reason men and all other creatures ever seek happiness. The Bliss of the reproductive power of males and females manifests in their bodies only at the time of sexual union. At this time ignorant men remain intent only on gratifying their passion, but Sādhakas, possessed of the knowledge of Kula, then meditate on the Yoga-blissful (Yogānanda) form (Mūrti) of S'iva and S'akti present in the hearts of males and females and, calling to mind the meaning (Artha) of the Mantra of their Iṣṭadevatā, do Japa of it. In the Kālikulasarvasva, S'rī Sadāśiva says, 'By doing Japa of Mantra and by adoration of Bhagavatī, the consort of S'iva, at times of sexual union, a man becomes, like S'uka, free from all sins.' In another place He says, 'The consort of S'iva should be worshipped by becoming S'iva.' True S'akti-sādhanā consists in considering all girls and women, old and young, and of all castes, as the visible forms of one's own Iṣṭadevatā and (according to one's means) worshipping them with clothes, ornaments and so forth; or bowing to them as mothers with the Iṣṭamantra in mind and not treating them with neglect or contempt under any circumstance. In the Kaulāvali-Tantra, S'iva says, 'One should make obeisance on seeing a young woman of a Kaula family. One should bow to any female, be she a young girl, or flushed with youth, or be she old, be she beautiful or ugly, good, or wicked. One should never deceive, speak ill of, or do ill to, a woman and one should never strike her. All such acts prevent the attainment of Siddhi.'

At the present time a measured use of wine, flesh and so forth and a thorough respect for woman as for the Devatā are particularly seen in the civilized society of the West. Satisfied at this, the Mahādevi, who is the Queen of Queens, has granted to the people of the West the light of science and sovereignty over the whole world. S'rimat Ādinātha Mahākāla has, in the 'Karpūrādi Stotra' called the Svarūpa-Stotra, briefly described the Mantra, Yantra, Dhyāna and Sādhanā of S'rimati Dakṣiṇa-Kālīka who is Parabrahman (Parabrahmarūpiṇi). This Supreme Tattva is hard to attain even by such Īśvaras as Brahmā, Viṣṇu and Rudra. Mahākāla Himself says, 'Neither Dhātā nor Īśa nor Hari knows Thy Supreme Tattva.'

However, in accordance with the teaching of my Paramaguru, Mahāmahopādhyāya and most worshipful Rāmānanda Svāmi Siddhāntapañcānana, the crest-gem of Tāntrikas, now gathered to the feet of S'iva, I write this Svarūpa commentary under the name of

'Vimalānandadāyini,' of this Karpūrādi Stotra, in consonance with the views of Tantra and other S'āstras.

PRAYER

AT THE FEET OF S'RĪ S'RĪ KĀLIKĀ

May the Mahā Devī who is called Kālikā,
Because She is without beginning or end,
Whose Body is imagined to be blue of colour,
Because like the blue sky She pervades the World,
And because She is Cidghanā [1] Sattvaguṇamayī
Who is imagined to be black,
Because She is colourless and above the coloured Guṇas,
Whose hair is dishevelled (Muktakeśī)
Because though Herself changeless She binds infinite numbers of Jīvas by bonds of Māyā, symbolized by Her dishevelled hair and because She makes liberated (Mukta) Brahmā, Viṣṇu and Maheśvara who are Keśa, [2]

---

[1] This is a play on the word Ghana which means mass and black or dark blue cloud. Cidghana is massive, compact, unmixed, pure Consciousness (Cit). Again She is Nirguṇa and stainless but is also Meghāṅgī (cloud-bodied) because through Adhyāsa of the three Guṇas She appears varicoloured just as a cloud in itself colourless appears white, blue, and so forth by contact with the sun's rays. So Devī-Purāṇa says, 'Just as the uniform cloud appears as of many colours, so does She too through the instrumentality of the Guṇas.'

[2] Keśa = K + A + Īśa. And K = Brahmā, A = Viṣṇu' and Īśa = Rudra. The Niruttara-Tantra says, 'Kālī who is Aniruddhasarasvatī, is the great desire-granting tree, the sole Cause of Enjoyment and Liberation for Brahmā, Viṣṇu and Maheśa.'

Who is imagined as having the Sun, Moon and Fire as Her three eyes,

Because as the Virat, the Witness of the world past, present and future She sees everything,

Who is pictured as wearing the dead bodies of two boys as Her ear-ornaments,

Because as said in Āgama and Nigama the childlike and unperturbed (Nirvikāra) Sādhaka is very dear to Her, who being the sole Creatrix, Preserver and Destructress of infinite millions of Worlds, has on Her Body the mark of the Yoni signifying creation, full and high breasts denoting preservation, and a terrible visage signifying the withdrawal of all things,

Who is said to have large teeth, and a lolling tongue and to hold in Her hand a cup made of human skull,

Because the Cinmayī Mahādevī drinks the wine of delusion arising from the Tamas Guṇa of Her Sādhaka by means of Sattva-pradhāna rajoguṇa,[1]

Who is pictured as wearing a garland of severed heads,

Because She is Sʹabdabrahman (Sʹabdabrahmarūpiṇī) and the heads are the fifty letters,

Whose upper and lower right hands are seen to be making the Abhaya and Vara Mudrās,

Because She both destroys the dangers, and grants the desires of Sakāma-Sādhakās,

---

[1] White Teeth stand for the white Sattva Guṇa, the red Tongue stands for the red Rajo-Guṇa and Delusion is the Tamo-Guna. The meaning is, the Mahāvidya is represented with a lolling tongue because She first destroys the Sādhaka's Tamo-Guṇa by increasing his Rajo-Guṇa, and large teeth because by increasing his Sattva Guṇa and suppressing his Rajo-Guṇa She grants him the state of Nirguṇa-Brahman. In the Dhyānā of Tārā it is said, 'Ugratārā Herself destroys the *Jādya* (unconscious nature) of the three worlds by putting it in her skull-cup.'

Whose upper left hand is depicted as wielding a sword,
Because She severs the bonds of illusion for the Niṣkāma-Sādhaka,
Whose lower left hand is seen to hold a human head,
Because She grants him Tattvajñāna,
Who is called Digambarī (space-clad)
Because being Brahman (Brahmarūpinī) She is free from the covering of Māyā [1] and unconcerned (Nirvikāra), [2]
Who is pictured as having a waist-chain of human hands,
Because hands are the principal instrument of work (Karma) and at the close of a Kalpa all Jīvas with their Karmas are merged in the Avidyā S'akti of Mahāmāyā,
Who is seen standing on the breast of corpse-like S'iva,
Because the Supreme State (Paramapada) and Svarūpāvasthā or Mahādevī (one with Siva) is Nirguṇa and changeless (Nirvikāra),
Who is seen in Viparīta-maithuna [3] with Mahākāla,
Because at the beginning of a Kalpa She who is ever blissful (Nityānandamayī), and being united with S'iva, feels pleasure in the work of creation which She effects by bringing the changeless Paraśiva under Her dominion (Vaśībhūta),
Who is again said to live in the cremation ground,
Because when at the end of a Kalpa all things in the universe from Brahmā to a blade of grass are

---

[1] In the eighteenth century work of Kamalākānta called Sādhakaranjana it is said : 'Of the Nirākāra-Brahman, understand, Māyā to be the Ākāra' (Nirākāra brahmer ākāra dekha Māyā). The S'ūnya has no form until encircled by Māyā.

[2] Vikāra is also 'change'. She is then in Her changeless aspect.

[3] Coition in which the woman assumes the dominant role. S'akti is active and S'iva is the passive principle.

dissolved in Mahākāla, She is in and one with that Mahākāla, who may be thus compared to a cremation ground, and because at the death of Jīvas She exists as the individual (Vyaṣti) Jīvātmā in the burning ground,

Whose Yantra for worship is composed of a circle symbolizing Māyā, an eight-petalled lotus denoting *the eightfold* Prakṛti, *three* Pentagons *representing* the fifteen Avayavas and a Bindu denoting S'iva-S'akti,

Because She is, as Paramātmā, in the gross and subtle bodies consisting of the three Guṇas and twenty-four Tattvas,

Whose Bīja 'Krīm',[1] the Queen of Mantras is pure Sattva Guṇa, and consciousness (Caitanyamayī) and grants both Enjoyment and Liberation,

Who is worshipped as Dakṣiṇā because She alone grants the full fruits of all forms of Upāsanā and Yajña.

May She, this Mahādevī, who is Saccidānandarūpiṇī and forgiveness itself, pardon all offences committed by me in the explanation of this Her Hymn.

S'ambhu with His five mouths is unable to relate Thy qualities.

Pardon all my childishness. Be propitious.

Guard my life, guard my repute and guard my wife, sons and wealth.

And at death grant me Liberation.

O Mother of the World, obeisance.

S'RI VĪMALĀNANDA-S'VĀMĪ

---

[1] The S'vāmi also points out that the 'Kr' sound in this Mantra is also to be found in the word Christ and in the Mussulman's Karīm. See Māyā Tantra Ch. vii for the Yavana-Bīja.

HYMN TO KĀLĪ

(KARPURĀDI-STOTRA)

VERSE 1

O MOTHER [1] and Spouse of the Destroyer of the three cities,[2] they who thrice recite [3] Thy *Bīja* [4] formed by omitting from *Karpūra*, the middle and last consonants and the vowels, but adding *Vāmākṣi* and *Bindu*,[5] the speech of such, whether in poetry or prose, like that of men who have attained all powers,[6] issues of a surety with all ease from the hollow of their mouth, O Thou who art beauteous with the beauty of a dark rain cloud.[7]

COMMENTARY

(INNER SENSE)

With respectful obeisance to the beauteous feet of Svāmī Rāmānanda I write this Svarūpa-vyākyā named the Grantor of Pure Bliss (Vimalānandadāyini). [8]

'Oh Mother' (*Mātah*)

The root Mā = to measure, to which is added the suffix tṛch = Mātṛ: that is, She who measures out or gives: She who grants enjoyment or Liberation according as the Sādhaka is desire-ridden or free from desires.

'Spouse of the Destroyer of the three cities'

The three cities are three bodies, gross, subtle, causal. She is the S'akti of Him who grants Liberation from these bodies. As the Power holder (S'aktimān) and His Power (S'akti) are one, it is She who is grantor of such Liberation. Kaivalya-Upaniṣad says, 'From the Ātmā, the root, the bliss, looking on all alike, who abides within the three cities, is born the multiple and various world and into Him these three cities are merged.'

'They who recite'

That is meditating on the same as being one with the Ātmā of the Sādhaka. Kālikā-S'ruti says, 'One should always think of Ātmā as Kālī. Those who do, attain the fourfold Puruṣārtha whether directly desired or not.' Todala-Tantra (Ch. vi) says 'Oh Devī, K grants Dharma, R grants Kāma, Ī grants Artha and M grants Mokṣa. Oh Beloved, the recital of these combined gives Nirvāṇa Mokṣa.'

'This (Etat)'

Thy Sattva saccidānanda aspect denoted by the Bīja 'Krīṁ'.

'Triple (Trihkritang)'

That is the triple aspect Sāttvika, Rājasika, Tāmasika.

'Bīja'

Denotes the aspect in which Thou art the Cause of the World. Although as Saccidānandarūpinī Thou art Nirguṇa when free of Māyā, characterized by the Karma of Jīvas and Kāla, Thou, becomest the seed in the creation of the world, what time Jīvas must enjoy the fruit of their Karma. In the Devīgītā, Devī says 'Then I who am Ātmā, Cit, Para-brahman and called the "One" assume the Bīja (seed) aspect through union with My own S'akti. The causal body of which I have aforetime spoken is Avyakta in which the world exists as seed (Bīja) from which issues the subtle body.'

'Karpūraṁ'

Saguṇa-Brahman, the Kalpaka or fashioner of the World.

'Omitting therefrom'

Omitting from Mūlaprakṛti composed of Sattva, Rajas, and Tamas Guṇas the middle Rajas Guṇa which is Ū and the last

Tamas Guṇa which is M. It is thus composed of Sattvaguṇa alone. The Jñānasaṁkalinī-Tantra says, A 'is Sāttvika, U is Rājasa, M is Tāmasa. Prakṛti is these three.'

'Adding'

Powerful to give Nirvāṇa Mokṣa and by Māyā to grant the desires of Sādhakas; and in whom the pure Sattvaguṇa predominates. The Tantra Kalpadruma says, 'K on account of its brilliance is the Citkalā, Jñāna. 'Associated with the fiery letter (R) She is auspicious and full of all Tejas. As "I" She grants the desires of Sādhakas. As Bindu She grants Kaivalya.'

'Beauty of dark clouds'

Thou who should be meditated upon as of a dark (Nīla) colour because Thou art Cidākāsa and dost possess the compact Tejas S'uddhasattvaguṇa. In the Nirvāṇa Prakaraṇa of Yogavāśiṣṭa it is said, 'Because S'ivā is Vyoma She is seen as black.' Tripurāsārasamuccaya says, 'As being Liberation, She who is attained by devotion (Bhakti) should be meditated on as being like the sky itself free from clouds.'

Notes

[1] The Divine Mother of the World in Her aspect as *Dakṣiṇa kālikā*, that is, the beneficent Grantor of *Nirvāṇa*.

The *Kālikāhṛdaya* says: 'I worship *Kālī* the Destructress of *Kāla* the Shining One, who is the *Bīja Krīm*, who is *Kāma*, who is beyond *Kāla* and who is *Dakṣiṇakalikā*.' *Gandharva-Tantra* says: 'Hrīm, I bow to *Mahādevī* who is *Turīya* and *Brahman*. He who remembers Her does not sink in the ocean of existence.' *Caṇḍī* says: 'Oh Thou whose Body is pure *Jñāna*, who hast three divine eyes, who weareth the crescent moon, to Thee I bow for the attainment of all good.' (V)

[2] *S'akti* of Maheśa who destroyed the *Asura* named *Tripura* (*Tri* = three; *Pura* = city) along with his three cities in Heaven, Earth and the Nether regions (V).

[3] Recite (*Japanti*); utter repeatedly with mind fixed on the meaning of the *Mantra* (V). Lit, 'make *Japa*.' The word 'recite' is employed as the nearest English equivalent, but is not accurate, in so far as in *mānasa Japa* the action is purely mental,

and in *Japa* of the next lower degree (Upāṁśu) there is movement of the lips only, but no utterance.

[4] The 'seed' *mantra. Bija* is seed, this cause of the *Mantra* body (V). According to the Nityā-Tantra, *Mantras* are of four kinds—*Pinda, Kartari, Bija* and *Mālā* according to the number of syllables, See as to *Bijā, The Garland of Letters.*

[5] That is, *Karpūraṁ*, less the vowels *a, ū, a*, and the consonants *pa* and *ram*=*Kṛ*+*Vāmākshi* ('the left eye' or long vowel *ī*), with the *Nādabindu* superimposed=*Krīṁ* which accomplishes all desire (Tantrasāra), is *Mantrarāja* (S'yāmārahasya-Tantra) (K. B.). Tantrarāja says, 'letter *Ka* is Thy form.'

[6] *Siddhi*, or success. *Siddhi* is that which is sought for (*Sādhya*) and is the result of *sādhana*, the training of the higher psychical and spiritual faculties. It includes the eight great powers, *Aṇimā, Laghimā*. etc., the power of motion 'and suspension in space, and others mentioned in the Skanda Purāṇa and other works. The Devī is Herself *Mahāsiddhi* (Lalitāsahasranāmam, v. 55).

[7] *Dhvāntadhārādhararucirucire*. Just as dark clouds, by shedding nectar-like rain, cool the earth parched by the sun's rays, so too dost Thou, by shedding the nectar of Thy Grace, give immortality to *Sādhakas* tormented by the three forms of pain (*Ādhyātmika, Ādhibhautika, Ādhidaivika*). The *Rudrayāmala* says, '*Devī* is Supreme *S'akti* and delivers from all difficulties. She is dark with the refulgence of a million suns and is cooling like a million moons.' (V).

[8] Vimalānanda is also the name of the Commentator.

VERSE 2

O MAHEŚ'I,[1] even should one of poor mind[2] at any time recite but once another doubled *Bīja* of Thine, composed of *Iśāna*,[3] and *Vāmaśravaṇa*,[4] and *Bindu*;[5] then, O Thou who hast great and formidable ear-rings of arrow form,[6] who bearest on Thy head the crescent moon, such an one becomes all-powerful,[7] having conquered even the Lord of Speech[8] and the Wealth-Giver,[9] and charmed countless youthful women with lotus-like eyes.[10]

COMMENTARY

'*Maheśi*'

Possessor of the great Power of creating, preserving and withdrawing.

'*At any time*' (*Kadacit*)

Durgārāma-Siddhāntavāgiśa is of opinion that by the use of Kadāchit it is meant that unlike other religious Karma which can be done only in a state of purity (S'uci), Japa of the Mantra of Kālī can be done at any time whether one is in a state of purity or not (S'aucāśauca-kāla). Here he says one should not give up the worship if there be a birth or death in the house. The Tantra-S'āstra says that one should do Japa of the Mantra, whether one is in the state of purity or not, and whether walking, standing or sleeping.

'*Recite*' (*Japati*)

Meditate upon.

'*Of dual aspect*' (*Dvandvam*)

Having the dual aspect of S'iva-śakti. The Tantra-S'āstra speaks of the King of Mantras being generated by the union of S'iva and S'akti.

'*Another Bija*' (*Bījamanyat*)

Thy causal (Kāraṇa) aspect which is the Bīja Hūṁ. In the Yāmala it is said, 'It is with the double S'abdabīja (which is Hūṁ) that She awakens the mass of S'abda.'

'*Iśāna*'

Is Iśvara. Kaṭhopaniṣad says, 'Puruṣa is the size of only a thumb. He is like smokeless fire, the Iśāna of what has been and will be. He is to-day and He is to-morrow. This is That.' Indu is immortality. Vāmaśravaṇa is the power of granting speech and of attracting forms (Rūpa). The Tantrābhidāna says, 'Ū is Bhairava, subtle, Sarasvati....attractor of forms.'

Who dost grant Nirvāṇa liberation. The Mahānirvāṇa-Tantra says, 'The forehead of Her who is Nityā, Kālarūpā, Arūpā, and S'iva Himself is marked with the moon on account of immortality.'

'*Dost bear the half-moon*' (*Candrārddhacūde*) '*Earrings*'

Whose earrings (things very dear) are formed of two Sādhakas who are like Maheśvara and simple as boys; that is child-like simple Sādhakas who have true knowledge are dear to Her. In the Vivekacūdāmaṇi it is said, 'Just as a boy plays with toys heedless of hunger and other pain so the wise man plays, happy, unattached and selfless.' Such a Sādhaka attains all forms of knowldge and riches and can charm the whole world.

(*Mahāghorabālāvataṁse*)

There is however another reading given by Durgārāma-Siddhāntavāgiśa namely Mahāghorābāṇāvataṃse, that is whose earrings are formed of frightful arrows (Bāṇa).

Notes

[1] *S'akti* or *Maheśa* the Lord of even *Brahmā*, *Viṣṇu* and *Rudra* (V). The *Devī* as Iśvari, (Ruler), of the Universe and Spouse of Nirguṇa Maheśvara. Iśvara, according to the Liṅga Purāṇa, when associated with *Tamas*, is Rudra the Destroyer; with *Rajas*, the One born from the golden egg, Brahmā; and with *Sattva*, Viṣṇu.

[2] *Mandacetāh* who is not capable of devotion to thy lotus feet according to Commentator K.B.; for, as the Brahmāṇḍa-Purāṇa says, all sin is expiated by remembrance of the feet of the Supreme S'akti.

[3] That is, *Ha*.

[4] The 'left ear,' or long vowel *ū*.

[5] *Nāda-bindu*—that is, *H+ū+ṁ* = *Hūṁ Hūṁ*. He who makes Japa of *Hūṁ* is more praiseworthy than Deva or Asura (Viśvasāra-Tantra) (K.B.)

[6] Worn by Kālī: reading Bāṇa instead of Bāla as to which see *post.*

[7] Viśvasāra (K.B.)

[8] *Bṛhaspati*, *Guru* of the *Devas*.

[9] *Dhanada*, i.e. *Kubera*, Lord of Wealth, King of the *Yakṣas*; according to one account the son, and, according to another, the grandson of Pulastya (see Muir, O.S.T. iv, 481, v, 488; v, 483; i. 492).

[10] That is, to them are given eloquence and learning, riches and beauty.

VERSE 3

O Kālikā, O auspicious Kālikā [1] with dishevelled hair,[2] from the corners of whose mouth two streams of blood trickle,[3] they who recite another doubled *Bīja* of Thine composed of *Īśa*,[4] *Vaiśvānara*,[5] *Vāmanetra*,[6] and the lustrous *Bindu*,[7] destroy all their enemies, and bring under subjection the three worlds.[8]

Commentary

' *Kālikā* '

Ka is Brahmā, A is Ananta, La is Ātmā of the universe, I is subtle, Ka is Brahmā, A is Ananta. (Tantrābhidāna). Thus it is said that Mahādevī is the subtle, beginningless and endless Ātmā of the universe. ' Thou who art Brahman without beginning or end.' In the Asitāstotra in the Adbhutarāmāyaṇa S'rī Rāma says, ' I bow to that Thine aspect which is Puruṣa without beginning and end, the unmanifest Kūtastha superior (to Thine aspect) as Prakṛti, the Ātmā of the universe appearing in multiple and differing forms.'

[Durgārāma-Siddhāntavāgīśa derives the word Kālikā as follows :—He who dissolves (Kālayati) the world is (Kāla or S'iva). And She who shines (Dīvyati) that is plays (Krīdati) with Him is Kālikā. Kāla + ikan + ā = Kālikā.]

' *With dishevelled hair* ' (*Vigalitacikure*)

That is one who is free from all Vikāras such as the passion for arranging the hair and so forth.

' *Stream of blood* ' (*Asradhārā*)

This blood indicates (the red) Rajas Guṇa. Mahādevī is without that for She is S'uddha-sattva-guṇa.

'*Recite*' (*Japati*)

Meditate upon.

Of dual aspect (*Dvandvaṁ*)

The Bījā Hrīṁ is both S'iva and S'akti. In the Devīgītā Mahādevī says, ' H is the gross body, R is the subtle body, Ī is the causal body. I am Hrīṁ the Turīya.'

'*Īśa*'

Who is the aspect of subtle Bīja.

'*Vaiśvānara*'

Which is full of Tejas.

'*Vāmanetra*'

That is, with Māyā consisting of pure Sattva-Guṇa.

'*Indu*'

That is, the S'akti which gives immortality.

Three syllabled Dakṣiṇē'

Dakṣiṇé is Dakṣiṇa in the vocative, and the latter is the Saccidānanda aspect which grants Kaivalya and is indicated, by the three-syllabled Mantra. Nirvāṇa-Tantra says, 'The Sun's son (Death) is established in the south (Dakṣiṇa). The name of Kālī makes him flee in all directions with fear. Hence She is called Dakṣiṇa in three worlds.' Kāmākhyā-Tantra says, 'Just as guerdon (Dakṣīṇa) given at the end of a rite, causes it to be fruitful and gives Liberation, so this Devi grants the fruit of all Karma and hence She is called Dakṣiṇa-Kālī.' The same Tantra also says, 'Puruṣa is on the right (Dakṣiṇa) and S'akti on *the left. The left conquers the right and becomes the grantor of* great Liberation. Hence She is called Dakṣiṇakālī in the three worlds.

[Durgārāma construes these words as follows: Dakṣiṇé tryakṣare ati (by Saṁdhi tryakṣare'ti) that is Dakṣiṇé ati tryakṣare. As Upasargas can shift their position 'ati' has been placed in the verse after Tryakṣare. Atitryakṣare is the vocative of Atitryakṣarā. Atitryakṣarā means Atikrāntah (Adhahkṛtah or placed under) Tryakṣarah (S'iva) yayā (by whom) She: that is, She who has placed S'iva under Her. The whole then means 'Oh Dakṣiṇé who dost stand on S'iva.' Tryakṣara literally means the three lettered one which is the Praṇava (Oṁ) and is used for S'iva. The Mahimnastotra (see *The Greatness of S'iva* calls S'iva 'Oṁ' and another Stotra calls Him Tryakṣaramaya.

The same commentator then says that there is a different reading for Dakṣiṇé tryakṣareti, namely, Dakṣiṇé Kālīketi which he explains in two ways (*a*) Dakṣiṇé Kālike'ti = Dakṣiṇé

Kālike ati=Dakṣiṇé atikālike. The last word is the vocative of Atikālikā which means Atikrāntā (Sadṛśikritā, made similar to) Kālikā (Meghajālaṁ; a bank of clouds) yayā (by whom) She—that is, She who looks like a bank of clouds; the whole then meaning 'Oh Dakṣiṇé who hast the appearance of a bank of clouds' (*b*) Dakṣine Kāliketi=Dakṣiné Kālike iti which means Oh Dakṣiṇa Kālikā. The word 'iti' is Svarūpārthaka that is simply indicates that She is addressed as Dakṣiṇa Kālikā. Examples of the elision of 'I' after 'E' in Saṁdhi are S'akuntaleti and Meghajāle'pi Kāliketi.]

NOTES

[1] The Devī. See Mahānirvāṇa-Tantra, chap. xiii and chap. iv, verse 31: 'At the dissolution of things it is Kāla who will devour all, and by reason of this He is called Mahākāla; and since Thou devourest Mahākāla Himself, it is Thou who art the supreme primordial Kālikā'.

Kālikā is *Brahmarūpiṇi* (V).

[2] *Vigalitacikure*, as is the worshipped *nāyikā*. See *post*.

[3] *Sṛkkadvandvāsradhārādvayadharavadane*. Kālī is so represented as having devoured the flesh of the demons. The Māhānirvāṇa-Tantra, chap. xiii, verse 9, says: 'As She devours all existence, as She chews all things existing with Her fierce teeth, therefore, a mass of blood is imagined to be the apparel of the Queen of the *Devas*.' Esoterically blood is Rajas Guṇa.

[4] That is, *Ha*, as to which see Kāmadhenu-Tantra, chap. ii; and Prānatoṣiṇī, 53 *et seq*.

[5] Lord of Fire, whose *Bīja* is *Ra*.

[6] 'Left eye,' or fourth vowel long *ī*.

[7] *Nāda-bindu*; the *Bīja* is thus *H+r+ī+m=Hrīṁ Hrīṁ*. In Svatantra-Tantra H*a* (*Vyoma*) is said to denote manifestation; *Ra* (*Vahni*) is involution; and Ī maintenance of the worlds.

[8] The earth, upper and nether worlds (see Viśvasāra-Tantra and Phetkāriṇī-Tantra). *Tribhuvanaṁ*, that is *Devas, Men, Nāgas* and so forth inhabiting *Svarga* (Heaven), *Martya* (Earth) and *Pātāla* (Nether world) (V).

VERSE 4

O DESTRUCTRESS of the sins of the three worlds, auspicious[1] Kālikā, who in Thy upper lotus-like left hand holdest a sword;[2] and in the lower left hand a severed head;[3] who with Thy upper right hand maketh the gesture which dispels fear,[4] and with Thy lower right hand that which grants boons; they, O Mother with gaping mouth,[5] who reciting Thy name, meditate in this way[6] upon the greatness of Thy mantra, possess the eight great powers[7] of the Three-Eyed One[8] in the palm of their hands.[9]

COMMENTARY

'*Sword*' (*Kṛpāṇam*)

The sword is knowledge (Jñāna) by which the bonds of ignorance of the desire-free Sādhaka are severed. See S'ivadharmottara.

'*Severed head*' (*Cinna-muṇḍaṁ*)

The human head is the seat of Tattvajñāṇa free of attachment.

'*Terrible countenance*' (*Prakatita-vadane*)

Her white teeth indicative of the white self-manifesting Sattva-Guṇa bite the red rolling tongue indicative of Rajas Guṇa and suppress both Rajas and Tamas by Sattva.

'*Precious Mantrās*' (*Manu-vi-bhavaṁ*)

The three 'Krīm' Bījas represent the Cidghanạ aspect of Devī, the two Hūm Bījas the Sattya-Guṇa aspect and the two 'Hrīm' Bījas the Rajah-pradhāna-sattva-Guṇa aspect.

[Durgārāma-Siddhāntavāgīśa explains this in the following different ways: (*a*) Manuvibhava = the Vibhava or Saṁpatti (precious possession) of Manus or Mantras. This precious possession is the name in the vocative case 'Dakṣiné Kālike.' The meaning of the passage then is that those who recite Thy name Dakṣiṇė Kālike, which is the precious possession of Mantras, and meditate on this Thine appearance possess the Powers and so forth. (*b*) Manuvibhava is the Vibhava of the Manu that is the twenty-two syllabled Mantra of Kālī. This possession is the name Dakṣiṇé Kālikā. (*c*) Manuvibhava = Manu (Mantra) vibhava (Ghataka) of which (the Devī's body) is the body of which Mantra is the generator. The bodies of the Devatās are produced by their Mantras. The passage thus means that, they who recite Thy name Dakṣiṇé and Kālikā and meditate on this Thine appearance generated by Mantra possess the virtues mentioned above.]

See last Verse.

Kālikā (*Kālike*)

'*Three eyed one* (*Tryaṁbaka*)'

[The same commentator (Durgārāma) offers three explanations of the term Tryaṁbaka used for S'iva (*a*) He who has three Aṁbakas or eyes is Tryaṁbaka, (*b*) He who has three Mothers or Aṁbās is Tryaṁbaka. The Kālikapurāṇa says, 'As Hara is born of three Mothers He is known, even amongst Devas, by the title Tryaṁbaka. (c) Todala-Tantra says 'the Vidyā Bhuvaneśvari is in Heaven, Earth and the Nether world (Pātāla). He who delights in the Devī as threefold in three places is called Tryaṁbaka. He is with S'akti and is worshipped in all Tantras.']

Notes

[1] *Dakṣiṇé*, the beneficent grantor of *Nirvāna*. (V)

[2] *Khadga*, the peculiar heavy sword with the blade curved at the tip so named, used to behead the sacrificial animals.

[3] The Devī is the destroyer of the wicked.

[4] The Devī is the dispeller of all fear, and makes with Her hand the *mudrā*. The right upper hand makes the gesture of dispelling fear, or the gesture of assurance of safety (*Abhaya-mudrā*) and the right lower hand makes the gesture of granting boons (*Varamudrā*). (V). The *Sādhakā* seeks fearlessness, which is the great gift of the Goddess, who is *Bhayāpahā*, 'remover of fear.' 'If thou art remembered in times of difficulty, Thou takest away all fear' (Mārkaṇḍeya-Purāṇa). At the same time it is she who fills the ignorant with terror (*Paśuloka-bhayaṁkarī*)—that is, those devoid of the knowledge of non-duality, for 'fear comes when there is duality' (Br. Up. 1-4-2, Lalitā, v. 99).

[5] *Prakatita-vadane* (see '*Daśa-Mahāvidya Upāsanārahasya*,' by Prasanna-Kumāra-S'āstrī). *Vimalānanda* reads *Prakatitaradane*, that is, with big protruding teeth. The *Yoginī-Tantra* says, 'Supreme eternal, large-toothed, smeared with blood.' The *Tārākalpa* speaks of '*Syāmā* of the colour of a new (freshly formed) cloud, with large breasts, terrible with protruding teeth. (V)

[6] As stated, that is, *Krīṁ Krīṁ Krīṁ Hūṁ Hūṁ Hrīṁ Hrīṁ* which with *Dakṣiṇe* makes ten syllables.

[7] *Siddhi*—that is, *Aṇimā, Laghimā, Garimā, Prāpti, Prākāṁya, Īśitva, Vaśitva, Kāmāvasāyitā*; the power of becoming small, great, heavy, light, etc., which are inherent in Īśvara, and are attainable by Yogis who become Īśvara and gain *Aiśvarya*. By realization of the self, that Divine state which is the universal Self is manifested, as also the eight-fold manifestation of the Divine power.

[8] *Tryaṁbaka* or *S'iva*. According to Tarkālaṁkāra's Commentary on Mahānirvāṇa-Tantra, *Tryaṁbaka* means the father of the three *Devas*, Brahmā, Viṣṇu, and Rudra. The Ṛgvidhāna uses it as an equivalent of Mahādeva. The Mahānirvāṇa-Tantra says: 'As She surveys the entire universe, which is the product of time, with Her three eyes—the Moon, Sun, and Fire—therefore She is endowed with three eyes' (*Ullāsa* xiii, verse 8). The Moon, Sun, and Fire are the *Icchā, Kriyā, Jñāna* and other *S'aktis* (see the Ṣatcakranirūpaṇa of Pūrṇānanda-S'vāmī) and *The Serpent Power*.

[9] 'By him who carries a flower its odour is enjoyed without seeking. By him who looks upon himself as the universal Self the powers (of Brahmā, etc.) are enjoyed' (Commentary of Sureśvarācārya on the tenth *S'loka* of *Dakṣiṇāmūrti Stotra*).

VERSE 5

O Mother, they who recite Thy charming *Bīja*, composed of the first of the group of letters,[1] followed by *Vahni*,[2] *Rati*,[3] and beautified by *Vidhu*,[4] thrice, the *Kūrca Bīja*[5] twice, and thereafter, O Smiling Face, the *Lajjā*[6] *Bīja* twice, followed by the two *Thas*,'[7] they, O Spouse of the Destroyer of the Deva of Desire[8] contemplating Thy true form,[9] become themselves the Deva of Love whose eyes are as beautiful as the petals of the lotus which Lakṣmī holds in Her playful dance.[10]

Commentary

'*Whoever*' (*Ye, ye*)

Even the most sinful. The Kālikularahasya says, 'Whoever he be who remembers Durgā with or without reverence is delivered from evil and attains the supreme end.'

'*Recite*' (*Japanti*)

Meditate upon.

'*Thy Bīja*'

[Durgārāma Siddhāntavāgiśa calls it the nine syllabled Bīja.]

First letter (*Vargādyaṁ*)

The aspect of Consciousness (Cinmayarūpa) which is the beginning of creation.

Placed on Vahni (*Vahnisaṁsthaṁ*)

Full of Tejas.

'*Associated*' (*Vidhu-rati-lalitaṁ*)

That is cooling and beautiful.

'*Thrice*' (*Trayaṁ*)

'That is the three aspects of Sattva, Rajas, Tamas.

'*Kūrca*'

Is S'abdabrahman.

'*Lajjā*'

Is Brahman associated with Māyā.

'*Two Thas*'

Svāha the revealing S'akti of Fire.

'*Smiling face*' (*Smitamukhi*)

Because She is always blissful.

'*Spouse of the Destroyer*' (*Smara-hara-mahile*)

S'akti of S'iva who is the Destroyer of passionate Desire ; that is She destroys the lust, anger and so forth of Her Sādhakas.

'*Thy true form*' (*Svarūpaṁ*)

That which is not different (in essence) from Jīvātmā. Svarūpa is explained here as the Rūpa of S'iva, that is Ātmā, meaning the Oneness of Paramātma and Jīvātma. Kālikā-S'ruti says, 'One should always think of Ātmā as Kālī'. Kālīkula-sarvasva says, 'He who worships the spouse of S'iva thinking that his Ātmā is Kālikā's Ātmā and meditating on the S'iva-like Guru is Sadāśiva Himself.' Yoginī-Tantra says, 'He who thinks, even if it were for a moment, "I am Brahman" to him the Devī gives unending fruit. One's own body should always be thought of as the body of the Iṣṭadevatā. And so the whole world should be considered as Her body.'

[Durgārāma explains Svarūpa in the following ways: (*a*) The true form is that indicated in the previous or following verses. (*b*) It is that of the nine-syllabled Mantra. (*c*) It is that indicated by the letters composing the Mantra. For instance Varadā-Tantra says that in 'Krīṁ', K is Kālī, R is Brahmā, Ī is Mahāmāyā, Nāda is the Matrix of the universe and Bindu is the Dispeller of Sorrow. In 'Hūṁ', H is S'iva Ū is Bhairava, Nāda means the Supreme and Bindu is the Dispeller of Sorrow. In Hrīṁ, H is S'iva, R is Prakṛti, Ī is Mahāmāyā, Nāda the Generatrix of the Universe and Bindu the dispeller of pain. Contemplation of Mantras constituted of these letters reveals their Caitanya. Japa of Mantra without knowing its Caitanya is useless.]

'*Become themselves*' (*Kāmarūpa bhavanti*)

They acquire the power of assuming whatever form they desire and of charming the whole world with their beauty.

NOTES

[1] That is, *Ka*.

[2] Deva of Fire, or *Ra*.

[3] S'akti of Kāma, God of love, or long Ī.

[4] The moon, or *Nāda-bindu*. The *Bīja* is, therefore, *K*+*r*+ī+*ṁ*=*Krīṁ*.

[5] That is, *Hūṁ*.

[6] *Hrīṁ*; literal meaning of *Lajjā*, is modesty.

[7] Or Svāhā, S'akti of Agni. The *mantra* is, then, *Krīṁ*, *Krīṁ*, *Krīṁ*, *Hūṁ*, *Hūṁ*, *Hrīṁ*, *Hrīṁ Svāhā* or the nine-lettered *Vidyā*, or feminine *mantra*, which ends with *Svāhā* (see Viśvasāra-Tantra).

[8] *Smarahara* or *S'iva*, who destroyed Manmatha with fire from his central eye of wisdom when the latter sought to distract him by passion from his *Yoga*. The Devī, according to the Brahma-vaivarta-Purāṇa, restored Manmatha to life (see as to this Bhāskararāya's Commentary on the Lalitā, verse 34).

[9] *Svarūpaṁ*, that is true form as described in the first and other verses (V).

[10] *Lakṣmī* is associated with, holds, and stands on the lotus, hence Her titles—Kamalā, Padmā, Padmālayā, Padmadhāriṇī (see Lakṣmīstotra in Tantrasāra, p. 577, Rasik Mohan Chatterjee's edition).

VERSE 6

O Devī [1] of full breasts, [2] whose throat is adorned with a garland of heads, They who meditating [3] recite any one or two or three of Thy very secret and excelling *Bījas* or all thereof [4] together with Thy name, [5] in the moonlike face of all such the Devī of Speech [6] ever wanders, and in their lotus-like eyes Kamalā [7] ever plays. [8]

Commentary

'*Devī*'

The self-manifest one.

"*Full breasts*' (*Pīnastanāḍhyā*)

The milk of these is the food with which She nourishes the world and the drink of immortality with which She liberates Her Sādhakas.

'*Whose neck*' (*Muṇḍa-sragatiśaya-lasat-kaṇṭi*)

She who is S'abdabrahman consisting of 50 letters. Niruttara-Tantra says, 'She is adorned with a garland of heads representing the 50 letters.' Kāmadhenu-Tantra says, 'In My throat is the wonderful Bīja of 50 letters.' Again 'I worship the Mother the source of the universe, S'abdabrahman itself, blissful.' Viśvasāra says, 'Blissful Brahman is adorned with S'abdabrahman and within the body is represented by all Mantras.'.

'*Bīja*'

Mūrti (appearance) in the individual aspect as Prājña, Taijasa, and Viśva and in the aggregate as Īśa, Sūtra and Virāṭ. Devīgitā says 'the causal self is Prājña, the subtle bodied one is Taijasa and the gross bodied one is Viśva.' Similarly Īśa is spoken of as Īśa, Sūtra and Virāṭ. The First is the individual (Vyaṣṭi) aspect and the second the aggregate (Samaṣṭi) aspect.

Eyes (*Netra*)

Not to speak of themselves being wealthy, the sight of them gives wealth to others. Bhairava Tantra says that Kamalā and the Devī of speech never forsake them for three generations downwards.

Notes

1 *Devī* which comes from the root *Div* to shine, is the Shining One (V).

2 *Pīnāstanādhye* (see also Bhairvīstotra in Tantra-sāra, p. 596). The physical characteristics of the Devī in swelling breasts and hips are emblematic of Her great Motherhood, for She is *S'rimātā*. See also as to the former, (Durgā-*Dhyāna* in Devī-Purāṇa, which speaks of her large and rising breasts (*Pinonnata-payodharāṁ*); the Annapūrṇā-*Stava* (*Vakṣojakuṁbhāntari*); Bhuvaneśvari-*Stotra* (*Āpivara-stanatatiṁ*); and the Saraswati-*Dhyāna* (*Kucabharana-mitāṁgiṁ*). The Annapūrna-*Dhyāna* (*Annapradāna-niratāṁ stanabhāra-naṁrāṁ*) speaks of Her limbs as weighted by Her breasts. The Mahābhāgavata describes Her as naked, terrific, with fiery eyes, full and erect breasts, and dishevelled hair; and the Lalitā (verse 15) says: 'Her golden girdle supports Her waist, which bends under the burden of Her breasts, thrice folding the skin below Her bosom' (*Stanabhāra-dalanmadhya-pattabhandha-valitrayā*).

3 *Bhāvayantah*, that is, meditating on the naked, full-breasted, black form with dishevelled hair as stated in Her *Dhyāna*, and which is the *Artha* of the particular *Mantra*. The *Bhūtaśuddhi-Tantra* says, 'A Mantra should be recited mentally meditating the while on the form of the *Devī* denoted by it' (V).

4 Any one of the aforesaid Bijas or the whole, that is, the whole nine-lettered *Vidyā* in full, which according to the Kumārī-Tantra cited in Tantraratna is *Krīṁ, Krīm, Krīm, Hūṁ, Hūṁ, Hūṁ, Hrīm, Hrīm, Hrīṁ*. S'yāmārahasya quoting Kālikā-S'ruti, says that the whole *Vidyā* should be recited once, twice or thrice, or the whole *mantra* with '*Dakṣiṇe Kālike* between the Bijas.' (K. B.) Thus, *Krīṁ, Krīṁ, Krīṁ, Hūṁ, Hūṁ, Hrīṁ, Hrīm, Dakṣiṇe Kālike, Krīṁ, Krīm, Krīṁ, Hūm, Hūṁ, Hrīṁ, Hrīṁ*.

5 *Dakṣiṇe Kālikā*.

6 *Sarasvatī*. The Bhāradvāja-Smṛti says Sarasvatī is She who ever resides in the tongue of all beings, and who causes speech.

7 *Lakṣmī*: for them is all learning, weallth, and prosperity (see Mahānirvāṇa-Tantra, *Ullāsa*, vii, verse 50).

8 In other words they become rich and learned.

VERSE 7

O Mother, even a dullard becomes a poet who meditates upon Thee raimented with space, [1] three-eyed, [2] Creatrix [3] of the three worlds, whose waist[4] is beautiful with a girdle made of numbers of dead men's arms, and who on the breast of a corpse,[5] as Thy couch in the cremation-ground, [6] enjoyest Mahākāla. [7]

Commentary

Dullard' (*Jadacetāh*)

One whose mind is smitten with passion for the world.

'*Poet*' (*Kavih*)

A great Jñāni.

'*Meditates*' (*Dhyāyan*)

'Who in mental vision sees Thee who art Saccidānanda-rūpiṇī.

'*Whose loins*' (*Bāhuprakarakṛta-kāñciparilasannitambām*)

At the end of each Kalpa all Jīvas abandon their gross bodies, and existing in their subtle bodies in which their respective Karmas inhere, form part of the Avidyā which is in the causal body of the Brahmarūpiṇī associated with Her own Gūṇās (Svaguṇa) until they are liberated at some future time after the commencement of the next Kalpa. Hence the girdle adorning the loins, lower belly and generative organ of the Mahādevi virāṭrūpiṇī, capable of producing children, is fashioned of the arms and hands of dead Jīvas. For these arms and hands were their principal instruments for the doing of work (Karma). The S'āktānandataraṅgiṇī says, 'With Karma is a Jīva born, with Karma he dies and in the next body again that Karma is attached to him.' Devīgitā says, 'In Her at dissolution Jīvas and their Karmas are merged in undifferentiated mass, just as all which is done (Vyavahārā) merges in dreamless sleep (Suṣupti).' Again the Devī says, 'It is I who create the whole world and enter therein with Prāṇa, Māyā, Karma and so forth.'

'*Raimented with space* (*Digvastrām*)

Raiment is the covering of Māyā. She is without that and above Māyā.

Three-eyed' '(*Trinayanām*)

Having knowledge of the three divisions of Time, past, present and future.

'*Creatrix*' '(*Vidhātri*)

She who at the beginning of the next Kalpa gives birth and enjoyment to Jivas according to their respective Saṁcita Karma.

'*On the breast of a corpse*' (*S'avahṛdi*)

The corpse is Nirguṇa-Brahman. The couch is the support (Ādhāra). On Nirguṇa-Brahman as Thy Ādhāra, that is, established in Thine own state (Pada) as Nirguṇa Brahman. Gāyatri-Tantra says, 'By the word corpse is indicated Brahman as the dead body (Preta).' Gandharva-Tantra says Sadāśiva is the couch on which lies the subtle Tripurasundarī.

'*In the cremation ground*' (*S'maśānasthā*)

The cremation ground (S'maśāna) is the great Ether (Mahākāśa) in which all creatures are merged as corpses in the Great dissolution (Mahāpralaya). In dissolution even the greatest of creatures are but corpses and hence it is a cremation ground.

'*Dost enjoy Mahākāla*' (*Mahākāla-surata-prayuktām*)

At the end of a Kalpa, there being no creation, She being inactive, and there being nought but supreme Brahman, She being inseparate from Paraśiva, experiences Herself as unlimited (Akhaṇḍa) Bliss.

Notes

[1] The Devī is naked, as is S'iva, for, like Him, She is clothed with space, and is the great void itself (Mahāśūnya).

[2] *Trinayanām.* The Three eyes are Sun, Moon and Fire (V). *Mahānirvāṇa-Tantra* says, 'Three eyes are attributed to *Kālikā* because She observes the whole world with such eyes as the Sun, the Moon, and so forth'. See as to the meaning of these three terms

which do not merely denote these luminaries and elements, *The Serpent Power* and *The Garland of Letters*.

[3] *Vidhātrim*, who provides Enjoyment and Liberation for all Jivas. (V).

[4] *Nitamba*, literally, buttocks but the girdle goes all round. Kālī is represented as so girdled.

[5] The corpse (*S'ava*) represents *S'iva* (V) because He is inactive whilst his *S'akti* it is who does everything. *S'avahṛdi*—that is, on the breast of S'iva (*Viparītarati*). The Devī is given the dominant position in her union with Her consort, because She is *Kartri* (actress), and He is *Bhoktā* (unacting enjoyer). According to Sāṁkhya, *Puruṣa is* neither producer nor produced, but passive, and a looker-on upon the actions of *Prakṛti*. It is not the *Puruṣa* who is active in the creation of the world, but it is She who, in the light of His gaze, dances the world-dance. So Kubjikā- Tantra says: 'Not Brahmā, but Brahmāṇī, creates; it is Vaiṣṇavi, not Viṣṇu, who protects; Rudrāṇī, not Rudra, who takes all things back. Their husbands are like dead bodies.' For in respect of power they are dependent on their S'aktis. As to the *Sādhana*, see Prāṇatoṣini 622, *Viparītaratau japtvā nirvāṇapadavīṁ vrajet*. Two corpses are sometimes pictured, the lower being the eternally quiescent S'iva, and the upper being the S'iva united with S'akti in creation. Similarly the Devī is represented as reclining on a couch made of five corpses, which are the Mahāpreta (see Bhairavayāmala, Lalitā, verse 174, etc). The *Mahāpretas*, whose *Bija* is is *Hsau*, are Sadāśiva, Īśāna, Rudra, Viṣṇu, and Brahmā.

[6] The site of certain forms of Tāntrik *Sādhana*, such as *S'avāsana*, *Muṇḍāsana*, etc., as to which the Phetkāriṇī-Tantra says that it is an excellent place for *Sādhana*. He who makes *japa* a number of times on a corpse in a cremation-ground attains all manner of success (*Siddhi*).'

[7] Parama-S'iva.

VERSE 8

THOSE who truly [1] meditate on Thee, the Spouse of Hara,[2] who art seated in [3] the cremation-ground strewn with funeral pyres, corpses, skulls, and bones, and haunted by female jackals howling fearfully; who art very youthful,[4] and art in full enjoyment upon [5] Thy Spouse, are revered by all and in all places.[6]

COMMENTARY

'*Meditate on*' (*Dhyāyanti*)

That is see with unperturbed mind.

'*Spouse of Hara*' (*Haravadhūṁ*)

Hara is He who removes (Harati) the threefold pains (Ādhyātmika, Ādhibhautika, Ādhidaivika) of Jīvas. His spouse is S'akti, that is She who grants Liberation to Jīvas and is Saccidānandarūpiṇi.'

'*Hast entered*' (*Praviṣṭāṁ*)

Art established.

'*Flaming*' *pyre* (*Prakaṭitacitāyāṁ*)

Cit-śakti On account of Her being self-manifested. Caṇḍī speaks of 'Her who pervades the whole universe as consciousness (Cit).'

'*Fearful*' (*Ghorābhiḥ*)

That is very powerful.

'*Jackals*' (*S'ivābhiḥ*)

That is Mahābhūtas which are auspicious (S'iva) before being made fivefold (Pañcīkṛta).

'*Skulls and bones*' (*Muṇḍāsthi-nikaraiḥ*)

The white colour of the skulls and bones indicates the white Sattva-guṇa. Hence associated with the Sattva and other Guṇas of the Jīvas dissolved in Mahāpralaya.

'*Ever youthful*' (*Atiyuvatiṁ*)

That is She is always the same, fresh, unchanging, and unwasting.

'*Satisfied with enjoyment*' (*Santuṣṭām-uparisuratena*)

She, after subduing Parama S'iva to Her will, has willingly enjoyment in the work of creation, preservation and dissolution. Nirvāṇa-Tantra says, 'The Vāmā (She who is on the left) is the Grantrix of Great Liberation after conquering the Dakṣiṇa (S'iva who is on the right).' Gandharva-Tantra says, 'She who is the Sun, Moon, and Fire and half of Ha (S'iva) puts down the Puruṣa and enjoys him from above.' Niruttara-Tantra says, 'When Nirguṇā Kali becomes Saguṇā She is engaged in Viparītaratī.' The Yogavāsiṣṭa in the Nirvāṇa-Prakaraṇa says, 'Natural unity is S'iva. Creation is (compared with it) unnatural.' That is the Mahādevī is Nirguṇa-Brahman in Her Svarūpa aspect and the subversion of this Svarūpa is the cause of creation.

'*Nowhere*' (*Kvacidapi na*)

In no birth.

'*Humiliated*' (*Paribhavah*)

That is they are not subjected to birth, death, and rebirth and attain Nirvāṇa.

Notes

[1] Commentator K. B.: where *param* is said to mean 'rightly,' or meditation alone without *japa*.

[2] *S'iva*.

[3] *Praviṣṭām*. 'Literally', entered.

[4] *Atiyuvatim*. She is without childhood or old age. The *Sāradātilaka* says, 'Although Thou art primordial, Thy youth is ever fresh'. (V)

[5] *Santuṣṭāṁ uparisuratena*, that is *viparītarati*, or *viparītavihāra* as to which see note 5 of last *śloka*.

[6] Commentator K. B.: Literally 'They nowhere suffer (*Kvacidapina*), that is, neither in this nor the next world defeat or humiliation.'

VERSE 9

WHAT, indeed, O Mother,[1] can we of so dull a mind say of Thee whose True Being[2] not even Dhātā,[3] Īśa,[4] or Hari[5] know ? Yet, despite our dullness and ignorance, our devotion towards Thee makes us talk of Thee.[6] Therefore, O Dark Devī,[7] forgive this our folly. Answer towards ignorant creatures such as we, is not befitting Thee[8].

COMMENTARY

'*Mother*'

Of us all including Brahmā, Viṣṇu, and Rudra. In the Devī-Sūkta, Viṣṇu says, 'One, subtle, and unchanged, and yet many, Thou dost give birth to millions of worlds. Who am I Viṣṇu, and who is the other S'iva and who are the Devas that we and they should be able to (fully) sing Thy praises?' In the Mārkaṇḍeya-Purāṇa, Brahmā says, 'When Viṣṇu, Īśvara and myself owe our appearance to Thee who has the power to (fitly) praise Thee ?' In Viṣṇuyāmala, Viṣṇu says to Devī 'Oh Mother none know Thy supreme aspect. The heavenly ones therefore worship that gross (Sthūla) aspect of Thine in the form of Kālī and the rest.' The Mahākāla-saṁhitā says, 'When Dhātā was not, nor Viṣṇu, nor Kāla, when the five Bhūtas were not, then Thou the Cause wert alone as the Supreme Brahman, the Being of all that is.'

(*Asite*) '*Unlimited*'

She is not limited by the Guṇas and is Nirguṇā.

NOTES

[1] *Jānāmi ;* origin of the three worlds.

[2] *Paramaṁ*, or 'reality' (Commentator K. B.).

[3] *Dhātā* is *Brahmā* who dispenses the fruits of *Karma*. (V)

[4] *S'iva. Īśa : Rudra* who wields the power of *Īśvara-hood.* (V)

[5] *Hari : Viṣṇu* who dispels the threefold sorrows of *Jīvas*. (V)

[6] *Tathāpi tvadbhaktir mukharayati. Tathāpi :* still, despite our dullness and ignorance (V) *Tvadbhaktiḥ :* inclination to sing

Thy praises (V). *Mukharayati* : impels to utter words in praise of Thee (V)

[7] This is literal but According to V, *Asite* = unlimited one. *Mahākālasamhitā* says, ' Unthinkable, unlimited, *S'akti* Itself, which is That on which all that is manifested rests, beyond the *Guṇas*, free of the opposites (*Dvandva*) to be apprehended only through *Buddhi* : Thyself alone art Supreme Brahman.' (V)

[8] As one does not become angry with animals (Paśu or animal and ignorant men also called Paśu) because they do wrong, so do not be angry with us. It is moreover, the part of the great to overlook the faults of their inferiors (Commentator K. B.).

VERSE 10

If by night,[1] Thy devotee[2] unclothed, with dishevelled hair, recites whilst meditating on Thee,[3] Thy *mantra*,[4] when with his *S'akti*[5] youthful, full-breasted, and heavy-hipped, such an one makes all powers subject to him, and dwells on the earth ever[6] a seer.[7]

Commentary

'Laya Yoga'

Is here described in this and following verses. Gheraṇḍa-Saṁhitā says' 'One should become S'aktimaya by doing Yoni Mudra. One should be in Paramātmā with sweet S'ṛṅgārarasa (love sentiment) and being Blissful (Ānandamaya) should unite with Brahman.' The Gorakṣa-Saṁhitā says, 'Raising the S'akti with the Jīva to the Lotus in the head one should become S'aktimaya and uniting with S'iva should think of all forms of happiness and enjoyment.' The Tantra-Kalpadruma says, 'One should meditate on Devī Kuṇḍalinī as Iṣṭadevatā, ever youthful, of the age of sixteen, full-breasted, dark, subtle, appearing as creation and in the form of creation, maintenance and dissolution (S'ṛṣṭi-sthiti-layātmikā).'

'Thy devotee' (Bhaktah)

Here the Divya Sādhaka who is a Yogin.

'By night (Naktam)'

That is, awaking in Brahmavidyā which (though Light) is darkness for all ordinary creatures. The Bhagavadgītā says, 'The self-controlled man awakes in what is night to all creatures.'

'Naked' (Vivāsāh)

That is, stripped of the covering of Māyā : that is awakened.

'Dishevelled hair' (Galitacikurah)

That is, with mind free from all restlessness. The word Cikura means both hair and restless.

'Meditating' (Dhyāyan)

On Thee as in enjoyment of Sāmarasya bliss with Paramaśiva.

'*Enjoying*' (*Ratāsaktām*)

By doing Laya of (merging) the Jīvātmā in Kuṇḍalinī-S'akti, the ever-youthful, all-pervading Genetrix and Preserver of all Jīvas. The creative and nourishing function of Kuṇḍalinī is indicated by the epithets 'heavy-hipped' and 'full-breasted.'

Notes

[1] *Naktaṁ.* At dead of night. The Phetkāriṇī-Tantra, 'By night, naked with dishevelled hair, in union with *S'akti*, by him is all *Siddhi*, gained'. The Kālīkrama says, 'The *Paśu* devoted to his own *Ācāra* should recite his *Mantra* a lakh of times by day. The *Vīra* or *Divya* should recite it a lakh of times by night.' Kubjikā-Tantra says 'Such as are in *Paśubhāva* are but *Paśus*. They should not touch a rosary nor recite *Mantra* by night.' (V)

[2] *Bhaktah.* Here a *Vīra-Sādhaka.* Niruttara-Tantra says, 'The *Mantrin* who has received *Abhiṣeka* should do *Kulapūjā*. Oh Devi the *Mantra* of *Kālī* does not become *Siddha* without *Kulācāra.*' (V)

[3] *Tvāṁ dhyāyan.* Mentally seeing Thee in his heart as ever in the Enjoyment of union with *Mahākāla.* (V)

[4] Thy *Mantra* is the aforesaid great *Mantra.* (V)

[5] He is *Ratāsakta,* the meaning of which is as follows: *Sa mantraṁ japati yadā sa śobhanāṅgapratyaṅgaśālinyā manohāriṇyāyuvatyā śaktyā saha maithunāsakto bhavati.* Whilst in union (*Maithuna*) the mind must be concentrated on *Devī Kālī* and *japā* must be done of Her *Mahāmantra.* The devotee should not think of aught else.

[6] So also Phetkāriṇī-Tantra (ch. x) says:

> '*Rātrau nagnah śayānas ca maithune ca vyavasthitah.*
> *Athavā muktakeśash ca tena syuh sarvasiddhayah,*
> *Staṁbhanaṁ mohana-caiva vaśīkaraṇaṁ eva ca.*'

Here *Athavā* means if the *Sādhaka* is without a *S'akti*; then recitation of *mantra* with dishevelled hair gives the same *siddhi.*

[7] *Kavi* which has not here the limited sense of 'Poet.'

VERSE 11

O Spouse of Hara [1], should (a *Sādhaka*) daily [2] recite Thy *mantra* for the space of a year meditating the while [3] with knowledge of its meaning [4] upon Thee, intent [5] upon Thy union [6] with the great Mahākāla, above whom Thou art, [7] then such a knower [8] has every pleasure that he wills upon the earth, [9] and holds all great powers [10] in the grasp of his lotus-like hands.

Commentary

'*Spouse of Hara*' (*Haravadhū*)

Charmer of Mahākāla.

'*Mentally recite*' (*Vicintya japati*)

The Kaulāvali says that mental (Mānasa) Japa is a hundred times more efficacious than verbal (Vācika) Japa.

According to Durgārāma the words may also mean 'recite' keeping in mind the Artha or meaning and so forth of the Mantra. For it is said that he who does not know the Artha of Mantra, the Caitanya of Mantra, and Yoni-mudrā is without success (Siddhi) even if he do Japa of the Mantra a million times.

'*Unperturbed mind*' (*Susthibhūya*)

The Kulārṇava-Tantra thus enjoins : 'Beloved ! when doing Japa of a Mantra one should be calm, pure, sparing in food, reverential, self-controlled, unaffected by the opposites (Dvandva), steady of mind, silent and self-disciplined.'

'*Meditating on Thee*' (*Vicintyatvām*)

The Kaulāvali-Tantra says, 'One should meditate upon the Spouse of S'iva before Japa and after meditation should again do Japa.' The Sādhaka who does Japa and meditation together soon attains success.

'*Upon Him*' (*Viparītam*)

(The original is 'Viparitah' in the first case and Durgārāma therefore makes it an adjective of the Sādhaka who he says unites with his S'akti in Viparita Maithuna. Vimalānanda however reads it as Viparītām in the second case making it an adjective of 'Thee' (the Devi) who is the object of meditation).

'*Great Powers*' (*Mahāsiddhinivahāh*)

Such as that by which is gained Sālokya, Sārūpya, Sāyujya and Nirvāṇa forms of Liberation.

Notes

[1] *S'iva.*

[2] *Sada :* Means 'always' here 'daily' (K.B.).

[3] *Vicintya*, that is, who has mentally thought of the letters of the *Bīja* and their meaning, which is mental *japa* (*Mānasa japa*), defined in Narasiṁha-Purāṇa (cited in the Āhnikācāra-tattva of Raghunandana) as the repetition in the mind, letter by letter, syllable by syllable, of the *mantra*, meditating at the same time upon its meaning.

[4] That is upon *Varṇa-saṁsthāna* or placing of the letters and their meaning and so forth.

[5] *Susthibhūya*—that is, whose senses are not directed to any other object (Commentary, K.B.).

[6] *Atiśayamahākālasuratām.*

[7] *Viparitam* (see *śloka* 7, note 5.)

[8] *Vidvān* whose sole aim is *Mokṣa.*

[9] Literally, 'wandering freely on Earth' (Commentary, K.B.).

[10] *Siddhi* (see *ante*, p. 295.)

VERSE 12

O MOTHER, Thou givest birth to and protectest the world, and at the time of dissolution dost withdraw to Thyself[1] the earth and all things; therefore Thou art Brahmā, and the Lord of the three worlds, the Spouse of S'rī,[2] and Maheśa,[3] and all other beings and things.[4] Ah Me! how, then, shall I praise Thy greatness?

COMMENTARY

'*Dost withdraw*' (*Saṁhārati*)

That is dost make the world lose itself in Thy Causal (Kāraṇa) body.

'*Dhātā*'

She is the creative S'akti of Brahmā.

'*Husband of S'ri*' (*Sripatih*)

She is the preservative S'akti of Viṣṇu whose spouse is S'rī or Lakṣmī.

'*Maheśa*'

She is the dissolving S'akti of Rudra.

'*All things*' (*Samastaṁ*)

Thou art both the material and instrumental cause of the world. The Triputā-Stotra says, 'Thou art Earth, Brahmā, and Creatrix of the world. Thou art also Water, Viṣṇu, and Preserver of the world. And thou art Fire, Rudra and the Dissolver of the world. As the Air of the world thou art Aiśvarya.' Another Stotra says, 'She assumes three forms of body for the purpose of creation, maintenance and dissolution. The world being constituted of the three Guṇas, Brahmā, Viṣṇu and Rudra are Her Vikṛtis.'

NOTES

[1] It is commonly said that She destroys but not so. Devatā does not destroy (*Na devo nāśakah*). Man does. She takes back what She has put forth.

[2] *Viṣṇu*, husband of *Lak*.

[3] *S'iva*. The *Trimūrti* is, in fact, Her manifestation.

[4] *Prāyah sakalaṁ api*, that is, all moving and unmoving things (Commentary, K.B.). For the Devī is *Viśvarūpiṇi* in that form of the whole universe. She is the objective world, '*jaḍātmika*' (Lalitā, verse 90), as well as its Cause.

VERSE 13

O MOTHER, people there are who worship many other *Devas* than Thyself. [1] They are greatly ignorant, and know nothing of the high truth, [2] (but I) of my own uncontrollable [3] desire for Thee approach Thee, the Primordial Power, [4] who dost deeply enjoy the great Bliss arising from union (with S'iva), [5] and who art worshipped by Hari, Hara, Viriñci, and all other *Devas*. [6]

COMMENTARY

'*Deluded*' (*Vimūdhāh*)

That is devoid of discrimination.

'*Enlightened*' (*Vibudhaih*)

The Bagalā-Stotra says, 'Oh four-armed, four-headed, worshipful Parameśvari, Oh Devi Aṁbikā who art ever worshipped with devotion by Kṛṣṇa, Oh Parameśvari who art worshipped by the Lord of the daughter of Himālaya, grant beauty, grant victory' and so forth.

'*Ādyā*'

Who art before and the beginning of the world.

'*Union*' (*Rati*)

Which is Viparita as above described.

'*Wine*'

That is Rasa.

NOTES

[1] That is, thinking that other *Devas* grant greater boons (Commentary, K.B.). Cf. also what S'aṁkarācārya says about the worship of other *Devas* in the fourth *śloka* of the *Devyaparādha-kṣamāpana-stotra*, and see Hymn to Jagadaṁbikā. V. 19., p. 142 *ante*.

[2] *Paramam*, that is, *Tattvaṁ*.

[3] For he is a devotee (Bhakta) whose desire for Her is so great that he cannot control but is controlled by it.

[4] *Ādyā.*

[5] *Rati-rasa-mahānanda-niratām.* The Devī delights in creation, which is the fruit of Her union with the *Puruṣa* (S'iva). 'Great Bliss,' for, as on the physical plane *yadrūpaṁ paramānandam tan nāsti bhuvanatraye* (Mātṛkābheda-Tantra, chap. ii), it is the counterpart on that plane of the ecstatic union which produced the Universe itself. It is the reflection of the higher Bliss attainable even here by the union of S'ivaśakti (in the form of Kuṇḍalinī) in the *Sahasrāra.* Some read *Rasikāṁ* for *Niratāṁ.*

[6] *Viṣṇu, S'iva,* and *Brahmā.* What, then, is the use of praying to *Brahmā, Viṣṇu,* and *S'iva* when they themselves worship Her? (Commentary, K.B.). Cf. also Devibhāgavata, *loc. cit.* The *Devi* is Mother of all, from *Brahmā* to the lowliest worm (*Ābrahmākhilajanani,* Lalitā 67).

VERSE 14

O KĀLĪ, spouse of Giriśa,[1] Thou art Earth, Water, Fire, Air and Ether.[2] Thou art all. Thou art one and beneficent.[3] What can be said in praise of Thee, O Mother ? Of Thy mercy show Thy favour towards me, helpless as I am. By Thy grace may I never be reborn.[4]

COMMENTARY

'*Kālī*'

Dispeller of the fear of Kāla or Death.

'*Thou art Earth*' (*Dharitrī kilālangshachirapi samīropi gaganam*)

Guptārṇava-Tantra says, 'Thou art Earth, Thou art Water, Thou art Fire, Thou art the Air of the world, Thou art Ether, Thou art Mind as Manas, Ahaṁkāra, Mahat (Buddhi) and Thou art Prakṛti. Thou art also, Oh Mother, Ātmā. Thou art the Supreme. Nothing is greater than Thee. Oh Devī of terrible form showing Thy teeth, may my sins be forgiven me.' The Triputā-Stotra also says, 'Thou art the Ādhāra-S'akti and the Ādhāra. Thou dost pervade the world and the world is in Thee.'

'*One*' (*Ekō*)

Without a second.

'*Beneficent*' (*Kalyāṇī*)

Because She grants Nirvāṇa Liberation to Jīvas.

'*Spouse of Giriśa*' (*Giriśaramaṇī*)

Spouse of S'iva. Or He who is in the Giri or Kūta is Giriśa that is Kūtaṣtha-Brahman ; His spouse or S'akti. Though changeless (Nirvikārā) Thou dost appear as the twenty-four Tattvas, namely, Earth and the rest through Thy Māyā. The Devīsūkta of the Ṛg-Veda says 'Thou who art one and many, subtle and the Vikāras (gross things) and giveth birth to millions of universes.'

'*All*' (*Sakalaṁ*)

S'ruti says, 'Verily all this is Brahman'.

'*Helpless*' (*Agatikaṁ*)

On account of liability to rebirth despite Sādhana.

Notes

[1] The Lord who inhabits the mountain, whereas, *Giriśa* is Lord thereof.

[2] Liṅgapurāṇa says, Devī becomes matter' (*Kṣetra*). She is *Kṣetra-svarūpā*, that is, the field or matter which is known by the soul (*Kṣetrajña*). See Lalitā Sahasranāmam (fourth hundred) for the Brahman who creates the visible world Itself enters into it (*Tat sṛṣṭvā tad evānuprāviśat.*)

[3] *Kalyāṇi*. According to the Padma-Purāna, *Devī* is worshipped as *Kalyāṇi* in the Malaya Mountain.

[4] *Bhavaṁ anu na bhūyān mama januh*, that is, liberated. The S'yāmārahasya reads *Bhavaṁ ananubhūyat*, using *bhavaṁ* as meaning *dukhaṁ* (pain), arising from *bhava* (the world) (K. B.).

VERSE 15

He, O Mahākāli [1], who in the cremation-ground, naked, and with dishevelled hair, intently [2] meditates upon Thee [3] and recites Thy *mantra*, and with each recitation makes offering to Thee of a thousand *Ākaṇḍa* flowers [4] with seed,[5] becomes without any effort a Lord of the earth. [6]

Commentary

'And' (*Tu*)

For Divya Sādhakas.

'Mahākāli'

Or Parabrahmarūpiṇī.

'Cremation-ground' (*S'maśānasthah*)

The cremation-ground is Parabrahman into which in the great Dissolution (Mahāpralaya) all beings go as though corpses. 'In the cremation-ground' therefore, means devoted to Parabrahman.

'Naked' (*Dikpatadharah*)

That is, free from the covering of Māyā ; whose Consciousness is untainted.

'Meditates on Thee' (*Dhyānaniratah*)

That is, upon Thy Saccidānanda aspect. The Rudrayāmala says, 'He who follows the Kula path should do Japa of Mantra seeking protection from Devī who is Consciousness, Bliss and Source of knowledge, who is all Tattvas, whose refulgence is that of millions of flashes of lightning.'

'Sunflowers' (*Arkānāṁ*)

Flowers of feeling such as compassion, forgiveness and so forth which are functions of the Mind called the Sun in the Brahmarandhra. The Jñānasaṁkalini-Tantra says, 'Oh Beloved, the mind is seated on the surface of the sun and life on that of the moon.' The Yājñavalkya-Saṁhitā says, 'The Moon is known to be in the Idā and the sun in the Piṅgalā (Nādi).

'*Self-produced Bīja*' (*Nijagalitavīryena*)

This Bīja is here the nectar which naturally flows from the thousand-petalled Lotus. The Mahānirvāṇa-Tantra says, 'The Heart-Lotus should be offered for seat, the nectar (Amṛta) shed from the Sahasrāra for water to wash the feet, the mind as the offering (Arghya), Memory (Citta) is offered by way of flowers, and the vital airs (Praṇa) as and by way of incense.' Jñānasaṁkalinī-Tantra says, 'Libation (Tarpaṇa) to the Supreme Liberatrix should be made from out the vessel of the Moon and Arghya should be given from out the vessel of the Sun. Compassion, wisdom, and forgiveness are flowers as is also control of the senses. So too are charity (Dayā) and religious merit. Non-injury (Ahiṁsā) to any being is an excellent flower. Bliss is a flower and so too is the worship of the Sādhaka. Whoever offers these ten flowers attains to the feet of the Liberatrix.' In this verse Savikalpasamādhiyoga is indicated.

Notes

[1] *Mahākālī*, *S'akti* of *Mahākāla*.

[2] *Susthah* : with undistracted mind. (V)

[3] *Tava dhyāna-niratah*, that is, Upon Thy form. (V)

[4] *Arka* = Sunflowers known as *Ākaṇḍa* (V) not the flower so called in English.

[5] *Nija-galita-vīryeṇa kusumaṁ*. Thus the offering is not only of the flowers of the *Ākaṇḍa* plant, *yatah sādhakah devyai svavīrya-miśritārkapuṣpāṇi samarpayati*. Durgārāma-Siddhāntavāgīśa cites the Mahākālasaṁhitā as saying that the *sūryapuṣpa* should be offered in the same way with *japa* of the *mūlamantra* (*svavīrya-miśrita-sūryapuṣpāṇi*). The *vīrya* does not, refer to the sap of the plant. *Nija* refers to the *sādhaka*. 'Along with, that is dipped in or that is spread over with.' *Mahākāla-samhitā* says, 'A *Kaula-Sādhaka* in the cremation-ground, naked, dishevelled and with tranquil mind, should offer a thousand sunflowers with seed reciting the while his *Mantra*. After meditating and worshipping with great devotion he should recite the Hymn' (V).

[6] That is, king or *rājā*. So the Phetkāriṇī-Tantra says that wealth, strength, eloquence, intelligence, and the love of women (*Sarvayoṣitpriyah*) is gained.

VERSE 16

O KĀLĪ, [1] whoever [2] on Tuesday at midnight, [3] having uttered Thy *mantra*, makes offering even but once with devotion to Thee of a hair of his *S'akti* [4] in the cremation-ground, [5] becomes a great poet, a Lord of the earth, and ever goes mounted upon an elephant. [6]

COMMENTARY

'*Kāli*'

Dispeller of the fear of Kāla or Death.

'*Whoever*'

Here a Divya Sādhaka.

'*Midday*' (*Madhyāhne*)

At noon.

'*Devotion*' (*Premnā*)

That is Parabhakti.

'*Offers*' (*Vitarati*)

Merges in Thee, that is, attains Nirvikalpa-Samādhi. Pātanjala-Sūtra says that Nirvikalpa-Samādhi is attained by suppression of the Vṛtti of mind.

'*In the cremation-ground*' (*Citāyām*)

In thee as Consciousness (Cit).

'*Bīja*'

That is here nectar which issues on the enjoyment of the union of Kula-kuṇḍalinī and Paramaśiva. The Gandharvamālikā-Tantra says, 'Oh beloved One, the Queen of Devas unites with Paraśiva and in a moment, Oh Devi Parameśvari, nectar is forthwith produced. That nectar, Oh Devī, is like the juice of of lac. With it, Oh, Mistress of the Devas, libation (Tarpaṇa) should be offered to the supreme Devatā.

'*At home*' (*Gṛhe*)

In the thousand-petalled Lotus (Sahasrāra).

'*Hair with its root*' (*Cikuraṁ Samūlaṁ*)

The mind with its functions. It is such Sādhaka who gains both enjoyment and Liberation.

Notes

[1] *Kāli* is destroyer of *Kāla* (V).

[2] 'Whoever' is here a *Vira Sādhaka*.

[3] *Madhyāhne*. Noon or (here) midnight. *Kakārakūtarahasya* says, 'Whoever naked and with dishevelled hair, on a Tuesday, at midnight, does *Homa* in the cremation-ground with hair, nails seed and whatever adheres to the *Sammārjanī* and offers them after having uttered the *Mūlamantra* and recited Thy name a thousand times attracts to him the Lord of the Earth' (V).

[4] The offering is stated in the words *grihe sammārjanyā parigalitabījam hi cikuram samūlang madhyāhne vitarati citayām kujadine*. These words have received various interpretations, of which the two chief alternatives are given. *Gṛhe* is by some translated as 'at home,' in distinction from the cremation-ground to which, according to this rendering, the *sādhaka* subsequently goes to make his offering. This, however, is said to be erroneous, as the *sādhanā* takes place not in the house but in the cremation-ground. Others (see Calcutta edition) translate it as the equivalent of *grihinī*, or wife. *Sammārjanī* is by them read to mean 'comb.' *Parigalita* is translated 'removed,' in the sense that the curling of the hair of the wife is 'removed or straightened with the comb. *Bījam* given either its primary meaning, or as the equivalent of *vīrya* is said to mean *kautilyam*, or curl of the hair. *Cikuram* is 'hair,' and *samūlam* qualifies it, meaning pulled out, taken off at the root. The meaning is, then, an offering is made of wife's hair, the curls (*kautilyam*) of which have been straighgtened out with the comb (*sammārjanyā*), and some of which has at the root (*samūlam*). The correct rendering, however, is according to K. B. *S'aktisādhakayoh gṛhe maithunasamaye yoniliṁgasaṁgharṣavaśāt śaktiyonipatitaṁ vīryaliptaṁ loma devyai samarpitaṁ bhavati*. *Gṛhe* thus doesnot mean 'at home,' but *manmathagrihe*. The hair is from the same. *Saṁmārijanī*=*S'iśna*. *Samūlaṁ* qualifies *cikuram* in the sense of 'come off at the root' under the circumstances stated. *Parigalita* is 'dropped'—referring to the *vīrya*.

According to *Vimalānanda*, *Gṛhe parigalita-vīryaṁ*, is that produced by union with the *Sādhaka's svaśakti* or wife (V).

Of the words *Gṛhe sammārjanyā parigalita-vīryaṁ cikuraṁ samūlam* the Commentator Durgārāma Siddhāntavāgiśa gives the two following alternative expressions: (*a*) *Sammārjanyā* means with a comb with which the hair is put in order. *Parigalitavīryam cikuram* means hair of which the *Vīrya* or crookedness has been removed. *Gṛhe* means in the wife: for it is said the wife is the home. The whole phrase then means Wife's hair, root and all, combed out straight with a comb or (*b*) *Sammārjanya parigalita-vīryaṁ* means *S'ukra* produced by *Sammārjani* here meaning *Liṅga* of the *Sādhaka*; *gṛhe* means in the abode of *Kāma* that is *Yoni* of *S'akti* together with hair, root and all.

The English translation is somewhat abbreviated with the object of giving only so much as all renderings are agreed upon. But in practice *Vīrya* is used by most in its literal sense, this is the gross meaning. The inner sense is given in the *Svarūpa vyākhyā* which follows.

[5] According to some, the offering is made on the built-up pyre, and, according to others, on the fire after the body has been consumed. *Citā*, however, is really used as a synonym for the burning ground (*Smaśāna*). The Niruttara-Tantra (Ch. I) speaks of two Kinds of *S'maśāna*:

S'maśānaṁ dvividhaṁ deva citā yonih prakīrtitaṁ.

[6] That is, he becomes a *Rājā*, and has no longer to go on foot like common folk.

VERSE 17

THE devotee [1] who, having placed before himself, [2] and meditated and again meditated [3] upon, the abode, [4] strewn with flowers, [5] of the *Deva* with the bow of flowers, [6] recites [7] Thy *Mantra*, Ah! [8] he becomes on earth the Lord of Gandharvas, [9] and the ocean of the nectar of the flow of poesy, [10] and is after death in Thy supreme abode. [11]

COMMENTARY

'*Devotee*' (*Bhaktah*)

The Sādhaka who is a Yogi on Divya path.

'*The Abode*' (*Kusumadhanuṣo mandiram*)

The triangular Yoni Maṇḍala in the Mūlādhāra. Nirvāṇa-Tantra says, 'In the triangle, the abode of Kāma, the Liṅga is Maheśvara.'

'*With its own flowers*'

Adorned with the Svayaṁbhu-linga which is compared to a flower. Gorakṣa-Saṁhitā says, 'He is truly wise who knows the supreme Tejas in the Yoni called Svayaṁbhuliṅga. Others are but beasts of burden.

'*Lord of Gandharvas*' (*Gandharva śreṇipatih*)

A great singer. It is said 'there is nothing better than a song.'

'*Poesy*' (*Kavitvāmṛta nadi nadinah*)

He becomes like the great poet Kālidāsa.

Is great' (*Prabhavati*)

He attains Nirvāṇa on being united with Thee who are Saccidānandarūpā. Kūrma-Purāṇa says, Brahmavādis have learnt in all Vedas and Vedāntas the one, omnipresent, subtle (Kūtastha), immovable, absolute, endless, undecaying Brahman, the sole supreme Niṣkala-Tattva higher than the highest, eternal, auspicious, wondrous.' Devigītā says 'Oh Mountain, he in whom Parabhakti is thus generated becomes merged in Pure Consciousness.'

Notes

[1] *Bhaktah*: here the *Vīra Sādhaka* (V).

[2] *Purah*: that is with the *Maṇḍala of Kāma* before him (V).

[3] That is, with intensity. *Dhyāyan dhyāyan*, repeatedly meditating (V).

[4] *Kusuma-dhanuṣomandiraṁ*. The Deva with the bow of flowers is *Kāmā* whose abode is the *Madanāgāra*. *Tantrakalpadruma* says, 'He who recites the *Mantra* ten thousand times meditating on the flower-covered *Yoni* (*Svapuṣpairākīrṇam*) of *S'akti*, of a certainty charms all with his poesy.' *Svapuṣpa* is called *Svayaṁbhukusuma* in *Tantra-śāstra*; *Mātṛkābheda-Tantra* says, 'Oh Lady of *Maheśa Svapuṣpa*, which charms all is the *Rtu* which first appears in a married girl (V).

[5] *Svapuṣpairākīrṇam*. The word *svapuṣpa = svayambhupuṣpa*— mentioned in the Tantras. The word *puṣpa* has here, and in ordinary parlance, a figurative sense, as in English. For *puṣpaśabdena atra ṛtur ucyate, mātṛkābheda-tantra-pramāṇānusāreṇa anūḍhāyāh kanyāyāh, prathama eva ṛtur atra ucyate. Tantrāntare tu vivāhitāyā eva, bālāyā ṛtur atra vivakṣitah*. The S'yāmārahasya reads '*supuṣpa*,' which literally means pleasing fragrant flower, but which is possibly a misprint for *svapuṣpa*. The meaning of the passage is as follows: *Sādhakah svasya puvobhāge śaktiṁ saṁsthāpya tasyā ṛturudhirasiktāṁ yoniṁ avalokayan san devīmantraṁ japati*.

[6] That is, *Kāma*, the *Deva* of Desire, whose bow and arrows are made of flowers.

[7] *Japati*. Recites ten thousand times (V).

[8] *Aho*. 'Ah' an exclamation of wonder (V).

[9] Celestial spirits (*devayoni*), who play and sing at the banquets of the *Devas*. According to the Viṣṇu-Purāṇa, sons of Brahmā 'born imbibing melody.' The *Sādhaka* thus becomes a master of dance, music and song. *Gandharva-śreṇipatih*. He becomes a great singer and a master of melody. The *Sāhasānka* says, '*Hāhā* is called a *Gandharva* and singing also makes a *Gandharva*' (V).

[10] He becomes a *Paṇḍita* in all literature. The Kāli-Tantra, quoted in the Kālikalpalatā, says that in strength he becomes like

the wind, in wealth of gifts like Indra, and in the musical art like Tumburu (K.B.)—a *Ṛṣi*, master of music and inventor of the *tambūr*.

[11] *Paramapadalinah prabhavati*, that is, he attains *nirvāṇa* (K.B).

Prabhavati : becomes capable of creating and so forth on being merged with Thy Supreme Feet (V). The word literally means 'Excels.'

——

VERSE 18

HE who at night, when in union with his *Sakti*,[1] meditates with centred mind[2] on Thee, O Mother with gently smiling face, as on the breast of the corpse-like Síva, lying on a fifteen-angled yantra[3] deeply enlisted in sweet amorous play with Mahākāla,[4] himself becomes the destroyer of the God of Love.[5]

COMMENTARY

'*Mother*' (*Janani*)

The Progenitrix.

'*At night*' (*Naktaṁ*)

Midnight. Brahannīla-Tantra says, 'He who is intent on meditation at midnight or early dawn surely sees the supremely blissful aspect of Devī.'

'*Meditates*' (*Dhyāyet*)

'On Thee as not different from the Sādhaka's own Ātmā, who art Cidābhāsa in his body as a Yantra.' Gandharva-Tantra says, 'He who is in Advaitabhāva, and thinks of the self as Devatā in the three forms of body thinks of Her and his Ātmā as one. He should worship the Devī as Ātmā with the articles prescribed. The Yantra which is one's own body should be considered the best of all Yantras.' Again 'He who meditates on the Nirguṇa, unattached pure Atmā of Tripurė as not being different from his own Ātmā becomes one with Her.'

'*Thee* (*Tvāṁ*)

That is Brahmamayi.

'*Smiling face*' (*Smera-vadanāṁ*)

Because She is ever blissful, being Bliss itself.

'*On the breast*' (*Mahākālenoccāih*)

On the breast of S'iva who is inactive like a corpse. She divides Herself into two parts like a grain of gram, namely, S'iva and S'akti by means of Māyā associated with Iccā, Kriyā, Jñāna, whilst at the same time remaining established in Her Nirguṇa-Brahman state.

'*Fifteen-cornered seat*' (*Tripāncāre pithe*)

This is the Sādhaka's own body conceived as the Yantra in which Avidyā is the encompassing circle, the eight-fold Prakṛti consisting of Earth and so forth is the eight-petalled lotus, the five Jñānendriyā, the five Karmendriyā and five Prāṇa are the fifteen Triangles and the Bindu which is Consciousness reflected in Māyā composed of pure Sattvaguṇa is the adorning Bija. The Gandharva-Tantra says, 'The Cakramantramaya is the Devatā's Supreme Body which is S'iva-śakti.' The Bhagavadgītā says, 'Earth, Water, Fire, Air, Ether, Manas, Buddhi, Ahaṁkāra, these Tattvas constitute my eightfold Prakṛti.' Gandharva-Tantra says, 'The subtle body composed of uncompounded (Apañcīkṛta) Bhūta and equipped with five Prāṇas, Manas, Buddhi and ten Indriyas is the vehicle for Enjoyment. Unbeginning and undefinable (Anirvācyā) Avidyā is the causal Upādhi. Know Atmā to be different from the three-fold Upādhi.'

'*Deeply enlisted*' (*Madanarasalāvaṇyaniratām*)

Always united in the reverse (Viparīta) way with Paramaśiva the Saguṇabrahman. The Gandharva-Tantra says, 'When that Supreme S'akti by putting that Puruṣa down, of Her will appears as the universe then She becomes passionate. And then becoming Herself active the Devī rises upon Bhairava and enhances Her own bliss with waves of natural pleasure."

'*Himself also enjoying*' (*Svayam api ratānandaniratah*)

Enjoying the bliss of union in Laya with Paramatmā by Yonimudrā and becoming S'aktimaya himself. The Gheraṇḍa-Saṁhitā says, 'He should do Yoni mudrā and himself become S'aktimaya. He should move in Paramātmā with the good S'ṛṅgārarasa. Becoming Ānandamaya he should be one with Brahman.'

'*Destroyer of Kāma*' (*Smarahara*)

The Advaita-sādhaka attains Kaivalya by being merged in Thee who art Paramātmā.

Notes

[1] *Svayam api ratānandaniratah*, of which the meaning is as follows: *yadā sādhakah śaktyā saha maithunakriyāsakto bhavati, tadā sa ślokokta-dhyāna-prakārānusāreṇa devīṁ dhyāyati.*

[2] *Samāsaktah*, concentrated on Thee.

[3] Kālikalpalatā says it is a kind of *yantra* (diagram).

Tripañcāre pīthe. The *Yantra.* The *Kāli-Tantra* says, 'First draw a triangle. Outside it put another. Next draw three triangles. In the centre draw the *Baindava-Cakra* adorned with the *Māyā Bīja.* Draw a circle outside the six cornered figure. Next draw the eight petals attached to the outer circle and *Bhūpura.* He who knows this great *Yantra* surely attains liberation.' *Bhūpura* is the gross body composed of the five *Bhūtas* (V). It is made with five triangles superimposed.

[4] *Mahākalenoccair-madana-rasa-lāvaṇya-niratām.* *Mahākāla* is *Paramaśiva* (V). *Madana-rasa-lāvaṇya-niratāṁ* refers to *Viparītarati* (V).

[5] *Smarahara.* The destroyer of *Kāma* is *S'iva* Himself (V).

That is, he becomes *S'iva* Himself, who destroyed *Smara* the *Deva* of Love (Kāma), with Fire from His central eye, when the latter, by the excitation of desire (towards Pārvatī), sought to detract him from his *yoga.* Or it may be translated 'excels in beauty the God of Love.'

VERSE 19

O Dark One,[1] wondrous and excelling in every way,[2] becomes the accomplishment,[3] of those worshippers[4] who living in this world[5] freely make offering to Thee in worship[6] of the greatly[7] satisfying flesh, together with hair and bone,[8] of cats, camels, sheep,[9] buffaloes, goats, and men.[10]

Commentary

'*Oh Black one*' (*Asitā*)

Asitā means free from bondage. Sitā means bound. Asitā is therefore 'not bound' or eternally liberated. The root So, means 'to bind.' Amarakośa gives the meaning of Sitā as 'bound.'

'*Wondrous*' (*Apūrva*)

Best.

'*At every step*' (*Pratipadam*)

In succession, step by step.

'*All Powers*' (*Sarvasiddhi*)

The five Siddhis which are the five forms of Liberation. The S'ivagita says, 'Sālokya, Sārūpya, Sārṣti, Sāyujya and Kaivalya. Know these to be the five forms of liberation.'

'*The flesh of*' (*Palalaṁ*)

These animals represent the Six Enemies (Ripu) or Vices which are specially characteristic of the following animals: The goat stands for Lust (Kāma) 'as lustful as a goat (Chhāga),' the buffalo, Anger (Krodha) 'as angry as a buffalo (Mahiṣa),' the cat, Greed (Lobha) 'as greedy as a cat' (Mārjāra), the sheep, Delusion (Moha), 'as stupid as a sheep' (Meṣa), the camel, Envy (Mātsarya) 'as envious as a camel' (Uṣtra), Man, Pride (Mada) 'the Pride and arrogance of man' (Nara).

The Ānandakalpa says, 'Worship should be done by making offering of lust as goat, buffalo, and so forth'. Offering is made to Thee who art Cidrūpā of lust and other vices as articles of offering (Upacāra) in worship with the object of ridding oneself of them. Bṛahannila-Tantra says, 'In the fire of Ātmā which flames with the ghee (Havih) of Dharma and Adharma, I ever offer in Homa by the Suṣumnā path, with the mind as ladle, all the functions of the senses—Svāhā.'

'In worship' (*Pūjāyām*)

In mental worship according to the manner prescribed.

'With hair and bone' (*Loma, asthi*)

That is the whole without omitting any part. Such Sādhakas attain the Sālokyā and other forms of liberation.

Notes

[1] *Asitā*: That is Kālikā *v. post.*

[2] *Pratipadam.* The S'yāmarahasya-sārasaṁgraha reads *pratidinam.* (every day) (K.B.), which seems preferable, for, as K.B. says, the worship (*pūjā*) is the general daily *pūjā*, upon which daily advancement in *siddhi* would follow.

[3] *Siddhi*: success in work; accomplishment of all which is desired (V).

[4] *Sat*, that is, *sādhu* (wise, good, pious). *Satāṁ=Sādhakānām* (V).

[5] That is, among men.

[6] *Pūjāyāṁ api* (see note 2), *ante.*

Pūjayāṁ: Naimittika or occasional worship (V). The force of the particle *api* is that the offering is not confined to special *Sādhanā* but is made in ordinary worship also. (K.B.)

[7] *Param* (K.B.).

[8] That is flesh and all.

[9] *Maiṣaṁ.* The S'yāmarahasya-sārasaṁgraha gives also *mauṣam,* of rat's flesh. The Phetkāriṇi-Tantra has both sheep and rat's flesh (K.B.)

S'yāmārahaysa says, 'To him who makes offering of the flesh of cats, sheep, camels, and buffaloes together with bone, hair and skin *Dākṣiṇe* is ever beneficial like a Mother.'

[10] As to this human sacrifice, K. B. says that Kings alone, and not any other, are entitled to make human sacrifice, citing the Yāmala quoted in the Kālikalpalatā (*Rājā naravalim dadyān nānyopi parameśvari*). For inner sense see Svarūpa-vyākhyā *post.*

VERSE 20

O MOTHER, he who, being a controller of his passions,[1] eats *haviṣyānnaṁ*,[2] and, being proficient in meditation on Thy feet, rightly recites[3] Thy *mantra* a hundred thousand times by day, and he who afterwards[4] naked at night, when united with his *S'akti*,[5] rightly recites Thy great *mantra* another such hundred thousand times, becomes on earth like unto the Destroyer of Smara.[6]

COMMENTARY

'*Naked*' (*Nagnaḥ*)

That is free from the covering of Māyā ; Nirvikāra.

'*Amorous play*' (*Nidhuvana-vinodena*)

That is enjoying the bliss of union between Ātmā and Parāśakti. The Kulārṇava-Tantra says, 'That is coition (Maithuna) in which there is the bliss arising from the union of Ātmā and Parāśakti. Others are but Enjoyers of women.'

'*Becomes*' (*Syāt*)

That is, becomes liberated whilst yet living (Jīvanmukta) like S'iva.

NOTES

1 *Vaṣī*. The first part of this *S'loka* refers to *Paśvācāra*.

2 That is, one who has undertaken the *Puraścaraṇavrata*, and eats pure form of food known as *Haviṣyānnaṁ* (K.B.).

Haviṣyāśanarataḥ : that is after the recitation (V).

3 Makes *japa* (see *ibid.*).

4 *Paraṁ* : that is, when he has been *Abhiṣikta* into *Vīrācāra*.

5 *Naktaṁ nagno nidhuvana-vinodena*, the meaning of which is *yadā sādhakaḥ śaktya saha maithuna-kriyāsakto bhavati, tadā sa mantraṁ japati*.

6 *Smarahara* or *S'iva* (see note 5 to *S'loka* 18, *ante*). The Tantra-kalpadruma says, 'He who eats *Haviṣyānnaṁ*, who keeping

Devi in mind recites the *Mantra* a hundred thousand times by day and is at night united with his *S'akti* becomes the Lord of the earth.' (V).

VERSE 21

O MOTHER, this Hymn of Thine is the source from whence originates Thy *mantra.*[1] It sings of Thy real self, and contains injunctions for the worship of Thy two lotus Feet. He who reads it at midnight or at time of worship[2] even his random talk[3] becomes the nectar juice of poesy.

COMMENTARY

'*Thy real self* (*Svarūpākhyaṁ*)

Speaks of the Dhyāna of both Thy gross and subtle aspects.

''*Reads*' (*Paṭati*)

That is recites aloud. The Viśuddheśvara-Tantra, 'Oh Devi, the reading of a Hymn (Stotra) mentally, or the recitation of a Mantra loudly is as ineffectual as water in a broken jar.'

'*Nectar of Poesy*' (*Prasarati kavitvāmṛtarasaḥ*)

He becomes full of the sweetness of Poesy. The Kālikula-sarvasva says, 'All whose difficulties and dangers are destroyed by a single reading, as it were flies in a flame. His speech flows like the Ganges full of prose and poetry.'

NOTES

[1] *Manusamuddharaṇajanuḥ*—that is, cause of *mantroddhāra*: formation of Mantra of Devī. The *mantra* is made known, and then impressed with the life and consciousness (*caitanya*) of the *sādhaka* (*mantra-caitanya*).

[2] *Pūjā.*

[3] That is, even his meaningless delirious talk, as in fever or madness, etc. (K.B.).

VERSE 22

NUMBERS of women with large eyes, like those of the antelope,[1] impatient for his love, ever follow him. Even the King becomes subject to his control. He becomes like unto Kubera[2] himself. An enemy fears him as if he were a prison. Living in continuous bliss[3] the devotee is liberated when yet living, and is never again reborn.[4]

Here ends the Hymn by S'rī Mahākāla, entitled *Karpūrādistotra*.

COMMENTARY

'*Liberated*' (*Jīvanmukta*)

And on death gets Videhamukti.

'*No rebirth*' (*Muktah pratijanuh*)

He gets Nirvāṇa in Brahman. The Mahākāla-saṁhitā says, 'Whoever constantly and with devotion reads this Hymn originating from Mahākāla, is free from danger, disease and death and in the end attains Kaivalya liberation.'

Here ends the Hymn named Svarūpastotra of S'rīmatī Dakṣiṇa-Kālikā by S'rīmān Mahākāla.
Here also ends its annotation and Svarūpavyākhyā entitled Vimalānandadāyinī.

NOTES

[1] *Kuraṅga*, which has beautiful large eyes.

[2] Lord of wealth.

[3] *Kelikalayā*, by the various entertaining acts (*parihāsādinā*) of which there are sixty-four. The meaning here is that there is continuous bliss.

[4] *Kelikalayā ciraṁ jīvanmuktah sa bhavati ca bhaktah pratijanuh.* The translation in the text reads *pratijanuh* to mean as K.B. says, *Janmanivritti* or cessation of birth. But *Pratijanuh* may also mean 'birth after birth.' According to this translation *jīvanmukta* would not refer to the state immediately preceding *Kaivalya* but, as K.B. says, *Jīvadavasthānubhūtadevatā-sākṣātkāramukha* in which case the

translation will be, He living in continuous bliss obtains direct Experience of the *Devatā* and is reborn life after life as Her devotee. According to the translation adopted complete liberation follows and in the other case some lower though happy state.

Obeisance

To Kāli the spouse of Kāla, who destroys all sin and is Kāla.[1] She who is Tārā the Saviour, the Supreme Brahmavidyā, who is adored by the lotus-born Deva.[2]

She who is S'rividyā, desirous of the welfare of Sādhakas on the path of Liberation, to whom Hari and Hara[3] make obeisance.

May that Devi the Mother, who appears in the form of all things, bring forth benefits for all such as sing Her praises.

Colophon

Of this King of Hymns wherein Mahākāla has described the true self of Kālikā, the Karpūrādya Hymn, untainted by worldly desire, which gives bliss to Devotees, the aforesaid Annotation containing its simple interpretation, as well as the Svarūpavyākhya (Commentary) which gives pure joy was prepared by me Vimalānanda Svāmi for the enlightenment of Sādhakas in the Saka year 1837. Mayest Thou *reside in the throat of him who* reads it.

OṀ, TAT SAT, OṀ

---

[1] The first Kāla is Mahākāla and the second is the produced Kāla.

[2] Brahmā.

[3] Viṣṇu and Rudra.